Computerizing

THE

Corporation

The Intimate Link Between People and Machines

Computerizing

T H E

Corporation

The Intimate Link Between People and Machines

Vicki C. McConnell
and
Karl Wm. Koch

The MENTOR Group

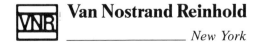 **Van Nostrand Reinhold**
_____ *New York*

Copyright © 1990 by Van Nostrand Reinhold
Library of Congress Catalog Card Number 90-12140
ISBN 0-442-31877-4

Printed in the United States of America

Van Nostrand Reinhold
115 Fifth Avenue
New York, New York 10003

Van Nostrand Reinhold International Company Limited
11 New Fetter Lane
London EC4P 4EE, England

Van Nostrand Reinhold
480 La Trobe Street
Melbourne, Victoria 3000, Australia

Nelson Canada
1120 Birchmount Road
Scarborough, Ontario M1K 5G4, Canada

16 15 14 13 12 11 10 9 8 7 6 5 4 3 2 1

Library of Congress Cataloging-in-Publication Data

McConnell, Vicki C., 1945-
    Computerizing the corporation : the intimate link between people
and machines / Vicki C. McConnell, Karl W. Koch.
        p.   cm.
    Includes bibliographical references (p.   ).
    ISBN 0-442-31877-4
    1. Management information systems.   I. Koch, Karl W., 1933-
II. Title.
T58.6.M393   1990
658.4'038—dc20   90-12140
                                                           CIP

TP

To George Beeler

Who reminded us that we are all family and that we
all need a meaningful future in which to live and
work in this age of rapidly advancing technology.

Contents

Foreword

The book you are about to read is not just another discourse on automation. Rather, it focuses on one of the most important and inadequately covered questions concerning information technology (IT): "How should organizations prepare, implement, and utilize IT more effectively to support the changing nature of human work and processes?"

Despite the increasing sophistication and "intelligence" of computers and ITs, many of us have come to believe that the systems we built are not living up to our expectations. Top managers of business and public-sector organizations feel that the costs of developing, maintaining, running, and upgrading such technical systems are exceeding the expected and perceived benefits of automation.

We have come to the full realization that ITs are automating a large part of our everyday lives. Computer chips are found in our homes, cars, watches, and most other material conveniences we have or need. Many of these we take for granted. Most of the time, they work very well. When they don't, we experience only minor inconvenience, since they are easily replaced.

But we are confronted with a different and much more elusive set of problems when we put computer and information systems in the context of people and organizations who use them directly or indirectly to perform their work-related tasks. These are the type of problems we read about in professional journals and the public press. These are the technology implementation problems often described as "runaway systems," "bugs," and other terms that give new meaning to the concept of a thesaurus.

This book is concerned with the class of technology and information systems which support the strategy, culture, and infrastructure of an organization. Its major thesis is that IT is advancing and changing at a rapid pace, with new opportunities of exploiting its potential in all forms of human endeavor. Therefore, there is a tremendous need to marry the technology potential to the human potential in new ways that were never seriously considered before.

Computers and their applications have passed through several epochs in the context of organizational evolution. The first epoch was automating or replacing clerical tasks such as payroll, accounting, and other finance-related systems. The 1960s were considered to be the initial wave of such automation.

As we entered the 1970s, the technology was applied to automating the controlling processes in manufacturing, distribution, inventory, and a multitude of logistical systems for industrial and service organizations. The third epoch is classified as the era of business transactions. Toward the beginning of the 1980s, organizations began to utilize computer technology and IT in ways which were previously not possible. Communications technology was combined with computer technology to allow the movement of information across organizational, national, and international boundaries at lightning speed.

Airlines, banks, and other financial service companies have led the way in applying these technologies to create new products and services. Of course, the presence of the personal computer (PC), with its plethora of new and improved software offerings, is now familiar to us all. Those who have not used PCs in one form or another are a vanishing breed. Computer technology and IT, in short, is now changing how we organize, relate, work, and compete.

There is little doubt that organizations need technical systems to perform many of their tasks. However, organizations also require human systems to work with the technical systems in order to survive and compete in the long run! What Vicki McConnell and Karl Koch present is a powerful and well-documented argument on how to successfully implement automation and information systems. The burden of their argument is that there needs to be a shift away from viewing technology implementation as a technological task and toward viewing it as an organizational task.

Rest assured, there are enough technologies out there to satisfy almost everyone's needs. However, there is very little work and thoughtful interdisciplinary probing of the complexities involved in preparing organizations (i.e., people, structures, culture, etc.) to live with institutionalized information system technologies.

The authors provide us with a new tool, the Technology Implementation Life Cycle™, which integrates technology systems building methodologies with their human counterparts. They evolved this method from the proven frameworks of technology and human systems integration in The McConnell Method™ and in Impact Management™. By citing actual experiences and real life situations, they are able to validate the implicit assumptions behind their process and philosophy. Technological systems and human systems must be built symbiotically in order to implement meaningful, responsive, and sustainable organizational systems.

This book sheds a new light on the often neglected problems of building an infrastructure (i.e., people, processes, systems, values, and practices) as technological systems become more deeply rooted and embedded in human work. This insight alone may give rise to a new vision of how we should go about tackling a critical and emerging phenomenon: Making very complex human and technological systems function to deliver benefits, while preserving the fragile nature and value of human dignity in the workplace.

M. H. NOTOWIDIGDO
Vice President, Information Systems
Wendy's International, Inc.

Acknowledgments

Vicki's

It is a well-worn but true statement that most accomplishments are not the work of one person but the combined effort of many. Although I have spent nearly 20 years developing The McConnell Method™, it was not achieved alone. Karl helped me to understand my own model in bigger and broader terms. He added and continues to add to my understanding of its power and impact. All of the outstanding colleagues who worked with me throughout the years are to be credited with executing and refining many of the method's tasks. There are three who I especially want to recognize: Patty Carpenter Forman, Mark Forman, and Susan Negrete Thomson.

A remembrance of the late Phil McLaughlin. You are missed by all who knew you. I only hope that they have bookstores in heaven.

A special thank-you to Dr. William Fagan, Irvine, California, who brought me back to physical health with his great kindness and skill.

A particular thank-you to my family for taking in the mail, watering the plants, and feeding Riley so that I could write this book.

A heartfelt acknowledgment to my son, James, who told me at the age of eight that he believed I would be "famis" one day. I cherish his love, encouragement, and faith in Mom.

A final lady's hat off to all the Mabels, Georges, Helens, Harrys, and countless thousands of working people whose spirit and dedication transcend any machine.

Karl's

I would like to acknowledge the gifts that others have given me. First and foremost, Vicki gave me the opportunity to start a business, develop a partnership in every good sense of that word, and share a vision of how people can be empowered through technology.

My good friend and colleague Donn Abdon had the patience to teach me how to reduce my theoretical jargon to understandable and practical language.

John Sherwood and other colleagues from Management Design, Inc., introduced me to the world of processes, change, and proactive management.

And then there are the countless scholars of human behavior, from whom so much has been learned.

A special thanks is due to my wife, family, and friends, who patiently bestowed the gift of time so that this work could be completed. My only regret is that one thank-you cannot be delivered. It is to my father, who always gave me encouragement in the gifts that he perceived I had.

Ours

Recognition should be given to those who have supported and aided us in this work. To our editor, Dianne Littwin, for the courage to bet on two new authors and the perseverance to see us through the process of completing this manuscript. To Hari Notowidigdo for his strength, wisdom, and constancy in all our endeavors. And finally, our thanks to the creators of personal computers and word processing. We would have quit the writing long ago without these marvelous tools.

Introduction

Three beliefs underlie this book. We believe in the full and effective use of computers and other information technologies (ITs). We believe in the full and effective use of people. We believe that people can be completely effective without technology but that the use of technology can never be full and effective without people. It is this final belief which is the real soul of this book. It is a belief that places IT in a servant's role. It does not mean that the need for new technology can be ignored. Far from it; organizations must make significant and rapid advancements in technological use. But they must first learn how to do so.

Successful technological progress will be achieved when organizational management rids itself of certain delusions. There is a fantasy abroad in the land that technology operates on its own. It is evidenced every time people talk about "computer mistakes," as if people did not cause them, and in the ubiquitous statement that "the computer is down," as if it were not our operational problem. Did you notice that no one ever says, "We broke it"? We concede that these expressions may represent only a style of speaking. Yet we believe that there is something more insidious behind them.

What lies behind them is an assumption that the technology itself is a new factor in human relationships rather than a new tool for people to use. When technology is treated as an equal partner in human affairs, it takes on a life of its own. Often it is presumed to be the answer to purely human problems.

Most of the published material on effective computer use describes technological advances and provides information about how to understand and use them. The implicit assumption is that people lack an understanding of technology. In our experience, the proper use of new technology is not inhibited solely by our lack of technical expertise, but also by our lack of people expertise. Many of the failures that organizations experience in technological use stem from human failures.

Management does not yet seem to know how to implement new technologies properly. We have noted that there is a general trend to bridge technical systems and

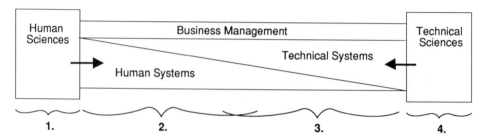

FIG. I-1 Published Materials on Computers and Management

Published materials fall into one of four categories. Categories 1 and 4 do not deal with problems of interaction between technical systems and human systems. Category 3 is found extensively in the literature, but it addresses the interaction problems primarily from a technical viewpoint. This book fits category 2.

human systems, with most of the effort coming from the technical side. Figure I-1 illustrates our point. There are books on the human sciences (category 1) and on the technical sciences (category 4), neither of which are concerned with business management. There are, increasingly, books on the use of technical systems within business management (category 3). These often provide material on how to support employee use of technology. Our book provides a new thrust in the development and expansion of category 2, which concerns the way human systems react to the introduction of technical systems.

When we began this book, we wanted to address problems of computerization. We soon realized that the ever-changing technology was about to advance beyond our subject. As the computer chip became part of every machine, the subject gradually shifted to automation. As the computer advanced in its design and applications, the focus gradually shifted to IT. We find it appropriate that we, as authors, should have one of the experiences about which we offer warnings. The technology will never stand still. It is always changing.

But the problems of implementing technology remain remarkably constant. They are management and people problems. Therefore, the principles of this book are universal ones which apply across the range of ITs. These include data processing, factory and office automation, personal computing, telecommunications, information and data bases, artificial intelligence, and expert systems. Past experiences in implementing computer technology are the basis for implementing newer ITs.

IT has another unique feature. It is invading every area of human life. This invasion is changing the manner of its use to such a degree that some older and familiar terms are now at risk. For many years we have distinguished between the technician and the "end user." As long as we had mainframe technology, with a centralized MIS staff, this distinction was easily made. The line is rapidly blurring, or perhaps transmuting to a new form.

We began to debate whether we should call the people who use these technologies "users" and "end users." To us the terms seem to belittle the person. The term "nontechnical user" is worse because it defines people in terms of what they are not. We have debated and discussed other possibilities: "owner", "client", "customer", "associate", "proponent", and so on. We do not have an answer, only preferences.

Vicki prefers "owner." She believes that MIS is a service industry and that technologies are delivered to clients or customers, who "own" them. Karl appreciates the term from another perspective. For him, there is a need to recognize that all members of an organization are owners. Thus, throughout this book, we stress that users are technology's owners (even when we use the term "end user")—a principle that underlies much of what we say. We are content to use the industry-accepted terms, "user" and "end user" until a better alternative is adopted. We do so because these words have the advantage of immediate understanding.

Finally, we have written this book with several hopes in mind. First, we hope to alarm the reader. We are greatly concerned when we observe the manner in which technology is thrown into the workplace. The prospects for the future are not good if we continue to do this. Second, we hope to provide a way out of this present dilemma. We believe in the adaptability of American workers and organizations. We believe in their future. And we assert that the future lies in the combined development of our human systems and our technical systems.

There must be a recognition of one truth if our hopes are to be realized:

> ***Problems of computerization and automation are management problems, not technical problems.***

That is why this is, at heart, a management book.

Computerizing

T H E

Corporation

The Intimate Link Between
People and Machines

Pitfalls of Implementation

If we could first know where we are and whither we are tending,
we could better judge what to do and how to do it.

—Abraham Lincoln

The George Beeler Story

George Beeler is the central figure in the February 1989 *Inc.* magazine article "The Last Shift."* This article tells the story of one man's gradually disappearing future as an automobile industry worker. George recounts his experience as the lead worker during the installation of a computerized screw machine which makes long, tapered automobile gearshifts parts. During the machine's installation, George encounters the following problems.

Problem 1: His trip to Germany for training on the machine's operation was extended to three weeks because the custom-built machine was not yet operating. As a consequence, he spent a lot of time fetching coffee and asking questions.

Problem 2: George helped the manufacturer translate the tags for the machine's 54-button electrical panels from German to English. Problem 3: The machine arrived in the United States three months later. Fortunately, George had retained enough knowledge to reassemble it. Unfortunately, he spent 75 hours the first week doing so.

---

*Reprinted with permission, *Inc.* magazine, (Feb. 1989).

Copyright © 1989 by *Inc.* Publishing Company, 38 Commercial Wharf, Boston, MA 02110.

Problem 4: Once assembly was completed, the machine would not start because its computer programming had been lost in transit. This forced George and three workers to reenter the 2,000-page computer program. Problem 5: The machine functioned smoothly for the first few days until the safety clutch gave out, an oil pump malfunctioned, and the fuse bank blew out.

Throughout this period, George Beeler persevered. He kept the machine running. He assumed responsibility for troubleshooting its problems. Somehow he kept the machine operating, even though fellow workers called it "the machine we have that doesn't run." He just wouldn't let them believe that this machine could not work. After all, George Beeler was a good worker, a dedicated employee. He knew that he was capable of growing and developing with new technology and new responsibility. All he wanted was a chance to prove himself.

What makes this account so meaningful is the context in which it is told. The article reveals the world of George Beeler. It tells about his hopes and aspirations as an adolescent, about trust and belief in the American automobile industry, and his confidence in the future. It speaks of his growing years in the Detroit area when the American automobile was king. It shows that he had strong confidence in the automobile industry. And it describes how he became a productive worker in that industry.

Now George, his family, and his friends find that auto industry jobs are scarce and the future is insecure. His present situation leaves him only with cautious optimism. Technological advances may have provided George a temporary advantage, a new job to do, and some hope for the immediate future. But even then he has no absolute security. This story clearly reveals the prevailing contradictions in George Beeler's life.

The author of the article (Hyatt 1989) comments, "This is not the world George Beeler expected to live in." To which we would add, very few workers today live in a world they were expecting. Instead, they find themselves confronted with more and more significant changes in the workplace. One of the greatest agents of those changes is the computer and the newly emerging information technologies (ITs).

How to React?

Is it possible to support automation, seeing its value and importance to the future, while honestly confronting the problems presently experienced by those who use it? That question is the driving force behind this book. It is also a question based on our dedication to constantly seek the truth about the way working people behave. We are concerned because the way people behave often turns automation into an obstacle to overcome rather than an advantage to seize.

Though human behavior creates the problems of automation, there are no villains or heroes in this book. There are only real, hard-working people, like George

Beeler, confronting one of the most momentous changes in human life: the arrival of the computer and the information technology that has developed from it.

There are many things about this relatively new tool that make it most uncommon. It is the first data processing device which is capable of exceeding the human mind in speed and accuracy of operation. It is the first communication tool which is interactive both inside and outside the mind of the observer. It is the one human tool most often linked to other human tools. One might conclude that our ability to develop what IT can do is exceeded only by the number of ways we can connect it to other machines.

Indeed, predicting what IT will next do is remarkably like trying to predict what a particular human might do next, given unbounded circumstances and resources. No matter how outrageous our predictions, the future reality always seems to exceed our estimate. An added perspective is developed when it is realized that the vast majority of IT developments are so positive and offer such hope for improving the conditions of human life. And, in countless instances, they deliver on their promise. But a nagging question remains—what happens when they don't?

For example: A large on-line computer system designed to speed up the claims processing of a major health care provider nearly bankrupted the company because it doubled the time needed to handle policyholders' claims. The problem was corrected as quickly as possible by reassigning a large number of computer personnel to develop a solution.

What is perplexing is why this problem arose with a basic computer application. After all, speed and accuracy are the hallmarks of computerization. The large number of existing computerized claims processing systems tell us that this task is not too complex or unique for computerization. This dilemma demonstrates that computerization problems are not always obvious and are seldom technical in nature. The next example makes it easier to see why problems arise.

Second example: A Fortune 500 fast food chain requires its programming staff to reprogram menu price changes for point-of-sale (POS) terminals quickly and repeatedly. This must be done so rapidly, in fact, that programmers have no time to thoroughly debug the price program before it is sent to the stores. In one case, a set of new price changes resulted in over 800 telephone calls in a 24-hour period to the management information systems (MIS) department's round-the-clock help desk.

An analysis of this situation is almost intuitive. The fast food industry has a corporate culture with some typical characteristics. It is operations-oriented, fast-paced, and staffed with managers who expect quick responses to their decisions and requests. It is easy, given that environment, for the MIS staff to overestimate their ability to respond. The corporate culture encourages this behavior. But recognizing the facts of the situation does not leave the computer staff free of responsibility in such circumstances.

We must be cautious as we analyze the contribution of MIS personnel to the POS problem described above. It is very easy to attribute the problem to a lack of analytical and programming skills. However, our study of the situation revealed that their difficulties lay in the area of management skills, not technical skills. These MIS professionals were quite capable of producing error-free software. They knew how to analyze, program, and debug. What they needed was skill in managing their situation and their end users, or clients. In this case, their client was company operations, which created the demand for instantaneous price changes to the POS software. Once the POS computer team began to focus on the problems of managing POS programming requests, they were able to bring the software problems under control.

These MIS professionals are not alone. This lack of management skill is also found outside MIS. The problems that result can be both serious and humorous.

Another example: A state bureau of motor vehicles cut back on computer equipment orders because of a tight budget. Management then assigned the few personal computers (PCs) they had to personnel who had little use for them.

Our study of this situation revealed that the decision was not ill-intended. Rather, once the budgeting process had passed out of the hands of operational managers, it was kept out of their hands. Budget cuts of PC purchases were initiated and controlled not by the affected managers but rather by fiscal and planning staffs. These staffs decided that it was more equitable to spread the PC purchase cutbacks evenly throughout the bureau.

Several managers told us that they would rather have seen selected departments computerized first, even if it meant waiting another fiscal year to receive their PCs. This was a management problem, not a computer problem. However, the effect of poor management decisions tainted and diminished all of the bureau's subsequent computerization efforts.

The problems of automation might be less troubling if they did not keep changing. That is, if only one set of problems were consistently encountered, then organizations might eventually blunder through to a solution. We have found, however, that as information technology continues to develop, it produces new problems of implementation. Companies even wind up with problem reversals like the following.

An example: The middle managers of a major southern hotel corporation acquired PCs and became very proficient in their use. Subsequently, they became disillusioned with the company's computer programmers. They discovered that the programmers could not respond to their requests as easily or quickly as they could by using their own PCs.

The traditional, centralized MIS department with large mainframe computers puts the control of computer functions *and thinking* into the hands of the computer professional. Historically, control of the computer and its uses was centralized. Only its products were distributed. This arrangement is no longer the norm; now computer power *and thinking* are distributed to the users. Lacking control over both the location and the uses of the technology, MIS professionals are often placed under extraordinary pressures.

These pressures demand that they become technological experts in an ever expanding and changing range of information technologies. MIS professionals also experience a drifting development of technology. That is, PC users may be drifting off in several diverse directions with their individual development in and use of ITs.

Computer technicians are expected to keep pace with this diversity while meeting the demands of the increasingly different uses of the technology.

Some organizations are addressing this PC "revolution" by placing their computer professionals in the divisions and work units that use their expertise. They are deploying their technical resources on the "front line." As these technical experts move out into the organization, they find themselves surrounded by coworkers whose unique expertise and value to the enterprise require that they, and not the technician, control the uses of the technology. As a result, control over IT is gradually shifting from those who are technically competent to those who are business competent.

This development will not ease the problems of technology implementation. Rather, it will distribute them throughout the organization, reaching as far as the technology is disbursed. Problems of technology implementation might be managed more readily and easily if they could be kept centralized and localized. Then a company could create one staff to resolve and manage them. But if implementation issues and problems were centralized, organizations might also continue a fallacious line of thought. They might think that the problems of implementation are technical, rather than managerial.

Sometimes a problem needs to develop to a critical stage before it can be given a proper and effective diagnosis. For example, doctors cannot always distinguish the real nature of a disease until it has progressed to its severest stage. The same is often true of technology implementations. American organizations have progressed to a more sophisticated and critical stage of automation. There is more technology in the hands of more people. As this has happened, the control of the technology has escaped from the technician. This widespread use of IT has caused the implementation problems to become more obvious and critical. Implementations, good and bad, are experienced from the executive suite to the corporate mail room. This highlights an old, often unrecognized truth: that technology implementation is a business problem, not a technical problem. Its success or failure lies with management.

The problems of technology implementation may be eased by adjustments in the technology. An example of this is the evolution of computer hardware design. Today one is more likely to sit down to a computer monitor that is equipped with an antiglare screen. Time and experience have shown that when the screen's glare and subsequent worker eye strain are eliminated, the worker is more productive and healthy.

Improvements such as antiglare screens will not totally eliminate or control implementation problems. They are a small and important convenience which makes the use of the technology easier. However, sometimes it is the attention to small considerations which builds a user perception that the larger task—the entire technology implementation—is going well.

As we review the development of this business problem, we see two reasons for the distress organizations experience in technology implementations. The first reason consists of social-historical tension points which affect the attempt to automate work. The four major points of tension are given in Table 1-1.

Table 1-1
Social-Historical Tension Points

1. A communication gap exists between technical and nontechnical people.
2. The technology itself drives the organization to use the technology.
3. Competition between firms escalates the drive to new forms of technology.
4. The technology is expanding into all areas of work.

The second cause of technology implementation distress is situation specific. It consists of the mistakes that organizations often, and typically, make when implementing new systems or upgrading old ones (Table 1-2).

We shall address these causes in the order given above, first presenting the social-historical roots and then moving on to the situation specific problems. There is no assumption that all of these causes will be found in every situation, much less that the reader would have encountered all of them. However, our experience has shown that they are among the root problems whenever computer implementation occurs.

Table 1-2
Situational Mistakes in Implementation

1. Oversimplification
2. Fragmentation of effort
3. Confrontation instead of collaboration
4. MIS overload or understaff
5. Inappropriate staff expectations
6. Treating computers as deliverables
7. Lack of behavioral expectations
8. Lack of resources
9. Misplaced assignments
10. No comprehensive planning for implementation

Social-Historical Roots of Computer Problems

The Communication Gap

The most common characteristic of computer problems is a deep and continuing communication gap between the technician and the nontechnical user. This seems incredible in the case of computers, considering that they have been in use for several decades. This gap can be demonstrated by the following examples:

Example 1: Many mistakes in programming occur in the requirements-gathering stage.

Systems analysts have been well trained in the science of their trade, but not as well in its art. As a result, grand assumptions of several sorts may be made in the requirements-gathering stage. The analyst may assume that (1) the user knows his or her requirements, or (2) the user can logically and cohesively state these, or (3) the analyst understands what the user is saying, or, finally, (4) the requirements stated are the ones desired or needed.

Even though the problem appears to originate with the assumptions of the analyst, the fault does not lie entirely with them or with the users. Handling communications between technicians and users is a management responsibility. Just pointing out the problem to the analyst or the user will not suffice. Wherever the problem surfaces, it exists because the technician and the user lack the skills needed to solve it. They, more than anyone else, may already know that the problem exists. A systematic way of communicating between them must be developed by management.

Karl learned how this communication problem could be handled while in charge of the development of Ohio's Home Energy Assistance Program computer system. A number of management and communication techniques were used to manage this project. For example, Karl held weekly meetings between end users and programmer/analysts. They were highly structured meetings with a preannounced agenda. All conversations were carefully managed so that computer users could be very specific in stating their system requirements and needs. Programmer/analysts were required to give feedback on how they understood requests to ensure a common understanding by all. This procedure helped to achieve the project's objective—the design and delivery of a system that performed exactly as everybody expected.

As more technology is distributed throughout organizations, the technicians and users may overcome these problems on their own. However, an intentional effort to overcome communication problems will ease this transition and lead to greater operational effectiveness and efficiency. A calculated program of communication will promote balance so that technicians and users develop a greater level of understanding about, and possible skill in, the other's area of expertise. Sound management principles suggest a role for middle management in supporting the resolution of this most familiar problem.

Example 2: Computer literacy remains a problem in the work force.

Almost a full generation has passed since computers entered the workplace. Yet, many workers are still uninformed about and unskilled in current technology. They are also grossly misinformed concerning the technologies of the future. "Bit" and "byte" remain mysterious words belonging to a language available only to the computer elite. Yet there is a continuing lack of concerted effort to improve computer literacy. At the same time there is a healthy curiosity about the technology. Because the technology is always advancing, computer illiteracy and ignorance will only worsen if steps are not taken soon.

The impact of computer illiteracy will be psychological, sociological, cultural, and national. The tendency for information technology to evolve constantly into more complex systems will only intensify these problems. We do not believe that the PC revolution will solve this problem. We do not believe that the spread of information technology into an organization will cause computer illiteracy to "self resolve" itself. We believe that the present levels of computer illiteracy, combined with the forced migration to higher levels of technology, will require ceaseless and consistent efforts to overcome the user's lack of knowledge and skill.

Computer professionals can become the front-line troops in the endeavor to supplant illiteracy with knowledge. However, they first need to acquire or develop the communication skills that many of them lack. The technician-to-user communication difficulties will only increase as the new technologies evolve, for they bring with them newer vocabularies and higher skill requirements.

Example 3: Nontechnical users complain that MIS professionals do not understand the organization's business.

A false pride has arisen among the computer elite, a pride that says, "It is sufficient that I know my trade. Others can manage the affairs of the business. I will tell them how to use this technology as they do their work." The recognition that some technical personnel have this attitude causes users a great deal of discomfort. It should be recognized that users have often fostered this attitude by their detachment from the technology. We have, in effect, two camps, one viewing the technology from the inside out, the other from the outside in. Someone needs to manage both of them so that they learn to share their differing viewpoints and differing areas of expertise.

Placing these two groups in a common front-line position will force them to talk to one another. But the problem will still remain if each group speaks from a different knowledge base. Cross-training and education will help. However, the ultimate solution will emerge as the organization develops job descriptions for the computer professional and the computer user that focus their work on the enterprise's mission and goals.

Example 4: Information technology implementation is always harder than we think.

We should learn to operate with this axiom: "The faster and better a new technology will work, the longer and harder it will be to shift to its full use." This axiom focuses on a reality about which we constantly deceive ourselves. Management tends to minimize the effects of automation on workers and their work. Managers often make the grand assumption that all humans are flexible regarding such changes. Since the decision to computerize is rationally sound, management comes to the "rational" conclusion that the change will be easy.

Our observations about automation suggest that there is at least one area of computerization/automation where the axiom is followed. In the manufacturing environment, management will ask for substantive and exhaustive studies on all the impacts of a manufacturing process change. At a minimum, a study will look at the personnel available to operate the new system, the time required to transfer to it, the costs involved, and the resources available. American business does not do as well in the automation of its other business functions. Perhaps there is a need for a "truth squad" which forces organizations to explore and prepare for the realities of technological evolution and change.

There is a need for a great deal of discussion and work before we achieve a true understanding of the communications gap created by technology. Some of the features of the gap can be linked to the characteristics of American society. The lack of communication between technician and user is part of a general lack of communication we observe across the organizational structures of many American companies. Since technology's vocabulary is a foreign language to the computer user, the difficulty may be an American antipathy to learning secondary languages. Another possibility may be the personality strengths and tendencies of those who are attracted to technical work. These persons may not be as well equipped by personality preference to deal with human communications and interpersonal sharing as to handle technical details. Whatever the social causes of the communication problem, it is management that must resolve them.

The Technology Drives Technology

The second common problem in using information technology is that the technology itself is often the driving force behind technological changes. That is, many organizations will change their technology because of pressures to adapt to the next generation of hardware or software. The impact of this change on their present form and style of management is often ignored or sublimated. The benefit to be derived from the new technology is assumed rather than demonstrated. The costs are often grossly understated or hidden. We have observed the following examples.

Example 1: There is a fascination with technology.

Many systems purchases are made unnecessarily. Someone in the organization, a technician or user, becomes fascinated with a particular technology and insists that it be bought and installed. Some computer hardware and software vendors encourage such behavior. However, we need go no further in seeking a cause than to admit that we Americans love gadgets.

Two axioms are often ignored in the rush to automate. First, there is nothing inherently wrong, bad, or inefficient about a manual system unless the business has a proven need for something better. Second, the business problem a company is facing may not be resolved with a change in technology. When these axioms are ignored, the

Table 1-3
The Ignored Axioms of Technology

1. There is nothing inherently wrong with a manual system.
2. Business problems are not always solved by technology.

move to new technology will exacerbate organizational problems rather than solve them. We call these truths the "ignored axioms of technology" (Table 1-3).

Example 2: Vendors often forced customers to migrate to new products.

Some computer vendors announce to their customers that the hardware or software product presently in use is due for replacement by a new or upgraded product. Therefore, customers are often forced to migrate to a new product because vendor support of the old product will soon be withdrawn. Vendors sell upgrades based on a new product's increased speed, lower cost, increased efficiency, and/or enhanced capabilities. In reality, the new technology may offer more in general, but never everything that the customer needs.

The decisions of vendors are often driven by their need to remain competitive. As service providers they will act to serve their clients, but clients must not assume that the vendor knows all of their business needs. Specifically, businesspersons should always assume that they know their own business far better than the computer vendor does. It is the business needs of purchasers that must drive their automation decisions.

Example 3: New toys are better than old toys.

One of the advantages of information technology is its "playfulness." A generation of youth has grown up with the computer as a toy. It should not be surprising that they continue to hold this view as they graduate to the working world. Having played with video games and computers in their leisure time, they are equally comfortable with the "toy" at work. Many younger nontechnical users of information technology arrive at work with this orientation. They are often very proficient in their use of technology, particularly PCs.

Others have a more serious orientation. They have studied to become computer experts, acquiring the skills of analysis, design, and programming. As they became computer experts, they discovered their ability to make the technology do all sorts of things. They could make it hum, whistle, stand up and salute. But many of them were good at these skills precisely because they came to the technology in a playful manner. They are totally unafraid of its capabilities and totally committed to their own ability to control and use it.

Both of these types of users work in American organizations. Their positive attitude toward IT encourages its broader use. On the other hand, they may drive an organization toward hardware purchases and software development that are not realistic or needed at the time. Today's firms find themselves in a complex and competitive business environment complicated by a ceaseless and growing array of technology. In such circumstances, organizations must understand all of their technological options.

The Competition Made Me Do It

This feature is most obvious in business advertisements. These ads create a looming fear that only those who have the best technology can win the competition for customers. Much of the advertising regarding technology focuses on this fear. Often what management asks of its technical staff is focused on the reality that "the competition does it that way." Some examples are as follows:

Example 1: Car rental booking systems have automated to capture repeat business.

Car rental agencies, particularly those located at airport terminals, have discovered that a significant amount of their income comes from repeat business. Automation of their service provides distinct advantages in capturing the attention and retaining the loyalty of those who repeatedly rent cars. With reliable, effective software, these automated systems can also overcome many of the scheduling and service problems of this industry.

Example 2: Automation of airline reservation systems provides a strong competitive advantage.

Major airlines that computerized their schedule, fare, and seat availability information gained a distinct advantage over their competitors. Though they were required by regulation to provide flight information on competitors, a few major carriers were able to provide their own information first through their automated inquiry system. This had the effect of directing purchasers, in more or less subtle ways, to their services.

Example 3: Medical technology is an important component of hospital care.

Hospitals in major cities are vying to own the latest in medical technology. With that technology comes prestige and the ability to attract doctors who are developing new forms of patient treatment. Unfortunately, available funds are not always sufficient to cover such expenditures, nor are there always sufficient patients to justify them. There is now a movement, in at least one midwestern area, to require regional planning for the purchase of new medical technologies. This will ensure that patients and their insurers will not be unduly burdened by a wasteful duplication of sophisticated technology.

Technology can provide an advantage to the organization that works in a competitive environment. But it must be positioned within the total strategy of the business. The "glitz" of an ad campaign may attract customers, but only the reality of performance will keep them. Performance is much more a people issue than a technology issue. Computers can bring consistency to customer service, but only people can perform in a caring manner. It is the combination of these two elements that produces effective service, thus providing the true competitive advantage.

In his book, Scandinavian Airlines President Jan Carlzon (1987) suggests that "moments of truth" occur when there is a "caring" contact between two people. It is such moments of truth that build the relationship between the client and the firm. Carlzon recognizes, and we agree, that technology can enhance and upgrade this interpersonal contact. In fact, the eventual success of such contact may hinge on the availability of technology that can quickly provide accurate and meaningful data. However necessary and vital the technology is, the business goal remains—to assist two persons in developing their relationship. That's what builds a business.

The same can be said of governmental agencies. The technology should be designed and implemented to enhance the interpersonal contacts between staff and clients. In her book *The Electronic Sweatshop* (1988), Barbara Garson states that just the opposite is happening in some social service agencies. She finds that social work personnel are being used to enhance the relationship between clients and the agency computer. Where this happens, the social agency has changed its goal. Previously, its goal was caring for and supporting people. Automation appears to have changed it to one of keeping people in the social services system indefinitely.

Technology Invades New Areas

The fourth technological tension point pertains to the types of functions we are *now* automating. IT has moved away from the automation of easily defined office functions (e.g., bookkeeping, typing, record keeping) to more complicated areas of management. Three stages of development have been identified by David R. Vincent (1989) in his book *The Information-Based Corporation*, as noted in Table 1-4.

Table 1-4
Stages of Computerization/Automation Use

1. People replacement, where the technical system replaces large staff functions, such as bookkeeping.
2. Enablement, where the system is designed to facilitate information sharing.
3. Socioeconomic change, where the systems so pervade the organization as to change its mode of operation and its economic base.

Example 1: Automation has been applied to manufacturing.

A frequently cited example is the movement of technology into the management of certain manufacturing functions where mid-level managers previously handled the details now controlled through computers. Integrated computer-aided design and computer-aided manufacturing (CAD/CAM) can control all facets of the manufacturing process from design of the product to its delivery.

Human participation is found at most stages of the process, but the computer literally ties the entire system together. The technology manages the just-in-time inventory control of materials and/or product components. Frequent meetings of large support staffs are no longer needed. Detailed, intricate planning methods can be programmed so that computer-aided decisions can be completed in a timely and effective manner. The use of advanced technology drives the entire system of operation.

Example 2: Technology is used to streamline middle management.

There is another driving force behind the spread of IT. That is the desire to reduce the expense of mid-level management, to streamline the organization and its decision making, and to make the organization more responsive to changing market conditions. The risk in making these changes is the possibility of overlooking other equally important mid-level management dynamics. Many of the interpersonal working relationships of an enterprise focus on middle managers. While it is true that new relationships can serve as well as old ones, there is a need to plan for this change.

Example 3: The PC has increased the impact of automation.

The impact of automation on American organizations has been compounded by the arrival of the PC. Some persons suggest that the PC eases employees' transition to more effective computer use. And unquestionably, many benefits are derived from microcomputer expansion into organizations. But not without some recurring problems.

Many managers are quite adept at using the PC. As a result, they begin to believe that the difficulties of running a large mainframe system have been grossly exaggerated. Some begin to depreciate the value of larger mainframe systems, believing that PCs will do all they need. Inevitably, these managers make the same implementation mistakes characteristic of their mainframe counterparts. They fail to develop a system that fully integrates technical, work, and interpersonal functions. One of the symptoms of this lack of integration is the development of individual data bases by middle managers.

This occurs when there is no plan for the integration of technical and human systems. Three activities should be completed before automating any work tasks, including automating with PCs: (1) defining the nature of the work tasks, (2) stating the full range of data required for these tasks, and (3) developing the computer systems to serve these tasks and provide the data. This sequence of activities will place PCs within a frame of reference. It will integrate their uses and value with the work and values of the business.

Summary: Social-Historical Roots

The four underlying points of tension noted above are found throughout American society and business. They are pervasive and are at the foundation of automation problems. An adequate response to each will require a great deal of effort. Initially, each organization will need to assess to what extent its automation decisions have been the result of conscious choice or social pressures. Organizations cannot eliminate social conditions, control the behaviors of computer vendors, regulate their competitors, or halt the advance of computer technology. But a necessary precondition to any rational control over organizational behavior is knowledge of the outside conditions influencing the organization.

Situational Mistakes in Implementation

Social problems themselves are enough to demand our attention. Unfortunately, management has also acquired certain bad habits, certain habitual behaviors, which compound the dilemma. The following discussion of inappropriate behaviors has been accumulated by the authors during the past 20 years. We have been involved in computer system implementations as employees and as consultants. We have condensed a great deal of data into an exhaustive yet brief list. The items in this list are presented in no particular order of importance.

Habit 1: Oversimplification

Senior managers lack an understanding of the complexities of technology implementation. It is not uncommon to hear them comment that their users will have an easy time adjusting to the new system. Alternatively, conceding that the users will have some problems, senior management underestimates the resources that will be needed. Quite to the contrary, our experience has shown that the task of computer implementation is complex and requires a much greater resource commitment than is generally understood or acknowledged. To illustrate this, examine the list of skills in Table 1-5 that can be used in implementing a new technology.

Table 1-5
**Skill Areas Used in an Effective Selection,
Development and Implementation of an IT**

Accountant
Business strategist/planner
Decision maker
Educator of adults
Ergonomics expert
Graphics designer
Marketing and sales representative
Owner
Project manager
Psychologist
Public relations practitioner
Sociologist
Technician (hardware and software)
Trainer
Writer/reporter

The skills presented in this list are used in varying degrees in implementing any technical system. However, each skill area will be used whenever an effective implementation is achieved. How this will happen and why each skill is needed is the subject of the remainder of this book. At this point, it is important to read the list carefully and note the breadth of skills presented. Many of these are not readily found among either the computer staff or the user departments. Finding, assembling, and using these skills in technology implementation will be of continuing concern to those senior managers who desire effective technology implementations.

Habit 2: Fragmentation of Effort

There is often a remarkable lack of strategic thinking in planning IT development. This problem most often occurs because the company has no established process for this type of planning. Since the process is haphazard, so is the planning. Thus, it is not uncommon for different departments within an organization to have incompatible information systems while possessing data of common interest which could or should be shared. Even though technology could help them coordinate their efforts, these departments continue to operate as separate fiefdoms. But that was a problem that existed before computers. Now the problem has been computerized. And the computerized problem will be solved only when we learn to solve the organizational problems first.

A similar lack of integration occurs with most computer system implementations. The system is developed and delivered. Then systems analysts and trainers are turned loose on the users. In general, no systematic process of implementation has been developed because no strategic thought has been given to the need for planning the implementation. The implementation focuses on achieving limited goals because it lacks the planning and foresight that would integrate the computer into the user's system of work.

Habit 3: Confrontation Instead of Collaboration

Too often, what management hoped or presumed would be a smooth implementation turns into a silent, or not so silent, confrontation. Technology users treat the technicians as intruders. Technicians confront the apparent recalcitrance of the users. Turf issues arise because there has been no advance vision of how an implementation should occur. That vision is critical if a smooth and gradual transition to any information system is to occur within a *planned process*. Employees usually want to cooperate with a technology change, especially when they see that it serves the organization's general interest. Yet the collaboration that would ensure a successful change is often stifled under a cloud of negative perceptions and attitudes.

Habit 4: MIS Overload

In typical American style, we rush to find a solution when business problems and technological possibilities are combined. As a result, MIS departments are often overstaffed and overloaded at the same time. The absence of strategic planning leads to a scattered and uncontrolled demand for services that causes companies to inflate their technical resources. At the same time, a lack of priority planning leads to an underestimate of the resources and the time needed to meet user demands. In addition, a lack of understanding about the complexity of technical system development and operation leads to exorbitant expectations of what changes and improvements are possible.

Habit 5: Inappropriate Staff Expectations

Many computer professionals begin a new implementation believing that the users will be pleased with the new technology being installed. After all, they think, the new technology "makes their work so much easier." Then come the users' responses. They complain. They express anxiety over the "newfangled" computer. They say that they weren't really expecting what they got. They feel totally overwhelmed. At this point, the technicians feel unappreciated. Worse than this, they may come to believe that computer users are uneducable, untrainable, and ungrateful.

The other extreme is the users who believe that the new technology will solve all of their work problems and take their troubles away. Unable to see the difficulties of automation and the problems of converting their old work habits to new ones, they feel betrayed. The new system has not rescued them as they thought it would. As a result, users feel that the technicians have held out false hopes and come to believe that they cannot be trusted. Users now believe that technicians do not live up to their promises or commitments. Or worse, some users start believing that the use of a computer or other technology always creates more problems than it's worth.

Habit 6: Technology as Deliverables

Computers and other ITs are often viewed as deliverables. Buy the machines, install them, and turn them on. This method may work with simple machines; however, the computer is not a simple machine. The end result of this approach is the new management game called "damage control." When using this "deliverable method," organizations scramble to (1) find the training, (2) explain and justify the changes, (3) smooth ruffled feathers, and (4) try to find a way to integrate all of its efforts. But the most important thing to remember about this game is that it can also be called "playing catchup."

Habit 7: Lack of Behavioral Expectations

Whenever a new system of work is designed, there must be specific and measurable work behaviors that are expected. If there are none, there can be no evaluation of the new system. We find that information systems are often proposed without any evaluation criteria. Therefore, when evaluating computer implementations, we recommend at least three categories of behavioral expectations: (1) proficiency, (2) efficiency, and (3) productivity. Proficiency is a measure of the number of computer system functions that the user can use. Efficiency is a measure of how the computer system affects overall levels of output. Productivity measures the comparison between time and output when using one computer system function.

Few plans for computerization include such explicit behavioral expectations. Some of the most comprehensive measurements are benchmark records of a user's key strokes or other quantitative measurements of work. Such measures are reminiscent of factory efficiency calculations. A shortage of planning in this area will not lead to an enhancement of human potential in the workplace. We believe that computers can greatly enhance human potential. We also believe that few American organizations have thoughtfully and thoroughly planned how this shall occur. Management must manage computer power to expand human potential.

Habit 8: Lack of Resources

American organizations are investing millions of dollars in the purchase and development of computer technologies and ITs that operate their enterprises. That consumption trend shows no sign of diminishing. The only significant change in purchasing habits is the move from larger machines, such as mainframe computers, to mid-size minicomputers to desktop microcomputers.

While the commitment to purchasing technology resources continues, the commitment to adequate implementation resources to support it has not kept pace. Some point to the birth and evolution of the information center as a response to the need for better implementation and user support. In our opinion, many information centers operate as delivery systems for hardware and software solutions. They are not, in mission or function, given the role of corporate change agent for automation. As a result, they often operate with a woeful lack of understanding and commitment to the task. They also lack the time, money, people, and facilities needed to do the implementation job correctly.

The situation is not much better with dispersed information systems and PCs. Managers who supervise departments using these smaller, distributed systems often complain that they must find their own resources for education and training of their personnel. In most instances, this means the use of outside consultants and training companies. The result is that the staff receives very good training in the use of an application, but little support is offered after training when the employees return to the job. There is a woeful lack of computer user education. User reference materials and documentation are either poorly written or nonexistent. Often workers do not know whom to call with system problems. This type of implementation simply doesn't give the computer user all of the support needed to deal with the new way of working. The end result may be chaos and frustration. In every such case, there will be underutilization of the system.

Habit 9: Misplaced Assignments in Implementation

A good systems analyst or programmer does not automatically make a good documentation writer, computer trainer, or communicator. Yet there are countless instances in which programmers and systems analysts are expected to provide user documentation, training, and general support. To their credit, some have discovered that they have a natural knack for these tasks.

But no matter how well they manage these assignments, their talents and skills are being improperly used. They are computer professionals who are highly competent in the analysis, design, and coding of computer systems. Their traditional work assignments and pay scales reflect that fact. Assigning them to implementation tasks is an ineffective use of their talents. In addition, when they lack implementation skills, users are shortchanged. They do not receive the type of training, documentation, and basic support services they require.

One reason that organizations fall into this ineffective use of MIS staff is the belief that the end user needs technical assistance. This is not so. The end user needs practical assistance, including basic technical competence. However, information system users have a greater need for assistance from professionals skilled in adult education, training, and documentation rather than technical areas.

Habit 10: No Comprehensive Implementation Planning

Literature reflects the reality of life. For example, the literature about computer implementation problems focuses primarily on fragments of the problem and is mainly episodic in nature. The closest we have found to a comprehensive statement of the problem is an article about the Rand Corporation study (Mankin 1988) which recommends a process approach to implementation. While we concur with its conclusions, they cover only parts of the problem. To date we have found that those who observe societal and business difficulties have yet to portray the entire problem of implementing new technologies.

The views of those inside the organization are hardly any better. Management is now beginning to understand the breadth of the problems and needs in technology implementation. As a result, management is developing some initial understanding of the amount of planning that is needed to do effective technology implementations.

This book proposes a step-by-step process for technology implementations, including the critical elements of data gathering and planning. Through our experience and research, we have identified 28 steps in data gathering and 35 steps in planning. These important steps are included in each of the phases of the Technology Implementation Life Cycle™* as set forth in Chapters 5 and 6. There likely are others that we have not discovered. But no matter how many more there are, we know that effective implementation requires a highly structured and well-planned effort supported by complete and pertinent data.

There are three requirements for the effective implementation of information technology: (1) structure, (2) planning, and (3) data. The lack of structure in implementing new technologies is due to the lack of data and planning. The lack of planning grows out of faulty assumptions about the complicated nature of the implementation processes. Management has assumed for too long that implementing new technologies is a simple task requiring minimal efforts. The facts that emerge from past effective implementations prove that minimal efforts will not do. The complex nature of human needs requires a change in management's assumptions, habits, and performance when involved with IT implementations.

Continuing to focus on individual bad habits does not provide more than minimal improvement in implementations. The true need is for the development of a general management methodology for all technology implementations. Such a methodology can address all of the bad habits while managing the underlying implementation problems.

---

*Trademark application pending in the name of The MENTOR Group, 700 Ackerman Road, Suite 110, Columbus, Ohio 43202.

This book is predicated on the need for such a general management methodology. In fact, we believe that this book is much more about management, and its systems and processes, than it is about computers and information technologies.

Justification for a General Management Methodology

The 1980s might be called the "rediscovery of management" decade. From the weighty tomes of academia to the popular book *In Search of Excellence*, the emphasis has been on the rediscovery and reassertion of management principles that win. At the same time, this decade witnessed some of the most significant new applications of IT. Studies of these applications have also shown that technology can make winners. Thus two dominant assumptions have arisen about developing a winning organization (Table 1-6).

Table 1-6
Effectiveness in Organizations

1. The best technology wins in the long run.
2. The best management wins in the long run.

When these two assumptions are examined together, the distinct impression emerges that technology will emerge as the driving force. At present, this is often true. *The Electronic Sweatshop*, (Garson 1988), referenced earlier, points to the power of advancing technology to change how we work. It reveals how computer systems overturn management systems, converting white-collar professions into lower-grade clerical staff. At the same time, these systems drastically alter the power structures of even the most complex organizations. Part of technology's power to claim control over our work results from the different qualities of technical and management systems (Table 1-7).

Management is confronted with a continuing and increasingly difficult problem. The relationship between technical systems and human systems is one of constant impact. Management systems impact on the ability of technical systems to deliver their potential. Technical systems impact and undercut the potential development of

Table 1-7
Distinguishing Qualities of Technical and Management Systems

1. Technology advances regularly, by its own initiative, and in ever-increasing degree.
2. Management systems tend to be at rest, and change only under external pressure — most often a crisis.

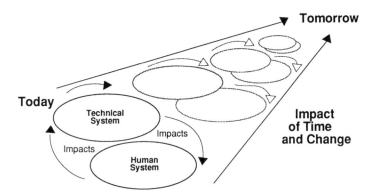

FIG. 1-1 A Flow Diagram on the Need for Impact Management

Impacts occur between technical systems and human systems, with good or bad results for an organization. Technical systems can overwhelm human systems because of their tendency to expand and develop continually.

human systems. We believe that a general management methodology can be developed to control these impacts. We call it Impact Management™*.

Figure 1.1 portrays the need, not the solution. It suggests that organizations will be confronted with two interacting systems, one technical the other human. The technical system is portrayed above the human one for two reasons, as stated in Table 1-8.

The human system is not always recognized as foundational, particularly in this age of the corporate raider. But there are those who understand the importance and greater value of all human aspects of an organization. The growing concern with our environment and ecology is a reflection of this value. It is an expression of an ethical approach to interrelating technical and human systems.

Ethics, in this case, must be supported with a model for action. That model must include the existence of technology, and it must be positioned in relation to human systems. We assert that an effective interaction between technical and human systems requires that the human system be foundational. The second element of this ethical stance must operate with the recognition that technical systems are by nature

Table 1-8
Assumptions of Impact Management

1. For an effective interaction the human system is viewed as foundational.
2. The technological system expands at a faster rate and "smothers" the human system.

*Trademark application pending in the name of The MENTOR Group, 700 Ackerman Road, Suite 110, Columbus, Ohio 43202.

more flexible and dynamic than human systems. Technical systems are more capable of change and can quickly materialize in new forms.

Management cannot control the relationship of technology and human systems until these two features of the model are accepted. Once accepted, management will be confronted with the reality that human systems must be developed to manage the impact of technology. Failing this, the human systems will fail. Only when human systems achieve some modifications in their behavior will they be empowered to use technology to enhance human endeavors and potential. The very power of technical systems forces human systems to adapt, change, and grow. The change in human systems must be centered in management systems and management methods. In Table 1-9, we have identified four basic principles of human systems operation which must be part of this modification of management methods.

Before proceeding further, we offer a word of encouragement for those readers who are technically oriented. Some of the skills needed to develop systems are remarkably similar, whether they are technical or human. But a word of caution is also necessary. The skills we propose will require some people to develop new and dynamic views of management. These views are not always found in organizations. Their acceptance and the development of new technology implementation skills will require a change in management style for many companies and many managers.

It is the contention of this book that such sweeping changes are needed. They are forced upon us by the technology revolution which is thrusting all organizations into the Information Age. The four principles noted in Table 1-9 provide an introduction to the change in management style that is needed for the effective implementation of all information systems.

Table 1-9
Impact Management Principles for Effective Systems Management

1. Proactive methods are preferred over reactive methods.
2. Integrated methods are preferred over fragmented methods.
3. Systems views are used to evaluate piecemeal issues.
4. Process management replaces problem solving.

It is of no small interest to note that the thesaurus in our word processing software contains the word "react" but not the word "proact." Proactive methods of management are anticipatory and future oriented. They allow the emergence of future problems through the establishment of management policies and procedures. They do not eliminate organizational problems. Proactive methods set up a systematic means for managing organizational problems with the least disruption of the enterprise's daily operation (Table 1-10).

A proactive style of technology management would have the technician seek out

Table 1-10
Impact Management

Principle 1 — Proactive methods are weighted over reactive methods.

users in order to understand their work and its requirements before users request assistance. At present most technicians are kept busy responding to users' requests, with little time to anticipate and plan for future needs. When future planning is done, it usually is designed around expected changes in the technology rather than expected needs of the human system. The problem with a reactive stance is that it is likely to do little more than patch new programs onto old ones.

Hari Notowidigdo (1987), vice president of information systems, Wendy's International, Inc., points up the problems created when computer programs are patched onto because of repeated user requests for changes and additions. He notes that these older, larger systems become increasingly difficult to change. Other information system managers have stated that they feel that some of these systems may collapse under their own weight or complexity. Programmers have indicated their concern about successive additions to older programs. They often wonder exactly what happens inside the machine each time they add a program.

It may be easier to establish a proactive stance in the world of the PC. Technical support for distributed or PC systems will lead to a more dynamic relationship between the computer professional and the computer user. The technical worker will be more intimately involved with the PC user and will not have a centralized MIS department to retreat to. But even in that circumstance, the temptation will be to react to users' inquiries, requests, and/or purchases rather than to assist in the design and support of human systems.

The reactive stance is more comfortable because that is the usual management style in most organizations. In general, technicians will follow the reigning management style. The solution will be found in the improvement of management's ability to manage its use of technology in a proactive manner. If management sets the style, others will follow.

Table 1-11
Impact Management

Principle 2 — Integrated methods are preferred over fragmented methods.

There are very few things in life that do not overlap with something else. This reality is experienced by all programmers, particularly when users come to them and ask, "Just add a little more to my system." The user will often state, "All I want it to do at this point is . . ." Imagine technicians trying to explain to an unschooled user that adding one small thing may change the way the whole application operates. At this point, the programmer knows that a fragmented approach doesn't work as simply as the user thinks it should (Table 1-11).

The use of integrated methods in technical systems and human systems also implies that some elements will not work unless they are made part of the whole. There are many separate problems in using technology, but there are very few isolated problems. We have listened repeatedly to the complaints of programmers about end user managers who want a "quick and easy" solution to a specific problem from a computer application. There generally is little understanding of the complexity of the programming solutions that are needed for the user's "simple" requests.

Human systems and management systems operate within the same rules and constraints as technical systems. It is just as disturbing to the human system when the technician presents a "simple computer solution" to a management problem. Too often these solutions do not account for the need for integration into a larger organizational or management framework. The managers of the human system will not always understand this fact. Or if it is spotted, they will not always be able to explain the need for integration.

One of the integrating factors in an organization is its culture. New components, whether technical or otherwise, must conform to the reigning culture of the organization. For example, a company may pride itself on informal communication between its executives and senior managers. It may foster breakfast meetings, encourage casual contacts, and generally rely on managers to seek out one another informally. The introduction of computerized forms of communication into this environment will create a significant challenge to the existing corporate culture. There will be a need to integrate the new style of communication into the larger pattern of organizational communication.

Table 1-12
Impact Management

Principle 3 — System views are used to evaluate piecemeal issues.

The University of Cincinnati has used a laudable approach to building working relationships between its computer science graduate students and those who use their services for graduate research. The noncomputer graduate students were required to take a tuition-free, noncredit course in programming. All at once, the problems of programming confronted the computer illiterate. For example, they learned that a piece of a program is often embedded in a larger program (Table 1-12).

The nontechnical graduate students did not learn this lesson easily. Typically, they struggled for days trying to overcome the built in logic of the computer. Finally, they gave in. They began by asking the proper questions about how the program functioned, how its needs were addressed, and how it must be structured in order to operate. This illustration is used to convince technical readers that they too must make a similar journey to understand the built-in logic of human systems.

The technician must be schooled in the dynamics of human systems and the human enterprise we call business. For that reason, Chapters 2, 3, and 4 of this book present models of human systems at the operational, tactical, and strategic levels of business. They are designed to give the technician and the manager some common understanding of how technology can enhance and advance the development of human systems and business.

"Process management" is a methodology which examines the entire work process before addressing any problems that are a part of that process. "Problem solving" is a methodology that resolves issues and problems as they arise. Both methods are needed in business. The only real issue is to know when to use which one (Table 1-13).

Table 1-13
Impact Management

Principle 4 — Process management replaces problem solving.

When computer user managers come to the systems analyst, they may come for one of two reasons. They may ask for a "quick fix." In this instance, they are seeking problem solving. Alternatively, they may request the redesign of a process. In this instance, they are asking for process management. Skilled systems analysts will be adept at recognizing when one or the other method is appropriate.

Unfortunately, too many managers constantly ask for problem-solving approaches. If pressed on this issue, they will claim a lack of time to do the background work. They will claim that "all they need" is a solution to a specific problem. Systems analysts and programmers say that these managers never stop coming back with just one more problem. Problems, and the need for problem solving, will never disappear. But when it comes to computer implementations, there is a better way.

Process management has a built-in method for managing problems. It is a problem-controlling method. Problem control requires that enough time be spent examining a process to (1) understand it as a system and a subsystem, (2) know all the elements of the process, and (3) set controls for all process elements.

Effective process management always includes problem-controlling methods. This does not eliminate the occurrence of problems. It minimizes their impact on the organization. It aids an organization in achieving the future it has set for itself. It assists the organization in achieving its goals. It is a management method used by today's effective and successful organizations.

Chapter 7 presents a process model for technology implementation and use within an organization's human system. During the writing of this book, it was suggested to us that Chapter 7 should be presented earlier. We feel that it should remain in its present location for the sake of readers who need to look at all the parts of the problem before they examine the overall model. Those readers who prefer to start with the grand design and then move through its parts should read Chapter 7 following this one. All readers should first study the plan of the book, as described below.

The Plan of the Book

Chapter 1 has provided a general overview of the problems of computer implementation. Chapters 2, 3, and 4 cover, in respective order, the problems and solutions for technology implementation at the operational, tactical, and strategic levels. Chapters 5 and 6 describe and detail the Technology Implementation Life Cycle. Chapter 7 demonstrates the need for an incremental and cyclical process for technology implementation. Chapter 8 addresses basic attitudes and future projections required for the sound and effective use of the technology.

Why Do I Have to Change the Way I Do My Job?

If you want to make enemies, try to change something.

—Woodrow Wilson

From the top of the organization to the bottom, the social and emotional needs of all employees are very similar. In the next three chapters we will focus on the three needs that are most adversely affected by the radical changes automation brings: (1) the need for achievement or recognition, (2) the need for stability or consistency, and (3) the need for ownership or participation. Each of these needs can be linked to its respective level of traditional management (Table 2-1).

Although these needs existed before the computer and other forms of automation, each of them has been greatly affected by the computer and assorted information

Table 2-1

Linking Human Needs to Management Levels

1. The need for feedback through achievement: relates to operational management.
2. The need for assurance through consistency: relates to tactical management.
3. The need for ownership through inclusion: relates to strategic management.

technologies. We begin this chapter by discussing the need for feedback through achievement. Chapter 3 addresses middle management's role in the tactical support of the organization, specifically as the guardian of organizational consistency. Chapter 4 deals with the role of strategic management in maintaining a sense of worker ownership as automation proceeds. Each of these chapters describes how automation can "disempower" the worker and what specific action steps are needed. Chapters 5 and 6 tie all of these action steps into a common plan called the Technology Implementation Life Cycle.

Area 1: Operational Management

The most commonly used definitions of operational management relate it to (1) the daily tasks required for an organization to operate and (2) a method of monitoring employee activities and measuring their work results. These definitions commonly apply to both line workers and support staff. In reality, all employees perform operational tasks. Operational duties are what quickly come to mind when people are asked what they do at work. The answer they give usually describes their day-to-day work activities (Table 2-2).

This tendency illustrates how strongly employees identify themselves with their daily tasks. It shows how people perceive themselves in relation to their work. This perception can be one of the most powerful motivators in managing others. The underlying dynamics of effective operational management are based on understanding how strongly the individual worker's sense of personal worth is identified with a specific job or task. Effective managers recognize that workers feel a sense of pride in their work. They seek to reinforce inner motivations by using the worker's sense of identification with assigned tasks.

That sense of identification can produce negative or positive results, depending on its nature. Boring, unchallenging, and repetitive duties may cause burnout. The job is perceived as meaningless, which in turn creates a sense of personal meaninglessness. Given more challenging assignments, the worker is often reinvigorated and assumes a much more positive attitude toward work in general and toward the organization in particular.

The hidden truth is that people derive a great measure of their sense of personal worth from their work—especially work they count as significant. Work is, for many, the most significant part of their self worth. If their work becomes meaningless, their sense of worth lessens. If their work is disrupted, they turn to alternative sources of worth. When their work is changed, they resist until they are able to develop

Table 2-2
Operational Management
The process by which organizations monitor and measure the daily tasks and activities of their employees.

competence in new work. Then they can regain their sense of value and worth based on their new labor.

Automation can drastically alter work. The perception that technology can do this makes it threatening. The employee's experience with automation can be structured to allay this perception or to reinforce it. As an example, computers have been used to downgrade work to clerical and routine functions, but it was not the computers that made the decision to do so. It was a management decision that created the downgrading.

Likewise, management can make decisions to enhance the quality and nature of human endeavors. Technology doesn't make these choices. Management does. When management chooses to either downgrade or enhance work, it also chooses employee reactions to automation. Consider the case of a secretary who is resentful about the installation of a word processor. When this happens, it is her management who must first ask themselves: "What decisions did we make about word processors that caused this person's negative reaction?"

The Principle: Feedback Through Achievement

When an employee's duties are meaningful, the job becomes a motivator for effective and efficient work because it is seen as a source of worker self worth. Therefore, workers will seek feedback on how well they are performing (Table 2-3). They will seek assurances that their performance has been an achievement. They will seek guarantees that they are productive members of the enterprise. They will want to know that their contribution counts for something. And finally, they will want to know that the organization is succeeding. Knowing that the organization is successful amplifies the worth of their personal labors. It assures employees of a continued, valued role in the organization.

One of automation's difficulties is its ability to accidentally invert the situation. If the worker "serves" the machine, then it is the machine that is productive and successful, denying the worker this self perception. If the machine "serves" the worker, then it will enhance the worker's perceptions of self worth.

A worker will constantly seek assurance. These assurances are sought during the daily performance of work. Guarantees come in the form of reactions and supportive comments from fellow workers and superiors. Workers can tolerate a temporary decline in their work performance, such as occurs during a brief illness. In this case,

Table 2-3
Assurance Seeking

1. Have I achieved, according to some standard of performance?
2. Have I contributed? Did my effort add anything to the organization?
3. Is the organization succeeding? Will I have a place to continue my efforts and to receive recognition?

they expect or anticipate that returning to work also means returning to their previous level of performance.

However, a long-term reduction in performance seriously affects workers' self-perception. It challenges their perception of being a valued performer. It causes them to question whether they are making a strong contribution to the organization. And it causes them to wonder if they have a permanent place with the organization. Automation can raise the same apprehensions in the mind of the employee who is unfamiliar with newly automated work. A poorly planned and executed technology implementation will increase the worker's perception of threat. The following implementation episodes illustrate this point.

Example 1:   A major teaching and research hospital installed a computerized outpatient clinic scheduling system with the expectation that all clinic physicians would use the system to enter, view, and add to patient medical records, including entering patient prescriptions and laboratory tests. However, the physicians lacked the necessary typing skills to use the system. They viewed the computer work as clerical work. The system was never fully used by the doctors. Ultimately, major portions of this application designed for physician use were removed from the hospital's on-line computer system.

Example 2:   Some state government clerical workers were sent to PC training classes, although they had no familiarity with a standard typewriter keyboard or typing skills. At last report, these employees had yet to use the PCs installed in their work areas. Their perceptions of computerization caused strong anxieties about their value to the agency. After all, if they were valued employees, they would have been trained in keyboard use first, wouldn't they? To some it felt like a trap designed to flunk them in PC use so that they could be fired.

Example 3:   An on-line inventory control system was implemented in a midwestern farm equipment manufacturing company. The inventory control personnel who were expected to use the new system had little or no knowledge of basic computer terms and terminal operation. Before system implementation, they received no computer education and only minimal training. As a result, the inventory control system was not fully operational for 10 months beyond the original startup date. The cost of the system skyrocketed from $250,000 to $1,000,000. When the deadline delay and cost overruns were analyzed, management was shocked to discover that the cause was a failure to educate and train the system users. The users were frustrated and angry because they did not receive proper support during the system's installation. They did not understand what management expected of them, nor did they know how to relate to the company's MIS staff, who designed and implemented the system.

These scenarios represented a threat to computer users. They understood their old system of work. They knew how to do their job and what to produce. What they did not understood was the new system of work. It conflicted with their prevailing work style. The computer system made them feel awkward rather than skilled, ignorant rather than knowledgeable, incompetent rather than productive.

The typical management response has been that the workers will get used to the new system and will eventually learn how to use it. Such a response assumes that workers will ultimately accept and productively use the new technology. Unfortunately, this prediction is valid. Most workers will strive valiantly to overcome the obstacles that make it hard for them to get their work done. But it is improper to use this reality to avoid management's responsibility in supporting their workers during technology implementations.

It is management's responsibility to return the workers to their former productivity levels or to move them to the higher performance levels that are expected from them as they use a technology. The fact that employees do this alone doesn't mean that they *must* do it alone. Additionally, doing it alone is not the most efficient use of their time and talents. The responsibility for the transfer of new technology to the worker rests with senior management. It is they who should make sure that every technology implementation is handled as a cooperative effort between the technical staff and the user personnel.

Another reason why management is vital to the technology implementation process is that this is always a time of risk for an organization. When management fails to manage this transition, the risks associated with technology implementation are increased. Expecting workers to "do it for themselves" creates distance between the users of the technology and their firm at the very time when feelings of closeness and support are most needed. The bad taste of an unsupported or ill-supported implementation can linger for years, impacting negatively on the general productivity and profitability of the company. Unfortunately, most workers fail to recognize that the lack of support is management's failing. They usually fault the MIS professionals. This costs MIS personnel their credibility, which often causes their image and reputation to decline rapidly. Then they wonder why they suffer the bad rap.

Much of this problem is puzzling to the computer professional. Conversations with them reveal many mixed feelings on this subject. They feel a sense of betrayal because they have attained a high degree of proficiency in their work. Many profess outrage that nontechnical employees fail to concede to their technical skills and insights. They feel that they have done their job well and should not suffer the blame for the failure of others to fully utilize a new technology.

MIS workers are frustrated because they are aware, more than most, of the potential that automation offers to their company. They cannot understand the reluctance or inability of some employees to use new systems to become more proficient in their work. For some technicians, the matter is settled once they see or experience the efficiencies automation offers. For example, they know that computers provide employees with a better tool. Their personal feelings about computerization are often based on what they themselves can do with computers rather than on what they can do to assist the nontechnical personnel in dealing with computerization. MIS professionals often do not understand that all people cannot respond to computers as easily and competently as they can.

Some computer professionals may begin to feel a sense of detachment from their company because they relate more easily to the machine than to the people and the business. Ultimately this feeling grieves many of them because they are dedicated to their company, their profession, and their own high standards of professional performance. We have seen them gathering together, apart from other employees, in their own inner circle. There they complain about the company, about its lack of understanding and use of technology, and about the quality of their working relationships with users. Management has failed to integrate them and their technology into the organization. And that is the ultimate source of their grief.

Nontechnical Causes of the Bad Rap

The path out of this problem does not lie in introspection. It is found in a reconsideration of the technology user's predicament. If the technician brings feelings and attitudes to the problems of automation, so also does the user. We have identified five factors that contribute to human reactions to technology implementations. Some of these have to do with feelings and perceptions. Others have to do with the presence or absence of skills in managing change. All of them influence the effectiveness with which people adjust to a new technology.

Awareness

A study of nurses in a New York State medical center found that their negative attitudes toward computers were largely attributed to four reactions. Some nurses had had bad negative personal experiences with computer processing of magazine subscriptions, bank accounts, and department store bills. Others had read newspaper and magazine articles and cartoons which focused on the problems resulting from computerization. A third group recalled negative portrayals of computer use in radio and television programs and movies. Finally, many shared a lack of awareness of the great range of benefits of computerization, from space flight to worldwide airline and hotel reservation systems.

Personal Differences in Adaptability to Change

In a competition-driven work environment, most employees concede that change is inevitable and that new technology is ultimately part of their future. However, behavioral studies sponsored by the Carlson Learning Company, Minneapolis, Minnesota, have also shown that each of us develops a style of behavior that influences how we perceive and respond to change. Some of us will be off and running in support of any change. Others will require a more slow and steady pace to accept and adapt to change. Still others will make their final adjustment only after they have acquired great skill and competence in the use of a technology. And some will try to ignore the technology in favor of direct contact with people.

We have found the Personal Profile System™ (PPS) of the Performax Corporation in Minneapolis a very helpful instrument for measuring user responses to technology. Personality instruments, such as the PPS and the Myers-Briggs Type Indicator™, can provide technicians with insights into logical and sensible reasons why nontechnicians react as they do. They also provide technology users with explanations of their own behavior which may puzzle them as much as the technician. Such instruments also provide suggestions on how they can use their personality strengths to support the process of technology implementation. Sources of information on this subject are provided in Appendix C, "Personality, Behavior, and Change."

Differences in Corporate Culture

In their book *Corporate Cultures, the Rites and Rituals of Corporate Life*, Terrence Deal and Allan Kennedy (1982) identified four cultures: tough guy/macho, work hard/play hard, bet-your-company, and process. They are similar to four basic human personalities, each with a different tolerance of or approach to change. Each has different methods for adapting to technology. Indeed, each is likely to use a different form or degree of information technology. Our experience with computer installations confirms that, for greatest effectiveness, the implementation process must match the corporate culture and its manner of reacting to information technology.

Different Experiences with Changing Technologies

The past experiences of employees are reflected in their reactions to a pending change. Those who have had positive experiences will see nothing but good coming from it. Others who have had negative experiences will project their worst fears onto the change. The result is a feeling-based, emotional discussion that makes a rational consideration of a proposed technological change impossible.

The problem is heightened when technology professionals are locked into positive perceptions while users are locked into negative perceptions and feelings. Neither, at this point, is really involved in listening to the facts presented by the other. Nor are they capable of looking at the data needed to resolve the issues blocking an effective implementation. Some intervening force is needed. An outside consultant can facilitate new perceptions among technicians. However, a long-range solution requires the development of an organizationally supported process of technology implementation.

An effective process builds confidence between technicians, users, and management as it proceeds. It is one of the key recommendations of this book.

Differences in the Management of Change

A plethora of books have been published on the management of change. What is intriguing is the number of them related to computer change, to change toward information-based management, and to the need for a change-oriented culture in American business. But there is a tendency to talk about change in the generic sense, as if every change is comparable in impact to every other change. This is simply not true.

There is a need to recognize that we will not manage change effectively until management has a scale for measuring its impact. Once measured, management will need an explicit, detailed process of change management which leads the organization to normalization once the change is completed. One area of change which is in sore need of analysis is technology implementation, the subject of this book. That is why Chapter 7 presents a process model for the introduction and management of change in the implementation of technical systems.

Developing Technology Implementations at the Operational Level

In operational management, the focus is kept on the employees and their need for a sense of personal worth and importance to the organization. Companies which serve this need also serve their own interests for productivity and long-term survival. This emphasis is particularly crucial in planning technology implementations. These employee needs are served when three general areas of emphasis are part of operational management (Table 2-4).

Operational Emphases Which Serve Technology Implementation (Table 2-4)

Employee Skill Development

In his book *Organizational Development*, organizational consultant and author Karl Albrecht (1983) points out that one indicator of a healthy business is the ability of its

Table 2-4
Operational Emphases Which Serve Technology Implementation

1. Employee skill development
   a. Profiling the worker
   b. Training the worker
   c. Educating the worker
   d. Evolution of employee skills
2. Human systems prioritized over technical systems
   a. Human design
   b. Education
   c. Documentation
   d. Human communications
3. Support the employee in charge of the work

members to see opportunities for their advancement. Our own experience confirms this conclusion. Workers maintain higher levels of productivity when their managers support them in their desire for self improvement and advancement. We have identified four areas where user skill development is critical to technology implementation and use: (1) profiling the employee, (2) training, (3) adult education, and (4) skills evolution.

Profiling the Employee

Increased use of information technologies has heightened the need for a comprehensive implementation needs analysis. The emergence of the PC has accelerated this need. PCs have caused the drive for automation to shift from the technician to the nontechnical computer user. The overall result is the migration of the technology throughout the organization. All employees become potential technology users.

Since all are potential users, it is to the organization's advantage to profile all employees. A "profile" is a data-based analysis which provides detailed information. The profile format we recommend is multidimensional. This means that management takes a look at the employee from more than one vantage point. For the purposes of technology implementation, we recommend three dimensions (Table 2-5). Once these multi-dimensional data are gathered, user profiles can be compiled. The data from these profiles can be used to assist in information technology selection, development, and implementation.

Table 2-5
Dimensions of the Employee Profile

1. Hierarchical dimension
2. Functional dimension
3. Computer knowledge dimension

Dimensions of the Employee Profile (Table 2-5)

Hierarchical Dimension

The first dimension of employee profiling determines where each employee belongs in the organization's hierarchy. Table 2-6 shows six possible levels. There may be more or fewer levels in any organization.

Senior management represents the highest level of an organization, encompassing corporate chief executive officers (CEOs) and governmental directors. In some enterprises there may even be a need to profile the corporate board of directors. How far up or down the hierarchy people are profiled is determined by the organization's expectations concerning the use of information technologies.

Functional Dimension

The second dimension of profiling is based on a firm's functional areas. For example, a manufacturing company's functional dimensions might include the ones listed in Table 2-7.

Table 2-6

Hierarchical Levels for the Profile: An Example

Senior management
Middle management
Departmental supervisors
Production staff
Technical/professional
Administrative/clerical

Table 2-7

Functional Levels for the Profile: Manufacturing

Operations
Administraive support (i.e., finance, personnel)
Manufacturing
Marketing and sales
Distribution

Table 2-8

Functional Levels for the Profile: Financial

Personal banking services
Commercial loans and operations
Home mortgages
Business and other mortgages
Assets and investments
Operations (i.e., fiscal transactions)
General management/operations
Branch administration

For a financial institution the functional elements might include the areas listed in Table 2-8.

These tables are intended to be illustrative, not comprehensive. Each company must examine its own structures to determine the dimensions of their hierarchy and function.

Technology Knowledge Dimension

Having created a matrix which identifies each employee according to hierarchy and functions, a third dimension, technology literacy and competence, is added. This dimension provides data concerning an employee's level of skill in using information technology. Each profile must contain enough information so that an effective plan for technology implementation can be developed. The rapid advance in PC use has only increased the range of data available and required. These data should move in a logical sequence, from the simplest to the most complex. Knowing if computer users can type is an example of simple data. Learning how sophisticated they are in participating in the applications development process is an example of more complex information. The example of technology knowledge given in Table 2-9 is based on computer technology.

These data should be developed according to topics. For example, does the employee have experience in specific software applications (Table 2-10)?

There should also be experiential data which show the level of competence in computer use (Table 2-11). This information is vital if an organization intends to support computer user skill development.

Data gathering of this type does have its risks. There is the risk of gathering too

Table 2-9
Basic Computer Knowledge

Skilled in keyboard use (e.g., typewriter)
Resistance to computer use
Understands basic computer terminology
Understands computer hardware operation
Experienced in software applications
Experienced in applications development

Table 2-10
Topical Knowledge About Software Applications

Word processing
Database
Accounting and spreadsheet
Desktop publishing
Decision support
Financial
Personnel and human resource development
Engineering and science
Statistical

Table 2-11

Experiential Profile on Computer Use

Proficiency level	For example, how much of a specific software application has the worker mastered?
Productivity level	Once started on a specific computer task, how productive is the person in a given time period?
Efficiency level	How well can the person use all functions mastered in a given software application, moving from one task to another with ease?
Effectiveness level	How well can the person choose between options in mastered software applications?
Attitudinal level	Given past experiences with computers, how positive is the person's attitude toward present and future performance?

much and being consumed by the data-gathering task. There is the risk of doing too little, which is characteristic of most organizations. There is the risk of not being permitted to gather such data. This risk is the result of management's reaction. In order to avoid it, those in charge of profiling employees must impress senior management with the strategic importance and value of these data. And lastly, permission to gather data of this type may be denied by users. In order to avoid this difficulty, the gathering of data must be viewed by employees as being reasonably free of any personal risk.

The strategic-minded executive is more likely to authorize data gathering when it is clearly connected to the technology training function. The employee is more likely to support data gathering when it is clearly connected to the company's support of individual self-development, advancement, and security. For both the executive and the employee, there must be some payoff before data gathering is considered reasonable and proper. The most logical payoff is to connect data gathering to the results of training or other technology implementation steps. In other words, having a profile of employees must make observable differences in the performance of the organization and the worker.

Employee Skill Development (Continued)

Training the Employee

We define technology training as "instruction on how to operate a technological system to accomplish work-related tasks."

The definition can be examined according to its parts. "How to operate" means that technology training is task oriented. The intent is a change in worker behavior. It is not focused on creating user understanding, though it will be shown later that understanding is also important. "To accomplish work-related tasks" reveals that technology training is technology and application specific. For example, an employee can be trained to use a PC (the technology) and a spreadsheet software (the application).

Technology training is intended to be functional because it enhances or supports people's work. Training is the "how" of computerization, i.e., building a user's skill by showing the person how to use a system. It is not the "why" of technology, which is education. It is education that provides an orientation to or an understanding of technology terms and concepts.

Developing technology training within this functional focus provides support for bottom-line issues that concern management and employees. Both have survival, security, and participatory needs. Management sees these as the organization's needs. The employee sees them as human needs. A merging of their perceptions should be the ultimate goal of all corporate training. This can be achieved through attention to five items when planning training:

1. Recognize that user awkwardness with the new technology and fear and suspicion of it are significant obstacles to effective training. These will be overcome through knowledge and experience. They also require sufficient time for user comfort and acceptance to develop. Such human reactions cannot be changed in a hasty manner.

2. Technology training must be planned with the dominant culture of the organization and/or user work group in mind. Individual employees tend to adapt their work style to the primary culture of the workplace. Training must undergo a similar adaptation.

3. Technology training must be flexible. It must match learners' profiles. This may mean grouping learners according to certain characteristics, or it may mean developing lesson plans with sufficient flexibility to accommodate learner groups with various levels of computer knowledge. Attention should also be given to the personal development paths that individuals can follow to increase their skills and their value to the company.

4. Technology training must be based on specific standards and statements of expected terminal behavior. There must be a written statement of what the user will do with the technology upon completion of each training course. This end behavior should be supported by a clear understanding of the ongoing technical support that is available once the trained employee has returned to the job.

5. Written performance standards should be provided once sufficient time has been allowed for the transition from training to technology use. These standards spell out the criteria which will be used to evaluate the users of the technology. They should also inform the users as to when their evaluation will occur, how they will receive feedback, and what type of assistance will be provided during their first uses of the technology. Evaluation is greatly aided if all users are informed on how performance evaluation supports them in their personal development and advancement.

Two points need to be stressed about technology training. First, such training must be evaluated by a performance or productivity standard that is mutually valued by the organization and the employee. Second, training must be only one of several strategies used to bring about exemplary performance in technology users. Other techniques must also be used to cause higher levels of user performance and productivity. For a comprehensive review of this subject, the reader is referred to one of the most detailed and seminal books on this subject, *Human Competence, Engineering Worthy Performance*, by noted performance and instruction expert Thomas F. Gilbert (1978).

Gilbert stresses the negative effects of always falling back on training as the solution to productivity problems. Providing better performance expectations, setting clearer standards for performance, providing regular performance feedback, and providing on-the-job aids are equally effective tools. In many situations, these alternatives are to be preferred because they provide stronger reinforcement for the preferred outcome.

These alternatives to training also yield positive reinforcement of the worker's self-image and worth. They place the responsibility for change more squarely on the shoulders of the workers. Thus, any improvement in their work habits and performance contributes to their sense of personal capability. But these alternative methods, like technology training, need to be managed and guided as workers are transitioned to new technology.

Educating the Employee

Technology training should be measured according to specific outcomes which have been stipulated in advance. Education, on the other hand, is not as susceptible to measurement, and its outcomes are rarely predictable. Adult education is even less predictable. Yet a great deal is known about the impact of adult education on organizations. Organizations that suppress employee adult education become sterile in their imaginations, inbred in their thinking, and phlegmatic in their behaviors. Firms that encourage adult education among their employees foster the abilities and spirit that have recently been labeled "intrapreneurship."

An intrapreneur is one who works within the corporation to foster and use his or her creative ideas for the sake of the enterprise. It is someone who is personally growing and seeking to express the results of that growth through the company. Both the organization and the individual benefit in the process. This idea is nothing but a modernization of Douglas MacGregor's Theory X and Theory Y concepts. In his classic work *The Human Side of Enterprise*, MacGregor (1960) overthrew the old negative idea that workers needed to be driven to achievement. Instead he asserted that work is a natural part of their lives. He believed that employees have a high degree of imagination, ingenuity, and creativity. Companies that develop this spirit among their employees demonstrate, through corporate actions, that they value self-growth among their employees.

One difficulty management needs to overcome is their own attitude about employee education. Most of our educational experiences have been more akin to pedagogy, child education, than to andragogy, adult education. Adult education authority Malcolm S. Knowles (1973), with the Department of Adult and Community College Education at North Carolina State University, is expert at identifying the differences between pedagogy and andragogy. We have extracted six characteristic assumptions about adult education from the many concepts he has used in describing it. These are followed by six forms of behavior that management should exhibit in order to communicate its support of employee adult education.

Six Assumptions About Adult Education

1. It is built on self-direction. The learner is in charge, not the organization. It is assumed that the learner will make all the decisions about what he or she will learn or study.

2. It is built on past experiences. Adult education draws as much on experience with learning as it does on books, classroom lectures and discussions, and other factors.

3. It is life related. Adult learners seek to apply their new insights and understandings to real-life situations. They often do this at work.

4. It seeks to be task or problem centered. Adult learners love to develop skill and understanding by working on a specific project or problem associated with their work.

5. It is built on internal incentives. Adult learners acquire knowledge and skills because they want to do so, not because they are told to do so.

6. It thrives on curiosity. Adult learners are truly curious. They want to know why things work as they do and how they can make them work the way they wish.

Six Behaviors That Support Adult Education

Saying what it intends to do does not convince employees that management is sincere. Doing what it says it intends to do tells employees that management is serious about adult education. If organizations intend to follow through on the assumptions of adult education, the following must take place:

1. There will be opportunity and encouragement for formal and informal adult learning. In their formal training and educational programs, companies will conform to the principles of adult learning and not slip into pedagogy. They will use corporate communications to recognize and support the informal learning of their employees.

2. There will be mutual respect between the adult learner and others. The company's management and human resource development personnel will accept and respect the employees as learners. They will recognize their opinions and

knowledge regarding employee education and training needs, and will use these when developing an adult education curriculum.

3. There will be mutual negotiation and assessment. All adult learners will be permitted to negotiate their own learning process with management. An agreement will be reached on how this process will be evaluated, particularly on how the learning will benefit the organization.

4. There will be a project orientation to adult education. The employee/learner will be encouraged and supported in the use of work-related projects during times of formal or informal learning. The projects used will not take precedence over the learning process.

5. There will be a sequence to the learning process of each participant. The process will have its own natural order or logic. Each process will move at a pace matching the readiness of the adult to learn.

6. There will be opportunity for experimental activity. The education may be applied to a theory or to a real workplace problem. The organization will allow its resources to be used in reasonable support of experimentation in employee education.

A closing comment is appropriate. Management assumptions are communicated by management behavior. A management assertion of support for adult learning will lack credibility unless it is communicated by activities such as those noted above. This will be particularly true of technology implementation efforts because technology is often used as a replacement for humans. Corporate disclaimers will not convince employees that the new technology is intended to help them and not replace them. Only ongoing management support for and encouragement of adult education will convince workers that the company values them and their continuation with the firm.

This support for adult education will also prepare personnel in the event that new technology does replace workers. They can feel more secure because they are better qualified for transfer within the company or to another employer.

Employee Skill Development (Continued)

Evolution of Employee Skills

Every technological change causes the extinction of some previously valued skills and behaviors. When there was no intervention, the result was the devaluation of the person with the old skills and behaviors. Is it any surprise, then, that employees often rebel against technological change?

The Theory X management response is to insult the integrity of workers and challenge them to stop whining, get off their backsides, and modernize themselves. However, management attempts to stop the complaining will do as little as employee attempts to stop the technology. Both are retreats from reality. The reality is that people can and will change, but they need the cooperation and support of others to do so. The extent of the cooperation and support needed is increasing rapidly as organizations move to the distributed technology of the PC.

There is a general management principle that applies here: No problem was ever solved until someone assumed responsibility for dealing with it. Management must assume the responsibility for all areas of technology implementation, even though management did not cause all of its attendant problems. Many aspects of the problems are historically driven. Skills extinction is an example.

Skills extinction occurs because technology advances without anyone's approval. Mainframe computer advances occur because of computer vendor behavior or MIS recommendations. PC pressures come from every quarter. There has been a virtual explosion in the available software driving the expansion of this technology. The increasing affordability of PCs also drives its advancement. More and more, it appears that technology's growth will never be controlled. Management, however, must learn to manage technology's impact on its employees, who constitute the human system of the organization. Three things can be done to control that impact:

1. Skills evolution must replace skills extinction. All employees must be challenged to continually upgrade and develop those skills, attitudes, habits, behaviors, and qualities which enhance their own value to themselves and the enterprise. This advancement and development must be oriented toward the company's emerging technologies.

2. Skills evolution must include life planning. All employees must be encouraged to establish career and life goals which are compatible with their company goals. But support of employee skills evolution should also be reflected in the organization's strategic planning. This planning should include the development of a long-range vision and plan for the company's advancement and development. All employees should be able to see how they fit into that plan, especially as it relates to their evolving level of skills.

3. Skills evolution must include a clear opportunity and support for lifelong employment. This may appear to be a mimicking of Japanese employment practices. It is not. There are many laudable examples of American organizations that practice lifelong commitments to their employees. A sincere effort on the employee's part must lead to management assurances that this person is a valued and respected member of the company. All employees should believe that they will have a meaningful place in the organization for the remainder of their working years. It is one of the ironies of life that companies which make this commitment are likely to be the only ones that can keep it.

Operational Emphases Which Serve Technology Implementation (Table 2-4 Continued)

Human Systems Prioritized Over Technical Systems

In the past 20 years, many films and television shows have employed the plot gimmick of a computer which has taken over planets, space vehicles, or defense systems. What is intriguing about these tales are certain common characteristics. First, the computer was portrayed as having almost super-human qualities which allowed it to provide some distinct, unusual service to humans. Second, the computer almost always had excessive pride in itself and considered itself far superior to humans. And third, the computer inevitably lost its contest with humans exactly because it was not human. Perhaps the arts have something to teach us.

Unfortunately, the war between computer and human is not limited to the media. It is happening in corporate America every day. Some writers have even referred to it as the "war between the computer technician and the computer user." If a war does in fact exist, that is foolishness of the worst sort. If a war is to be avoided, two rules must be learned: (1) technology must be used and (2) technology must serve the human system. This is to say that the highest value must be placed on people, not on technology. We create the technology, not the technology us. For people to allow themselves to become servants of the technology is madness. For people not to use the technology is irresponsible. A responsible and sane use will involve a recasting of attitudes about four elements associated with computer implementation: human design, education, documentation, and human communications.

Priority Elements

Human Design. The term most commonly used to describe concern for human physiology is "ergonomics." We chose to use the term "human design" in order to avoid some of the narrow definitions applied to ergonomics. We define human design as all elements that contribute to the wellness of the human user of the technical system. In reference, for example, to the computer, this definition includes such factors as the following:

1. The computer hardware used by workers.
2. Computer software output, such as reports and screens.
3. Physical surroundings, including proper furniture, lighting, and ventilation of the computer work area.
4. Psychological and social environments.

In short, though worker wellness will support worker productivity, its focus is employee physical and psychological well-being.

The list of human design concerns grows daily. There is also another growing list: of absenteeism, of used sick days, of health damage claims, and of medical insurance settlements. Reports of these can be found in the daily newspapers, as well as in the professional computer magazines and journals.

Human design issues spring from the problems humans experience with use of the technology. These issues range from glaring computer monitor screens to poorly designed computer reports to offensive and glaring office lighting. Such poor human design can have a traumatic impact on the ability of any company to achieve full and effective use of its technology. Organizations cannot change the fact that technology may cause these problems. They can learn to identify and manage technology to minimize the impact of such problems, or they can await legislative action which will dictate how they will manage their organizations. Look at the present alternatives.

In a worst-case human design scenario, the employer and the employee stand in an adversarial relationship. The employer demands that the employee use the technology as is. The employee uses the force of law, or a union contract, to tell the boss what to do.

In a best-case human design scenario the employer and the employee stand in a collaborative relationship. Both recognize that the technology serves them and that no abuse of humans is to be permitted. While there are a number of ways that management and workers can collaborate, there is one criterion that is essential to an effective collaboration on this issue. Management must demonstrate, by its behavior, that decisions about technology will never be harmful to employee physiology and psychology. The employees must always feel secure when using technology or when reporting human design problems.

Education. There is a commonly repeated dialogue following many technology implementations. A new computer user, such as an insurance claims clerk, is sitting at a terminal working with a new system as a supervisor passes by. Turning to the supervisor, the worker asks, "why am I doing this?" or "where does this information come from?" or "where does this information go?" The typical response is, "don't worry, just do your job; you don't need to know why." If it is true that the worker does not need to know, then why was the question asked? The supervisor has missed the point. Good workers always need to know why. Part of what makes them good workers is their curiosity about the larger structure in which they work. Good workers want to understand what things are important and why they are important. This helps them to be good workers.

There are two important axioms concerning the importance of technology user education. These are presented in Table 2-12. For example, an aerospace firm with a history of laying off workers installed a computerized parts inventory and retrieval system. They failed to explain the system's purpose, which was to increase the efficiency of the present inventory personnel so that they could handle anticipated

Table 2-12
Axioms on Explaining a Technology Implementation

Axiom 1 -   When a technology implementation is not explained to workers, they will create their own explanation.

Axiom 2 -   When workers create their own explanation of implementation, it will always be the worst possible one.

new business and larger work loads. No layoffs or dismissals were planned. In the minds of the workers, one explanation predominated: The company planned to replace workers with the computer. As a result, half of the inventory department sought and found other employment before the new system was in operation. They did so because *their* explanation of the new system was that the company intended to lay off large numbers of existing staff through computerization. Naturally, those who left were the better employees.

Knowing why management decided to automate their work is important to most employees. That is why it is far better to introduce a new technology than it is to impose it. But it is also possible for a company to go beyond this minimally necessary step and assume a more collaborative posture.

The ultimate educational process would involve employees in the self-discovery of technology. Employees would be informed about the organization's future needs and would assist by suggesting ways to improve existing technologies. In this form of collaboration, the employee would become a partner of the organization in the decision to automate. There might be mixed responses to such an arrangement because not all employees would be equally equipped to participate. The advantage is that those who can would be given an opportunity, to the benefit of all. In addition, there would be a much greater sense of ownership of the technology by all.

The careful explanation of every technology advance and the encouragement of employee contributions to such advances convince employees that the human system has the highest priority. When the impetus and criteria for technological improvements come from the users, it is extremely easy to sell them on the new system. This is called "selling them what they're buying."

Documentation.   There are two problems with most documentation written for new technology users. The first occurs when it is not written. The second occurs when it is written. When it is not written, users are lost in their problems because they have no place to turn for help. When it is written, it is often done so poorly that users get lost trying to use it. Many computer users state that it takes longer to find the answer in computer documentation than it takes to read the answer once found. And that situation is based on the assumption that the answer is understandable to the average reader.

These problems arise because documentation is written as part of the development of a technical system rather than a human system. For this reason, technical documentation tends to be encyclopedic in style and content. This makes it highly instructive, often filled with technical jargon, and extremely complicated for the reader.

Fortunately, some improvement in user documentation has been seen in recent years. There has been a gradual shift away from explaining the technical system to describing the tasks that the user will perform with the system. No longer is everything about the system explained, as if all information about a system were important to the user. The newer trend is to explain what the user needs to know to use the system. There has also been a gradual shift from unwieldy technical jargon to ordinary English.

Much of this change in user documentation is due to the advent of the PC. Most PC software is sold directly to the computer user. Word soon gets around among PC purchasers when a software package is difficult to use, particularly when its documentation is burdensome or useless. As a result, the PC vendors have learned that they need to provide well-written, usable reference materials. Those who do not provide good documentation are more likely to lose sales, no matter how good their technology is.

The next improvement in user documentation will occur when it is seen as an on-the-job aid which assists in developing exemplary performers. In this next stage, documentation will be written in answer to the question "how can this documentation create the highest levels of employee productivity?" Viewed in this light, user documentation will never be adequate just because it explains the technical system or the human work system. It will be considered adequate when it supports desired levels of worker productivity.

It should be obvious that the development of this kind of documentation will be a team effort. It will require the combined skills of the technician, the computer user, the supervisor, and the competent writer. It will be a collaborative effort aimed at the highest return to the employee and the company.

Human Communications. The arrival of IT has created the need for special forms of organizational communication. This need arises for two reasons. First, there is a great disparity between different people in their understanding of technology. Second, there is an enormous range of available technology. In this situation, human communication is a priority. Sometimes it is the only answer to employee needs which are created by the automation of the workplace.

Two typical responses to the communication need are the computer hotline and the computer newsletter. The hotline allows the user to seek computer support by calling and talking to people expert in solving users' problems. A newsletter allows the MIS department to provide computer information to the user. However, more communication than this is often needed. The occasional visit of a computer programmer/analyst or trainer to the user's work area can be vital to a user's feeling of support.

Ultimately, the key to successful and effective communication lies not in a list of human communications activities but in the criteria used to structure these activities. The following six elements are found in effective human communications:

1. It is ongoing. Special communication may be needed in the course of an implementation, but there is also a need for continuous communication. This constant sharing encourages users to expand their use of technology.

2. It is interactive. There is a balance between information from technical staff to users and information from users back to technical staff.

3. It is assertive. Response mechanisms, such as hotlines, rely on the initiative of the user to seek information. The best human communication occurs when the technical staff takes the initiative, such as in the periodic visits to users mentioned above.

4. It uses a variety of tools. It employs open houses, user newsletters, system demonstrations, special new system installation events, bulletin boards, and a host of other options.

5. It is business oriented. It maintains an intentional focus on support of the employees during the use of technology, with the obvious intent to make the organization more effective, efficient, and productive.

6. It is well supported. Top management recognizes that such activities contribute to the company's profitability through a more effective use of technology. Recognizing this, the firm commits the necessary resources of skilled staff, time, and money to support the communication effort.

There is one additional criterion that is essential to human communications for improved technology use. Human communications should be evaluated by criteria that serve the organization's interests. This happens when the computer user receives effective help from MIS. It also occurs when MIS personnel are fully aware of the business needs served by a particular technology.

What is often overlooked is the fact that many MIS professionals are woefully ignorant about their organization's business. There is as much need to educate and train them about the business as there is to educate and train users about technology. Therefore, human communications efforts should focus as much on management and users communicating with technical staff, as it does on technical staff communicating with management and users.

It should be noted that this situation was not caused by the decisions of the technical staff. In most instances, it developed as a natural result of fragmentation of employee development. We live in the age of the specialists. When the organization expects technicians to specialize, it should expect that they will have gaps in their knowledge about the business. There is an axiom that is worth repeating: When the technology invades every area of the business, the technician must be schooled in all areas of the business.

A key issue is how an organization can educate its technical staff about the business. The most productive way to manage this is through a collaboration between technician and user during systems development. This requires that top management set the criteria for technology use and implementation. Two basic criteria must be established: that technology serve the product or service of the business and that it serve the organization's human system. Once these criteria are set, it will be possible for the technician and the end user to educate and train one another in the business of the organization. This task will take time and patience, but it cannot begin until the criteria are set.

Operational Emphases Which Serve Technology Implementation (Table 2-4 Continued)

Support the Person in Charge of the Work

Every worker reports directly to someone else. A supervisor has ultimate responsibility for the worker's performance. This is the administrative function—helping others to work. Any intrusion into the work functions of a business is also an intrusion into supervisory responsibility. Thus, when a worker's job is automated, both the worker and the worker's supervisor are affected. In fact, automation may intrude between the worker and the supervisor.

There have been cases in which offices have been automated with instructions given to the supervisors to whip their staff into shape. When this occurs, senior management has infringed on the authority and responsibility of the supervisor. There are real employee needs that must be met when automating, and the supervisors must be given authority and resources to meet them. Upper management may not always recognize the true nature of these human needs. Some of these needs are as follows: (1) to mourn the passing of the old way of work, (2) to adjust one's thinking to the reasons for the new way, (3) to use parallel systems operations until the new way

Table 2-13
The Functions of the Supervisor

1. To create and implement processes of work that can be repeatedly used
2. To create and implement systems that support these processes
3. To help people communicate better
4. To help people collaborate more effectively
5. To do all of the above:
   a. By being available for guidance
   b. And by providing necessary policies, procedures (which include operating manuals, e.g., documentation) and standards

is fully tested and normative, and (4) to adjust the work load to provide time for learning the new system. All of these needs occur in almost every technology implementation, and all of them influence the effectiveness of those who supervise. Most supervisors recognize and validate this list—particularly those who understand their function in the organization.

Table 2-13 provides a handy checklist for anticipating the potential impact of automation on the productivity of any employee. One can ask, what impact will technology have

On existing processes of work?

On existing systems that support the work?

On work-related communication between employees?

On work-related collaboration between employees?

On the supervisor's ability to provide guidance?

On the policies of the work group?

On the written procedures and manuals of the work group?

On the standards of the work group?

Hopefully, this list will cause some reflection concerning the complexities of technology implementations. It indicates the degree of intrusion and the capability for disruption of the supervisor-employee relationship. There has been a tacit recognition that systems design and programming is a complex task. Our purpose is to demonstrate that implementation is equally complex. Most organizations employ the traditional systems development life cycle to guide them in analysis, design, and programming. To us it seems vital that all organization also employ the Technology Implementation Life Cycle which starts where the systems development life cycle leaves off. We believe it is critical that the Technology Implementation Life Cycle complement and strengthen the efforts of the systems development process. That is the subject of Chapters 5 and 6.

A Closing Comment

A professor, expert in change management, was asked how one might move an ocean liner from one pier to an adjoining one. He said that one should not cut the ropes holding the ship to the first pier and let it drift across. It would move in an uncontrolled manner and could cause all sorts of damage. First, one should attach the ship by long ropes to the new pier, and then gradually loosen the old ropes and tighten the new ones. The ship will be transferred slowly and safely to its new moorage.

Effective technology implementation must be done in the same manner. Keep the employees secure in the old work style. Then run out the ropes and fasten them to the new way—the automated way. But don't move them too quickly. Gradually loosen their hold on the old system as you winch them across to the new one. Maintain their sense of security as you move them, recalling that they are secure in their performance and not in words of assurance. They will believe these words when they are safely and securely moved across to the new way, that is, when it has become the old way.

Take This System and Shove It

Mechanical means of communications have their important place; but they are only adjuncts. None of them can take the place of man-to-man contact.

—William G. Werner

American organizations are in the early stages of a massive IT invasion. This onslaught is leading to major workplace dislocations. We believe that the impact of this invasion will be felt most strongly by middle managers. The PC, robotics, artificial intelligence systems, and many other technologies are accelerating these dislocations beyond the control of individual workers. New and improved technologies coupled with skillful technicians are pushing automation onto the desks and into the hands of virtually all middle managers. Some welcome this change because it enhances their existing strengths and skills. Others delay their involvement as long as possible. But all middle managers are feeling the full force of advancing technology as it changes their work.

In the old guild system, where skilled craftsmen worked and controlled their work, no one imposed a new system of work upon them. They made changes, but over time. As individual knowledge and skills grew and as new methods and technologies became available, a guild member's work habits changed. This old-fashioned way of changing work practices was slower, yet was a more reasonable and satisfying way for the guild worker to deal with changing times and changing technology.

In the guild system, this was tactical management at work. The long-range goal was to promote the unity of the guild, to maintain its market position, and to cultivate a steady improvement in worker skills. The tactical goal was to do so with consistency. This meant maintaining an equilibrium among members and promoting economic vitality for all. And it worked for that time.

As American organizations are confronted with the rush to automation and the growth of information technologies, some equally effective tactical procedures are needed, procedures that do the following:

1. Provide consistency in work behaviors.

2. Maintain equilibrium between competing values in the workplace.

3. Support the vitality of the economic enterprise.

All of this is part of the task called "middle management." It is tactical management at work.

Area 2: Tactical Management

Of the three forms of management, tactical management is often the most difficult to define. It functions as a bridge between operational and strategic management. It is often thought of as the follow-up to strategic management. It is also considered the lead-in to operational management. But it lacks the physical feel of operational management and the intuitive feel of strategic management.

Tactical management takes a dream and defines how it might work. It moves corporate goals along until they become the realities of daily work life. It is often more complex and demanding than either strategic or operational management. It involves all of the complexities of planning. It seeks alternatives, evaluates each, and proposes solutions. It attempts to solve a variety of problems with one solution so that economy of effort can be achieved. Because it does all of this it can be defined as a planning function (Table 3-1).

In addition to its function of linking strategic to operational management, tactical management establishes and maintains the general systems of communication and coordination within an organization. In most companies, it is the middle managers who tie all of the functions of the enterprise together. Top executives may believe that they coordinate through their meetings, memos, and directives. Actually, they set the criteria for coordination. The daily work of coordination and collabora-

Table 3-1
Tactical Management: A Planning Definition

The process of rational planning by which organizations set out to achieve long-range goals.

tion is carried out by middle managers. From a personal perspective, this might be called "human relations in practice." From the organizational perspective, it is resource allocation and control (Table 3-2).

As organizations have grown in size, so has the number of functions assigned to middle management. This, in turn, has led to an increase in the number of middle managers. In many businesses, this has been the most rapidly expanding area of management. Some of this growth has been precipitated by external factors, which require careful record keeping and reports such as governmental regulation and labor contracts. Some has been brought about by span-of-control problems, where the number of employees under one middle manager have ballooned beyond one person's control.

As middle management grew in size and complexity it developed its own systems and processes for handling its work. The result has been the rise of "bureaucracy" within organizations, a word that causes many to recoil. The word "bureaucracy" often refers negatively to middle managers who are too controlling and slow, who obstruct progress, and who misunderstand everything.

The term "bureaucracy" can be used in a neutral sense, as we prefer to do here. It may be used to describe a work system created for the control of the organization's internal behaviors and external responses. Because middle management works to control internal behaviors and external responses we define it according to work systems functions (Table 3-3).

The definitions presented in Tables 3-1, 3-2, and 3-3 point to the three functions of middle management: (1) planning, (2) resource allocation, and (3) systems building and maintenance. These are ideal targets for IT. In actuality, they were automated in reverse order. Initially, it was easier to use large mainframe computers for the design and implementation of technical systems that would replace manual systems, such as payroll. There were many economies to be achieved in changing to computer systems. As the applications software developed in complexity and utility, it became possible to move into the other areas of middle management, into resource allocation, and finally into planning.

Economy, however, must not be the sole criterion by which the movement of IT into middle management is evaluated. There is, behind each of the tasks of middle

Table 3-2

Tactical Management: A Resource Control Definition

The process by which a balanced distribution of resources is achieved, through communication and coordination, and toward the achievement of organizational goals.

Table 3-3

Tactical Management: A Systems Definition

The system established for internal control of work-related behavior and for response to external environmental constraints.

management, a human dynamic that must be understood in order to make *effective* use of IT in middle management. As it performs its more practical and mundane tasks, middle management also serves many worker needs—principally the need for security.

The Principle: Assurance Through Consistency

One basic principle of human behavior is the need for security. This need can be satisfied in various ways. A stable marriage and home life provide security. The extended family and society in general also provide security if they are stable and significant parts of one's life. The workplace can be another key source of security. Knowing or sensing that the enterprise will survive and continue into the future is a part of each employee's sense of personal security.

Workers differ in terms of the indicators that convince them that their workplace is stable. Some perceive stability from general work conditions. Others need to see the big picture through company-released reports and official documents. Some are convinced if the paychecks keep coming on time.

These indicators must be present in a consistent manner if employees are to feel secure about their employment. Let there be one late payday, and questions will surface about the company's health. Let earnings drop in one quarter, and there can be talk of mismanagement and thoughts about the failing health of the enterprise. Even a change in management brought about by ordinary retirement can start the rumor mill.

Employee feelings of security are linked to the absence of negative indicators and the presence of positive signs of organizational health. No organization can eliminate all negative events or guarantee any positive ones. However, there can be a consistent effort to demonstrate organizational health. One of the unwritten responsibilities of middle management is the maintenance of this consistency. It is a responsibility that lies behind other assigned responsibilities. It is the task of always keeping things running as smoothly and effectively as possible (Table 3-4).

Those seeking security find more assurance in "business as usual" than they do in the midst of organizational change. Change of any kind replaces old, comfortable indicators of corporate health and security with new indicators. Since automation changes work modes, it can disrupt the sense of security that employees find in their jobs. The following incidents demonstrate this point. Note that the companies cited

Table 3-4
Definition: Assurance Through Consistency

Assurance through consistency occurs when the organization acts consistently to achieve its goals and to enforce its stated and assumed policies.

are not experiencing any real problems. However, their behaviors may lead their employees to perceive problems where none exist.

Example 1:   A computerized payroll system for a major publishing house was being designed and developed. At the same time, Harry who distributed the paychecks, was nearing retirement. He left the company just before the new payroll system printed the first set of employee paychecks. The new system was installed and running without the parallel operation of the old manual system to serve as a backup. When the new computer-printed paychecks were disbursed, it was discovered that Harry had left, taking with him one vital bit of information. Only he knew the employee preferences for paycheck distribution. For instance, some sales representatives preferred to receive their checks once a month, not every other week. During the computer analysis and design phase, no one had asked Harry about the old method of distributing paychecks.

Employee resentment and rebellion over the new computer system reigned until Harry was hired back as a highly paid consultant to advise on the redesign of the computerized payroll system.

Example 2:   An international publishing conglomerate bought a software company. The CEO of one of its publishing divisions had identified the prospective company and directed his financial staff to prepare an assessment of the purchase. Their report indicated that the purchase price would be recovered through software earnings within the first three years. The CEO's recommendation to purchase was forwarded to the conglomerate's chairman of the board.

The chairman also asked his financial staff to "work up the numbers" on the purchase. They stated that it would take 10 years to recover the purchase cost. The ensuing discussions between the CEO and the chairman revealed that the differences were caused by differences in the data that each had been using. Of course, both studies had been prepared on the PCs of their respective staffs. This situation is called "variations of the truth."

Example 3:   A programmer for a midwestern petrochemical company developed a computer program which would produce computer reports about required parts inventory levels for the company's exploration division. Visiting the user department to see how well they were getting along with the new program, he discovered that the secretary who was responsible for entering the data and generating the reports was also hand-calculating the information. Upon inquiring, he found that she was in fear of a computer error and was doing the hand calculations to "check the computer results." This situation is called "I believe what I can see."

These examples illustrate how automation can assist in damaging the employee's view of organizational consistency. The temptation is to view them as problems driven by automation. This is not the truth. The real driving force behind this kind of behavior is our marginal understanding of middle management and our equally poor ability to manage the changes that occur when we automate. And this is where we once again draw that important distinction: These illustrations are examples of business problems, not technology problems.

Most organizations do not know how to manage change when it affects middle management. Changes caused by IT are no exception. In fact, technology changes often exacerbate middle management problems because they bring these to the surface. Automation tends to point up the deficiencies of an organization in understanding its own system of middle management. Oddly enough, automation also offers ways of enhancing middle managers' potential. Hopefully, this tension caused by technology will lead to an examination of middle management functions. Hopefully, it will also cause the development of more effective and productive uses of technology by middle managers.

The key to the understanding of middle management will emerge through an examination of the consistency patterns which reveal how work gives assurances to workers.

A Pattern of Consistency

The concept of consistency is embedded in most, if not all, of the tasks of middle management. Four factors will be examined to show the *patterns of consistency* in middle management work (Table 3-5). Each is part of the process by which the organization's mission or purpose is translated into the daily operations of the organization. Each is part of the process by which middle management provides assurances about the health of the organization to its employees.

Planning: Consistency in the Use of All Available Data and Information

Mention the word "planning" and most people will think of behaviors that follow a decision rather than those that lead to a decision. This particular bias is most evident when American and Japanese decision makers get together. The typical Japanese approach is to explore all data and all options carefully and exhaustively. For them, this is planning. It happens before the decision. The typical American approach is to explore less and decide sooner. For them, planning occurs after the decision has been made. The correct approach to planning is closer to the Japanese model. Our concern is not to imitate them but to assert that planning must occur before decisions. And, planning must include the exploration of all options with the data and information needed to evaluate them.

A distinction must be made between data and information. Most rational thinkers would assert that decisions ought to made on the basis of data. In fact, they are

Table 3-5

Methods by Which Middle Management Gives Assurance of Consistency

1. Planning: Consistency in the use of all available sources of data and information.
2. Decision making: Consistency in the selection of preferred behaviors leading to goal achievement.
3 Structuring: Consistency in the use of middle management resources.
4 Continuity: Consistency through the presence and interpersonal activities of middle managers.

Table 3-6

Definition of Information

Information is data that has been given some meaning, value, or interpretation, often through the life experience of the interpreter.

not. Top executives indicate that many other things enter into their decisions. Many state that they use their intuition to settle on a final course of action. Truly effective decisions do not ignore the data associated with the issue, but they include other elements as well. Specifically, they include information (Table 3-6).

The process of decision making involves more than data because it is a very important act that must explore all options before settling on one course of action. To do this, it must have information. Information crosses over into human experience, perceptions, hunches, opinions, and a host of other non-data-based criteria. Information is data which have been weighted, evaluated, synthesized, or even "tweaked" and "schmoozed." Information is data raised to a higher level because they have been given value, meaning, or interpretation.

Karl teaches a course on statistics at a local university. A great deal of time is spent teaching the students that, by itself, no single number has any meaning, value, or interpretation. Increasing the volume of numbers does not give them meaning, value, or interpretation. Data have no meaning, value, or interpretation as long as they stand alone. They need a meaningful relationship to some other value, or criterion, or experience, or even some intuition. Comparing numbers to a criteria of importance to a person, a group, or an organization gives data these meanings, values, or interpretations. It converts them to useful information.

An excellent example is measuring a computer operator's key strokes. The data may reveal that a particular operator averages 200 key strokes a minute, but the question is: "In relation to what?" At this point, one begins to get involved in the "productivity debate." That debate focuses on what criteria to use to compare with measured key strokes. Some of the suggested criteria are the average of others, a chosen ideal number, the person's error rate, the hourly pay scale, and the potential profit to the company. The debate does not have to be settled to make the point. Put simply, numbers by themselves have no meaning, value, or interpretation. They must be compared to something.

Once compared, these numbers become something else called "information." Yet it is important that their origin in a group of data not become obscured by the transformation they have undergone. That would be unfortunate, for both data and information are needed for middle management functions. Data are needed to provide as broad a basis of facts as decisions require. Information is needed to provide as broad a basis of human experience and insight as decisions require. And this is the point at which the computer cannot help us—at least not yet.

There is a heresy abroad. It is that data are equivalent to information. It is supported by some computer professionals and vendors. It is also supported by some professional books and materials on data-based management. We do not believe that there is such a thing as data-based management, except possibly at the lowest levels of employee supervision. There is data-using management, management which seeks and gathers data in the course of its work. But the use of the data is built on previously developed information or on information that emerges as the data are examined. The value, meaning, and interpretation of the data are totally dependent on the human role in the analysis of data.

Yet the computer is often extolled because it creates, manages, and manipulates a large volume of numbers. Using this "logic of volume," an argument is made for the enhancement or even replacement of certain management functions with computer functions. Meetings are no longer to be held face-to-face; they are teleconferenced or conducted through electronic mail. Middle management decisions are no longer made by middle managers. They are preprogrammed and automatic. Inevitably when the technology is thrust forward in this manner, the argument is being made for the value of data over information. Having no other basis for giving the numbers meaning, the sheer volume of numbers is used. When this happens, we become players in the game called, "Having forgotten our original objectives, we redoubled our efforts."

There is no doubt that information technology can and will be used in middle management functions. In fact, the value of middle management functions can increase in worth and impact on the organization through supporting technology. But the technology cannot replace the process of middle management, for this is a human process. At present, it seems fair to say that IT cannot enter into human work, but that it can supplement and support it. This is presently true because the technology cannot participate in the process of converting data to information in the same way that a human can. We will make no prediction about how and when IT will develop this capability. Our goal at this time is simply to assert the need for humans to develop and use information.

The Recommendation

The resources of computers and other technologies can be integrated into the processes of middle management. They can be used for data gathering, for exploring alternatives, and for decision making. But their integration must be done cautiously so that the human skill of data interpretation can be developed and applied to new data. While we favor the use of IT we have seen situations where managers were literally flooded with computer-generated data, far in excess of their ability to use it.

Middle management will be more effective when the flow of data it manages comes at a steady rate and is capable of uncomplicated interpretation. Changes in data forms and sources make data interpretation much more difficult. These changes, in turn, make it more difficult for middle managers to advise and work with their subordinates. Change the data and middle management may flounder. It is bad enough when machines flounder, i.e., "the computer is down." It can be disastrous when managers flounder.

Decision Making: Consistency in the Selection of Preferred Behaviors Leading to Goal Achievement

When middle management expands and becomes a bureaucracy, it tends to muddy the waters of decision making. Everything seems to be slowed down in the hands of a bureaucracy. Objections are raised, issues are discussed repeatedly, and meetings are carried on interminably. Meanwhile, progressive managers are left wondering if this is an affliction caused by the personalities of middle management or by the bureaucratic nature of their work. In fact, it is neither. Rather, it is a logical behavior given middle managers' responsibilities. The fact that they operate dysfunctionally is due to their lack of skill in managing innovation.

Most organizations expect middle management to assume responsibility for making decisions, review the decisions of others, and approve and support those which maintain organizational cohesiveness. In this way, middle managers screen values which assist in keeping the organization focused on its basic tasks. In the book *In Search of Excellence* (Peters and Waterman 1982), this focus was identified as a success factor called "stick to the knitting." We identify it as one part of the pattern of consistency which assures employees that the organization is strong and healthy.

But healthy organizations also innovate. They develop. They change. And here, middle management can play a role. The decision to automate a manual system of work introduces a great deal of change into the workplace. A significant amount of creativity is used in the development of these automated systems. A large amount of resources is typically expended to make the new system the best one possible. But throughout all of this creativity, management has failed to note that the skill of implementing such systems is different from the skill needed to create them. The skill of implementation is called "innovation." It requires an entirely different set of abilities.

"Creativity" is the ability to develop an idea, process, procedure, or product that is entirely new or departs significantly from any previous one. "Innovation" is the ability to take a creative thought or product and put it to work in a new or existing way. People at all levels of an organization come up with creative ideas. But it is the middle managers who must implement them if they are to be used. In most companies, this means that middle managers must implement them in existing work systems. When there is a change in work systems, middle managers must have the analytical skills listed in Table 3-7.

The skill of innovation develops in an organization when two criteria are present: feed forward and creativity. Feed forward *is possible* when a company has a stated mission or purpose which drives its existence. Feed forward *happens* when this mission is linked to a constant drive for effectiveness. Effectiveness involves asking whether the organization has made the best possible choices in decision making. Middle managers flounder into bureaucracy because their work behaviors are measured solely by efficiency. Efficiency involves asking how well managers use the organization's resources in the behaviors it has chosen. Older, more habitual ways of

Table 3-7
Analytical Skills in Managing Innovation

1. To determine whether all of the old work will be done by the new system.
2. To determine whether all of the new work relationships can be developed to support the new system.
3. To determine whether the new system will be capable of integration with other, older systems, including the general system of the organization.
4. To study and evaluate any other problems of integration, consistency, or cohesiveness.

working will always appear more efficient to the middle manager than new behaviors which must be learned. However, when the issue of effectiveness is raised each worker must improve the old way or find the new or better way of working. When middle management is evaluated by effectiveness measures, it must learn how to innovate.

If innovation is a behavioral process, creativity is a thought process. Creativity can occur in isolation. Innovation requires people management skills. It requires the breadth and extent of interpersonal contacts typically found among middle managers. For that reason, middle managers can either accelerate or block the diffusion of innovation in an organization.

In our experience, there is an application here to technology implementation problems. For example, systems analysts and programmers are typically creative types. They are skilled at creating computer systems and applications of all kinds. But senior management makes a major mistake when it assigns responsibility for computer implementations to creative types. Implementation of computer systems is an innovative function and requires the skills of the innovative person such as the middle manager. Two examples come to mind.

Example 1:   Magazine and newspaper articles frequently talk about computer maintenance problems. These articles (Carroll 1988) have highlighted the hectic pace of applications development and the resulting nonintegration of software. Some of the computer professionals involved have described their systems as a "patchwork quilt" of programs. This is the kind of problem one expects when creativity is unchecked by standards of integration.

Example 2:   The other example is a citation from a recent issue of *Banking Systems and Equipment* magazine (August, 1988). Here Robert H. Spicer II writes about total branch architecture (TBA) and comments, "Of utmost importance to TBA is human engineering. The single most important concept of human engineering is consistency. This must extend from the manner in which the application interacts with the user to the hardware itself." Later he asks a rhetorical question: How does one react to the exponential complexity that will result from the interaction of in-house, distributed, and third-party applications? He points to the need for a computer infrastructure to support it.

Both of these examples point up a basic deficiency in the use of middle managers in the process of automation. Having developed information systems through creativity, we assume that the same skills can manage their implementation.

The Recommendation

This is the typical order in which American business operates: First, it introduces the technology; then it struggles to adapt the organization to the technology. In a March 1988 *Inc.* magazine article, computer authority Paul Strassman observes that the typical Japanese firm concentrates on changing its organization first. "They're continually innovating organizational forms." Then they seek the technology to support their new organization. They have learned that to harness the energy of the technology, one must first harness the energy of the organization. They employ the analytical skills needed to harness creativity and turn it into innovation—the ability to do those new tasks that have been created.

Structuring: Consistency in the Use of Middle Management Resources

Put an organizational resource into the hands of middle managers, and they will structure it into some kind of a system. They have to do it, because that is their function (Table 3-8).

Consistency in Structured Relationships. Middle managers accomplish a great deal of their work through structured relationships with other managers. Most of them have worked for a number of years to establish these relationships. Any change in work habits will influence the value and effectiveness of these relationships. Automation can change these relationships drastically. Sometimes this change is intentional, senior management having decided that new relationships will benefit the organization. Sometimes it is unintentional, the technology being allowed to set the pattern. Either way, it is disruptive of the old associations. It changes the power bases of the middle managers.

Some executives may say that this is good. They want to disrupt things. They want everyone to dance to a new tune. These executives must remember that whoever calls the tune must also pay the fiddler. The price the fiddler charges for this tune is very high. Change the power bases in an organization and you disrupt many things. The work and the work flow are altered. Workers will have identified their hopes for advancement with the old ways of working and will now find these avenues closed to them. The old relationships also presented an image of stability in the organization, a stability which some saw as strength.

This does not mean that the change is of little value and should be avoided. By all means, carry it out. But do not forget the true cost of such a change, a cost which all must pay. There will be a disruption of the "good old boys'" network and its informal communication pattern. Mentors will be disconnected from those they are developing. Channels of down-line support will be disrupted. New relationships of mutual support and encouragement will be required. In short, many hours of work time will be spent in developing a viable and supportive social system to replace the one that was disrupted.

Table 3-8
The Resources of Middle Managers
a. Structured relationships
b. Structured data and information
c. Structured analysis of data and information
d. Structured use of the manager's time
e. Structured expectations

Consistency in the Use of Structured Data or of Data Converted to Information. The work of middle management is also accomplished through the use of valuable information. Over the years, the data that middle managers have examined have been put through a process of being received, evaluated, and synthesized into a useful format. These data are now information, a tool for governing the processes of the company. In this form they can be communicated to senior executives, along with the individual and collective recommendations of middle managers.

When IT is introduced into this process, it generally speeds things up. It creates data faster than managers can convert them to information. This, in turn, affects the communications of middle managers to senior managers. Converting data to information and applying acquired wisdom to it takes time. The faster the technology works to create data the more this interpretation problem is worsened.

The technical response is to have the computer assist in the analysis of data. Now the technology not only creates the data, it also interprets them. Unfortunately, this causes an additional difficulty. Someone must set the criteria by which the computer will do such an analysis and even after the analysis, there will still be a need to apply the collective wisdom of middle managers to the computer's findings.

Ultimately, IT will be developed that can analyze their own data. They will be designed to function in the manner that human managers presently perform data analysis. There will be improvements in the technology. However, the starting place for developing this technology must be the present way middle managers analyze data through their manual systems and personal contacts. This means that organizations will first need to learn how to make the most effective use of their middle managers. They will need to learn exactly how middle managers convert data into information. Ultimately, it will be the human system that structures how the computer creates, analyzes, interprets, and uses its data. It must not happen the other way around.

Consistency in the Structured Analysis of Data and Information. A frequently overlooked feature of middle management is their need for shared experiences in the use of new data. Part of the ethic in healthy organizations is the team spirit which requires that managers share data and information in support of the business. Conversely, one of the initial impacts of the PC revolution was the creation of multiple data bases. The older process of communal data gathering and evaluation was sometimes set aside for a combative and one-upmanship display of knowledge.

This antagonistic use of data is not in the best interest of the company or its management. The use and value of individual insights and skills are increased when (1) all persons operate from common data, (2) there are common understandings about the definition and interpretation of the data, and (3) a spirit of cooperative truth seeking is present.

Consistency in the Structured Use of a Middle Manager's Time. Another difficulty arises when middle managers are excessively busy with new data. They lack the time to manage their subordinates effectively and to maintain the ongoing systems of the organization. The use of a manager's time to shift to a new form of data is linked to at least three factors: (1) the need to understand the new data, (2) the need to share an understanding of data with peers, and (3) the need to continue the management of ongoing systems.

The need for transition time, so that a manager can absorb new data, is not physically obvious. In operational work, the need for transition time can be more readily observed. The physical effort of learning to operate a new technology can be observed by others. The manager's efforts to learn how to use new data are not observable except by indirect methods. Yet, that kind of transition may require more time than any of the other transition needs of IT implementation.

Consistency Through Structured Expectations. Finally, managers have been accustomed to doing their work with skills that are not oriented to technology. Many do not know how to type. The use of a keyboard is foreign to them or is considered demeaning. "Secretaries type, executives write" is an old but long accepted canard. The times and the advancing technology are changing that belief. But much more will be changed than the need to "type." Senior management's expectations of middle managers are undergoing a significant major change. One indication of this changing attitude is the attempt to simplify the organizational structures and flatten the hierarchy. As a result, the development of middle management skill in the use of technology will require intensive and sensitive efforts.

Two examples of sensitive and effective handling of this issue can be cited.

Example 1: In Columbus, Ohio, a PC training company conducts public seminars. All students are in a common classroom but are in semiprivate carrels with their own PC. Carrel walls are high enough that the difficulties of an individual learner are not observable by other students. At the same time, students can see beyond the carrel wall to observe the instructor. The instructor can also view the progress each learner is making by accessing the student's PC screen on the instructor master monitor. This training company has found that such privacy, accompanied by personal attention, encourages managers and senior executives to attend their classes.

Example 2: Community Mutual Blue Cross, Blue Shield in Cincinnati, Ohio, has a department which develops computer-based training (CBT) software. All newly hired employees learn CBT quickly because the explanation of their benefits package is given to them as a CBT course. The company also provides guidance to its managers and executives if they wish to purchase a PC for home use. As a result, these managers often practice their PC skills and use the firm's CBT programs during their off hours. The managers avoid the embarrassment of appearing unskilled while acquiring the benefits of PC use.

The Recommendation

Turning middle managers into comfortable and skilled users of IT requires the recognition and servicing of special needs. There is a need for managers to retain the old structures of working until they can shift to the new ones. There is a need to retain their sense of competence, particularly in the eyes of subordinates. And there is a need to move ahead to acquire newer and more challenging skills, but to do so comfortably and within an explicitly stated framework of expectations.

**Continuity: Consistency Through the Presence
and Interpersonal Activities of Middle Managers**

Much of the value of middle management work results from the effective interpersonal relationships these managers have with superiors, peers, and subordinates. IT can create greater efficiency, but often at the cost of distancing these relationships. For example, electronic messages may replace live contacts with another person. The electronic medium will provide certain advantages in record keeping, detail, timeliness, and assurance of response. But a computer cannot replace all of the characteristics of the human interaction.

To demonstrate that point, we have developed a list of perceived differences between interacting with a computer and interacting with a human (Table 3-9). The list is not normative in the sense that every difference is verifiable by objective standards. The list is truthful, however, in the sense that it reports the perceptions people have given us. In organizational life, the perceptions of workers account for a great deal.

The informal comments of one systems programmer inadvertently supported these differences. He said that he was becoming concerned about his increasing preference for dealing with machines rather than people. It was a valid concern for him, and it represents a growing concern for countless others. It cannot be denied that the computer will improve life. However, we insist that management must set the criterion by which "improvements" are judged. One basic criteria will be whether the computer has improved the quality of human relationships, for life without human relationships is meaningless.

All of this is said to point up the trend of replacing human managers with technology. It is not enough to say that no one intends to replace middle management with computers. That presumes only a physical displacement. There needs to be an awareness that there is also psychological displacement of middle management activity. For example, how often do customer service representatives, bank tellers, and grocery store clerks comment to customers with a problem, "well, the computer made a mistake." There are several things wrong with this answer. First, it is most likely a lie. Second, if the computer made the mistake, there'll be no apology. Computers can't apologize; only humans can. And finally, when customers need assistance with problems, they want the assurance of caring, concern, and future consistency in their correction. They can't get that from a computer.

The Recommendation

Dumping the human problems of middle management into the lap of IT will only create new problems. IT always presents advantages and disadvantages when it

Table 3-9
Comparison of the Computer as a Replacement for the Mid-Level Manager

The Computer	The Manager
Machine	Human
Invisible data	Visible data
Closed-system communication	Open-system communication
Inflexible	Flexible
Nonnegotiable use	Negotiable use, interaction
Reportable, static	Readable, observation
Predictable	Changeable
Nonperceiving	Perceiving
Immobile	Mobile
Cold	Caring
Work based	Multiple-environment based
Sequential, serial	Ordered and random
Sensate	Intuitive and sensate
Logical	Supralogical
Capable of overload	Capable of stress
System oriented	Process oriented
Data receiver	Data generator
Presenter	Decider
A means to an end	The goal, or end purpose
Goal free	Goal setting
User driven	Mission, purpose driven
Task absorber	Task definer and assigner
Emotion free	Emotional
Staff	Line
Supports the organization	Is the organization
Stores and manipulates data	Creates and manipulates information
Quick and dumb	Slow and wise

replaces human functions. A careful progression must be used whenever human functions are to be replaced. This process must be closely followed and governed by senior management. Changing human functions into machine functions will always affect the values of the organization.

Management must first learn what makes the human functions of middle management effective. Then it must determine where technology can enhance these functions and where it can harm them. Particular attention should be paid to the impact of the technology on human interrelationships. The list of human vs. computer differences (Table 3-9) can be a forewarning concerning the potential impacts of technical systems on middle management. Follow this rule: "Do not implement technical systems in middle management until you have analyzed the impact of automation on the quality of the organization's human interaction."

There is often a great difference between those things which demotivate and those which motivate. The patterns of consistency must be acknowledged and served in order to avoid demotivation. When middle managers cannot operate within a pattern of consistency, they lose their ability to motivate themselves in productive work. Attention to the items covered in the patterns of consistency will not motivate managers to accept technology implementations. But it will remove the demotivators that block technology implementations.

Demotivators block action because they nourish depression. When organizational demotivators exist, the result will be organizational depression. Anyone who has ever suffered depression will attest to the fact that it fosters inactivity. Motivators will not motivate in the midst of depression. Once the demotivators are controlled, the process of technology implementation can proceed using the motivational principles which will now be discussed.

Flattening the Hierarchy

A great deal is being said and written today on the need to "flatten the hierarchy." There is also a great amount of support for this need. The argument is that organizations have become too fat in the middle. They need to be made lean. IT has proven to be a remarkable help in this process. In fact, at this time, automation is often carried out in order to flatten the hierarchy. The stated reasons often are that automation will cut the fat from management, speed up the flow of data, and eliminate roadblocks to decision making. All of these are laudable goals and can be achieved through automation. All of them involve some form of flattening of the hierarchy. But all of them also threaten the human functions of middle management and have the potential for disrupting the consistency with which the organization performs.

At this point one might think, "but the automation of middle management functions has gone on for years without producing that result." This is true, but it fails to perceive the change in *how* automation is currently operating. In most organizations, automation began with middle management functions that stood alone. As an example, a payroll function was typically computerized as a stand-alone system. Only later was it connected to other personnel and accounting systems.

Today technology has advanced to the point where it can capture, manage, and provide much of an organization's data in one integrated application. In the past, layers of managers were needed to oversee specialized data, such as accounts receivable, and to integrate them into the overall organization. The computer can now do that. But the computer can also make these data available to all other employees. And it can do so quickly and easily.

When technology is used to flatten the hierarchy, it will flatten the hierarchy with a vengeance. Most of the clerical functions can be immediately replaced. Many of the analytical functions will be replaced. Even though computers have far greater capabilities than ever before, they still lack the ability to replace all human functions. There will be a continuing need for some middle managers to oversee the human functions of the management system, even when their numbers are decreased. These

Table 3-10
Planning Technology Implementation for Middle Managers
1. Setting value-drivien goals
2. Changing their psychological mind set
3. Developing new competencies

managers will need a carefully planned transition to their new responsibilities. Three steps are needed to plan and effect this transition (Table 3-10).

Planning Computerization for Middle Managers

Value-Driven Goals

Middle managers are accustomed to being in the line of communication between top management and line workers. In this capacity, they are responsible for many of the decisions and behaviors that IT threatens to take over. Letting go of their control over communication will require a new set of values. Jan Carlzon (1987), president of Scandinavian Airlines (SAS), wrote in his book *Moments of Truth* what should become the classic narrative about a change in corporate values.

Carlzon's concern was to get closer to the customer. He wanted to place decision making in the hands of SAS employees who have 30-second contact with customers. His goal was to "manage the dickens out of those unique, never-to-be-repeated opportunities to distinguish ourselves." He recounts incidents in which employees were able to take the initiative under this new style of management. He also tells of those middle managers who saw their older, primary functions handed over to others. As a result, these managers tried to block the new style of customer service.

Ultimately, Carlzon succeeded to the extent that he was able to enforce the new company values down line from himself to others at SAS. The new values became the criteria for all new employee behaviors. Effective performers were those who lived up to the behavioral expectations of the new values, got close to the customers, and did whatever was needed to serve them. The new values became the criteria for the vertical integration of the organizational system. They told everyone what to do, from top management through middle management to front line employees.

The next discovery was that middle managers were now thrust into an unaccustomed role. They became facilitators and mentors to their subordinates. Accustomed to giving instructions, they were now expected to advise. Accustomed to deciding, they were now expected to provide data that informed others on how to decide. Accustomed to passing problems on to higher levels, they were now expected to handle problems themselves or to pass them laterally to those who could. This was not just a disruption of the normal patterns of work. It was the imposition of a new role. But it was a value-driven imposition. The new behavior was needed to serve a higher value.

Table 3-11
Components of the Value: Continued Development of Middle Management

1. The repudiation of knowledge monopolies
2. The support of employee growth through use of company resources
3. The evaluation of middle managers by their effectiveness in supporting subordinates
4. Open support for the principles of adult learning, that is, andragogy

Automation will have a similar impact on the middle manager's role. It, too, will need to be value driven if managers are to accept the new roles that automation imposes upon them. There is often a misunderstanding about the object of a middle manager's revolt. When the revolt follows on the heels of a new system implementation, it is assumed that it is directed at the new technology. In truth, it is often directed at the new work behaviors expected from the manager. The reason managers rebel at new behaviors is that they are often not driven by the same set of values to which they are accustomed.

The more dimensions there are to a behavioral change, the more values will be needed to support that change. If the computer will support the front line of corporate activity, then there must be a value to this change. If the new behavior requires the development of new skills and understanding, there must also be a value to this change. But the implementation of new technology goes beyond changes in specific work behaviors. Technology implementations often require the imposition of a value that encourages and supports the continuing development of every employee in a wide range of skills and behaviors. In the case of middle management, this new value will have several components (Table 3-11).

Repudiation of Knowledge Monopolies

The list in Table 3-11 does not come from some imagined theoretical framework. It represents observed reactions of managers to automation and/or to attempts to flatten the corporate hierarchy. The specialization of middle management functions had led to knowledge monopolies which were used repeatedly to protect the position and role of the incumbent. Knowledge had become an issue of turf rather than an open and available resource to the company. The flattening of the pyramid meant that the individual had to release control over knowledge, over a specific area of turf. The new value system had to assert that openness and sharing count for more.

Use of Company Resources to Support Employee Growth

The value of continued support for employee growth and skill development must be supported by the use of company resources. Few organizations have a stated and demonstrated value for the support of employee development. There must be stated organizational polices, procedures, and a budget. Firms which wish to give strong support to automation cannot slight this need. The organization wise in transition management will use its resources to aid employees in four ways (Table 3-12).

Table 3-12
Resource Use in Transition Management of Middle Managers

1. To understand the need and value of the new system
2. To acquire new skills
3. To shift gradually from old behaviors to new ones
4. To assist managers to contribute to the new way of doing business

Evaluation of Middle Managers According to Their Support of Subordinates

In the old style of work, middle managers modeled their behavior after that of supervisors. Supervisors' work expectations were such that they directed the workers in their jobs. Their role was to monitor both the work and the worker. Middle managers assumed similar work goals, though they may have exercised them in more indirect ways. Middle management control was exercised through established routines, procedures, channels, and approval mechanisms. This often led middle managers to make the ubiquitous statement that, "we've never done it that way before."

Changing this style of work with subordinates requires that managers accept a new value, support for subordinates, over the older value, control of subordinates. It also calls for a modification of how managers evaluate employees and how they expect evaluations to modify the subordinate's behaviors. This change in evaluation must be done in a fair manner. The expected work of subordinates must be clearly defined. The manager's support role must be stated just as clearly. There must be lucid and detailed statements of what constitutes effective support before middle managers can begin the transition to this new management style. And there must be corporate support throughout the transition.

Open Support for Adult Learning

In American firms there are ample opportunities for managers to advance in their specialization. There are few opportunities and little support for general skill growth. IT coupled with the flattening of the hierarchy will force managers out of the protective mold of their specialization into new areas of knowledge and skill. For managers this will be an experience of generalized learning. Two value-related elements are needed. First, the organization must value and reward generalized learning even when specific applications are not readily apparent. Second, the firm must explicitly state and reward those kinds of learning that it values.

Psychological Mind Set

When middle managers look at their work world, they see it as dominated by three things: economics, engineering, and technology. As they explore the implications of these factors, they develop an internalized value system, a mind set, that reinforces

Table 3-13

Psychological Mind Set of Middle Managers

1. Significant human relationships have to do with achieving an organization's objectives
2. Rational thinking is preferred over emotional thinking
3. Workers are best controlled by unilateral direction, coercion, and control

three basic "truths." The first truth is that the most significant human relationships have to do with achieving an organization's objectives. The second is that rational thinking is to be preferred over emotional thinking or feelings. The third is that down line workers are most effectively influenced by unilateral direction, coercion, and control.

This psychological mind set is traceable to the beginnings of our present economic structures. Much has been done to try to change this mind set. These efforts have done little to change the workplace. Managers' attitudes remain much the same, except for a little softening. The new type of corporate executive is called the "gamesman" by author Michael Maccoby (1976) in his book of the same name. Gamesmen have not changed their psychological mind set toward others. They are simply more adept at manipulating others through human relations.

This slight shift in attitudes is not enough for an organization. The term "gamesman" implies an artificial entity that does not meet the organization's needs. All enterprises need a realistic and positive approach to management in order to gain a realistic and positive use of information technology. There is a need for a new view of corporate reality, and with that a new mind set. Each of the components of the older mind set (Table 3-13) will be examined, and new components will be recommended.

Significant Human Relationships Have to Do with Achieving an Organization's Objectives

The new mind set does not require a replacement of this behavior. But it does require a redefinition of the organization's economic objectives. It is true that companies cannot survive for long without meeting their short-term economic objectives. The concerns of those called "bean counters" must still be met. But the long-term survival of the organization requires a flexibility and an innovativeness that does not immediately appear on the balance sheet. Or, more likely, it appears only as a cost to those with a short-range view of the business. This short-range mind set is encouraged by those who use IT mainly because of its ability to handle data efficiently.

IT, however, has the capability to serve both the enterprise's short-range and long-range needs. It has the capability to replace some human functions and to enhance others. It can do many things better and faster than people. But it can also assist people in doing their work better and faster. It is this mix of abilities which suggests the need for management to develop a mix of organizational goals and objectives. Among these objectives will be one constant—the continued development of technology and people.

Oddly enough, IT can be a valuable aid in this process. The goals of employee growth and organizational development are best served when there is effective communication and thorough record keeping. Both of these are natural tasks for the efficient computer.

Rational Thinking Is to Be Preferred Over Emotional Thinking

This second part of the old mind set will be changed through a recognition that the world is multidimensional. That is, life is both rational and nonrational. Multiple levels of cognition are open to humans, who may use data, reason, intuition, feeling, and emotion when understanding and responding to their surroundings. Note that there is no mention of irrationality. The new mind set does not work against rational thinking, behaving, and deciding. Rather, it contends that other ways of thinking must be joined to it.

Senior executives often make decisions based on a hunch. They use facts and rational thought to carry them just so far. Then they rely on the wisdom of their experience, their feel for the situation, and their best intuition regarding possible outcomes. They use all the elements of human cognition. This ordered and structured use of all facets of human cognition is needed in today's business.

Middle managers need development if they are to use this type of thinking. Too many of them have been involved only with the facts of their work. Facts are safe. They can be used to justify behaviors or decisions. They are immutable and unassailable. Yet, they are also insufficient. Facts will not explain *why* we are in a chosen line of work or why we enjoy serving people. The working world is multidimensional, and our patterns of thought should reflect that reality. In Chapter 7 we propose a process model that includes all these elements. This model also provides a process for technology implementation and use within the organization.

Workers Are Best Controlled by Unilateral Direction, Coercion, and Control

The third component of the new mind set is built around assumptions about human nature that are more positive. Decision making will be more broadly distributed in anticipation of technology's ability to distribute the data. But it will require the development of the middle manager's ability to be self-directed and self-controlled. It will mean the growth of skills that relate to technology's ability to facilitate communication with others. It will mean that the consequences of individual decision making will be distributed to those who decide.

A positive attitude toward human potential will be accompanied by a healthy skepticism about delivered goods. This will mean that middle managers will adopt a "show me" attitude concerning senior management's statements on the new mind set. At the same time, senior management will require constant supervision of the transition to this new psychology of work. Progress will be measured in quantifiable terms wherever possible. The old mind set required that managers direct, coerce, and control the behavior of others. The new mind set will require that they direct and control the results of behaviors.

The transition to this positive management of others will be achieved only with a full, dedicated commitment from senior management to long-term results. Immediate results will be slow and spotty. It will be a long-term *process*, and it will be costly. However, it should not be beyond management's capability. Management has found millions of dollars for the purchase and programming of computers because they were dedicated to the improvement of technical systems. They can also find the resources needed for this transition if they are dedicated to the improvement of the human systems.

Developing New Competencies

We believe that the only proper application of IT is that which extends the human capacity. Our interest is not in what the technology can do but in what people can do when supported with the latest technology. We recognize that the computer has either created or expedited significant changes in the competencies required of middle managers. We support these changes. They represent the next stage in the development of human competence in the work world (Table 3-14).

Decision Thinking: The Redefinition of Planning

Our first encounter with the term "decision thinking" was in Peter Drucker's book *Management: Tasks—Responsibilities—Practices* (1973). Drucker states that managers will need, more and more, to develop the skill of decision thinking rather than traditional decision making. His concern is to broaden the scope of the process of decision making and to construct a new role for the manager. Rather than focusing on making decisions, the manager is concerned with the process of thinking toward a decision. The manager's role is to assist others who enter the process of planning.

Decision thinking and decision making are part of the process of planning. The primary focus of planning needs to shift to identifying the questions and to carefully defining and describing all available alternatives for a decision. At present, most planning is a process of finding the "right" solution or answer to a problem or need.

Table 3-14
New Competencies Required by IT

1. Decision thinking: The redefinition of planning
2. Data interpreter: The supplier of new knowledge
3. Organizing responsibility: The new way to delegate
4. Frontline: The new management style
5. New knowledge skills: The real flattening of the hierarchy
6. Continuous learning: The ultimate challenge

There are several difficulties with this approach. First, it is entirely too moralistic. A decision reached on this basis dare not be abandoned, for that would be "wrong." Second, it frequently removes the decision from the hands of those who will implement it, thereby depriving them of responsibility for it.

Planning must be done as the search for effective answers. Please note the plural form. With this type of planning, many different responses will be effective, but each will have its advantages and disadvantages. Each will be effective in a different manner. In this type of process, the organization's planners assist the doers by providing them data and information on all available options. Now the doers will be equipped to make their own decisions and bear responsibility for them.

Data Interpreter: The Supplier of New Knowledge

Managers who participate in restructuring the planning process become interpreters of data and suppliers of new knowledge. The older method equipped managers to lead others and to provide their subordinates with needed data. Any innovations, new ideas, and new uses of data were to be filtered through the manager for final refinement and approval. The newer method equips managers so that they interact with their staff as mentors.

Mentors must first keep the corporate values before their subordinates. Subordinates must learn to find meaning through a comparison of data with the company's accepted values. Middle managers must learn to lead in this process of self-discovery. It is this process that changes data into information and prepares the staff for the next step. The next step is assisting subordinates to examine alternatives and the possible impacts of each alternative on organizational goals.

The exploration of potential impacts is a knowledge-based expertise. Information becomes knowledge when it is examined in the light of accumulated wisdom based on human experience. The wisdom is sometimes that of an individual and sometimes that of a group. Sometimes it is the accumulated wisdom of an organization. It is the ability to know, estimate, or intuit that certain things will follow from each course of action.

The advantage of mentoring others is twofold. When others make their own decisions based on commonly accepted values, they have fewer problems with owning these decisions and being responsible for their behaviors. When they acquire the accumulated wisdom of others, they have less anxiety about making decisions. They are comfortable with the possible consequences of their decision making and their ability to handle the outcomes.

Organizing Responsibility: The New Way to Delegate

Each employee needs a cohesive sense of what he or she does. The new way to delegate sounds a lot like the old one because certain principles are similar. A written job description is one way of organizing responsibility. It becomes part of the new way of doing things when it is focused on responsibilities rather than tasks. This delegation of responsibility has been avoided by organizations because it was viewed as a diminution of power. If employees are given an area of responsibility, they have control over their work. "We" no longer have power over "them."

Corporate CEOs are excellent examples of the truth that power and responsibility are not the same. Effective CEOs are very busy people with little to do. They are busy because they spend long hours at work. But they have little to do because they spend their time mentoring and assisting those who report to them. The most effective CEOs we know have very few stated responsibilities other than assisting down-line personnel. Yet they are very powerful people.

The CEO can be a model for managers throughout the organization. Effective managers who mimic them develop their own ability to organize responsibility for others down the line. This does not always mean an increase in the number of tasks the person handles. It means that more importance and value are delegated and loaded into these tasks because the employee is given direct responsibility for them. Now the role of middle managers is to assist subordinates to be high achievers.

Frontline: The New Management Style

It would be hard to imagine a successful organization that did not have as its stated value service to the customer. But to carry through on this value, the organization must identify the employees who provide services directly to their customers. Then the organization must know how to empower them to provide real service. In most organizations, it is the operational workers who have customer contact. These are the frontline employees. The success of the enterprise depends on them.

Middle management has responsibility for empowering and supporting the frontline. It can do so in several ways. First, middle managers are the chief representatives of organizational values. Several things compound this responsibility. Automation increases the volume and kind of customer contacts that one employee can handle or receive. This must be matched with an increase in the volume and kinds of communications about corporate values. If it is not, the technology may be allowed to act in ways that violate the service orientation of the firm.

The flattening of the hierarchy facilitates the sharing of corporate values. The values pass through fewer layers before they get to the operational worker. There is greater clarity about what these values mean. This requires middle managers to increase their skills in sharing planning and decision making with others.

New Knowledge Skills: The Real Flattening of the Hierarchy

Automation of middle management always involves learning new skills. How extensive these new learnings will be depends on how much the individual already knows about the system being implemented. But there is other learning that must occur. A newly implemented IT makes it possible to introduce entirely new data which may not be familiar to the middle manager. A manager in this situation has to acquire new knowledge about these data, about their interpretation, and about their effective use.

In addition, IT often makes it possible for middle managers to view the data of other middle managers. Newer computer systems can build one common data base for all managers to share. Recent developments in relating diverse data elements to one another create logarithmic increases in the knowledge available to managers. The extent to which this is a threat to managers is determined by the extent to which organizational planning and decision making are competitive rather than cooperative. Cooperative decision thinking allows managers to share expertise more comfortably and to school one another without personal threat or risk.

The middle manager's competence in an IT environment is based on four characteristics: (1) the manager's ability to use the technology, (2) the amount of new data a manager must use, (3) the complexity of the data base, and (4) the degree of cooperative planning and decision making in the organization.

Continuous Learning: The Ultimate Challenge

Most organizations know the value and benefits of offering employees education and training. Most of them also confuse this process with continuous learning. Educational and training programs can be part of an effort to promote continuous learning. They cannot be the entire effort. Continuous learning is something employees do, not what the company does. It is fostered in an environment open to growth and change. It is fostered down the line as senior managers model this value by their own efforts to continually learn and grown.

Education and training can be planned, offered, and scheduled. Learning occurs randomly and unannounced within an organization. The organization can control the offerings and results of formal education and training. Only the learner can control the process of learning. Education and training are offered when the company is motivated to provide it. Learning occurs as the individual is motivated to learn.

Effective organizations understand what motivates learning and provide incentives for learning to occur. Many of these factors are identified in Chapter 2. In Chapters 7 and 8, we will comment on the need for constant organizational development and technological improvement in the modern enterprise. Neither organizational development nor technological improvement is possible without employees who are continuous learners. And employees will not be continuous learners unless a learning environment is established and valued by the organization.

Summary

It is a delusion to think that IT can replace the dynamic interpersonal functions of middle management. It is wisdom to believe that they can assist in assessing, reviewing, and improving these functions. If, as we have stated, consistency in management is one of the primary functions of middle managers, then IT is uniquely equipped to aid middle managers. But it must support their work rather than preempt it.

4

This Is My Company Too!

The real problem is not whether machines think, but whether men do.

—B. F. Skinner

Daily newspapers, radio, and television accounts remind us how rapidly and relentlessly the world is being changed by technology. In general, each person can choose how much new technology he or she wants to buy and use. However, the same choices are not available to most workers. In the workplace, such decisions are made by others. Workers lose control over technology choices. They lose control over the speed at which automation overtakes them. There is a motivational principle involved in these two different choices.

In my personal life, I am motivated by the fact that it is "my life." I own it. This truth can be seen by all. However, in my work life, I am also motivated by the principle of ownership. That I "own" my position, role, and job duties is easily seen. What is not easily seen is that I am also motivated by my "ownership" of the firm. When the firm makes choices about "their" technology, they are also making choices about "my" technology. Unfortunately, in the process, the way the choice is made may support or undercut my sense of ownership of the enterprise.

Some executives demonstrate a commitment to worker motivation by fostering a sense of shared ownership in the organization. These executives encourage an attitude of family. Employees are told that they are an equal part of the team. Pay incentives are created to promote the feeling of ownership. Stock options are made available. Special year-end bonuses are linked to yearly profits. These are some examples of how employees are encouraged to feel ownership.

But employees do not need to be told that they are owners. Most, employed long enough with the same company, come to that conclusion on their own. Over time they come to feel that they own their jobs. They have a sense of protective ownership over the way they do their work. This is a reality of organizational life. We all begin to feel ownership after a while, even when it is not offered to us by any explicit word or action.

When workers own their jobs, they are integrated into the organization's social system. Workers have a place in the company, just as the company has a place in the larger society. And within this framework of ownership lies the worker's hopes for personal prosperity and company prosperity. It is also within this framework that management has its highest hopes for employee productivity and contribution to the future of the organization.

One of the responsibilities of strategic management is its support of the employees' sense of ownership. This form of commitment to each employee can come only from the highest executive levels. However, even with a total commitment to employee ownership, there are mistakes. Most of these begin with a mistaken understanding of strategic management.

Area 3: Strategic Management

One of the worst mistakes made concerning strategic management is the assumption that strategic thinking is entirely a rational process. Once this mistake is made, the result is long-range planning, not strategic thinking. With long-range planning, the emphasis is on using data to determine what the future will look like and, from that perspective, setting company plans. This is a natural, rational approach to an organization's future.

Long-range planning helps management anticipate the future as best it can. But strategic management is different. The basis of strategic management is not an attempt to anticipate the future. It is the setting of a corporate vision—a picture of what the organization wants its future to be (Table 4-1). The most effective leaders make sure that their employees share that future vision. These leaders hold that vision before their employees. It is a picture that includes all of them because they all will be asked to turn this future vision into a reality. They will be asked to own

Table 4-1
Strategic Management Defined

Strategic management is the process used to define the future that the organization chooses for itself.

the dream. They will be included in all the work that will make the future vision come true.

The best strategic management is built around this feeling of ownership. It addresses the survival, participation, and prosperity needs of employees and organizations. By combining these needs, management elicits the efforts of all employees in making the future happen. Individual employee responses are also based on these needs. Employees want to see the company attain its vision. They want to see the company move in its chosen direction. They also want to see the company back its employees by supporting their ideas about and contributions to the future vision.

The same confusion between long-range planning and strategic management occurs when new technology is selected. The MIS professionals push for the purchase or development of a particular computer because that's the direction in which the technology is moving. Armed with computer vendor promises and projections and MIS recommendations, management approves the latest technology acquisitions. At that moment, the participants in the decision are operating with the assumptions of long-range planning. One of these is that future technologies determine the future of the organization. The basic mistake of this approach is that it concedes control of the future to others.

Automation will not, in itself, disrupt the strategic management of an organization. However, improper management of technology implementation will, as the following examples show.

Example 1: A major West Coast retail conglomerate purchased a family-owned chain of upscale clothing stores. As part of the purchase, the chain became a division of the acquiring corporation and retained its former executives to continue the management of the operation. The intention was for the transfer of ownership to appear transparent to customers. Corporate management assured division management that it would be "business as usual."

Once the sale was complete, operations proceeded as planned. The one exception was the new computerized corporate accounting system that the division would have to adopt. As it was explained, this was the one common computer system that all divisions must use. However, once the accounting system's conversion took place, corporate management went back on its word. Using the information from the accounting system, they began dictating new policies and plans to division management. Among other things, division management was told that they could not continue building new stores because division profits were too low.

Example 2: A major midwestern manufacturer decided to computerize its production management systems. Approximately half of the affected employees greeted the change with pleased anticipation. The remainder were convinced that they would lose their jobs. They assumed that cost cutting and staff reductions were the main reasons that management had instituted the change. The installation of the new system caused a number of employees to retire or quit. Those who stayed rebelled against the new technology. This rebellion caused a fivefold increase in the cost of the system and an extra seven months of installation time.

Example 3: An international fast food chain introduced a computerized system for retrieving store operations information. The system was intended to move information up through the organization to senior management. Instead, the information jumped management levels and was sent directly to corporate headquarters. As a result, senior managers had much greater detail on store operations than the store managers. The information was used by some to reprimand store managers' performance.

Example 4:   A state bureau of motor vehicles computerized license plate records and sales information. At the same time that their large mainframe system was being implemented, some PCs were installed. During the planning phase, the administration solicited the ideas and opinions of line workers and supervisors. Although their input was used, no feedback was ever given them on the value and use of their ideas. They came to the conclusion that it was a waste of their time because management didn't ever listen to them anyway. This experience reinforced their opinion that there were two levels of staff in their agency, the workers and the managers. They viewed themselves as the real workers and owners of the agency. The rest, middle managers and up, were just temporaries.

Example 5:   A leading northern California bank bought a bankrupt factoring company. It appointed its own executive vice president to this newest division. He immediately began examining its past and present operations. While the operation appeared to be well run on the surface, he soon discovered that it was drowning in a sea of paper. Receivables were as much as six months in arrears. Cash application of client payments was extraordinarily slow. His solution was to computerize the entire financial process.

Although a necessary and reasonable solution, the idea met immediate resistance and resentment when the credit department heard about it. When asked to explain their reaction, they said that credit checking was a work of art, not of numbers. It is more likely that their real feelings and hidden agenda were expressed by the question, "who will own client credit decisions—the computer or me?"

The Principle: Ownership Through Inclusion

One thing should be noted from all of these examples above. The technology did not create the chaos. It was the behavior of senior managers that led to the problems. It was they who neglected the principles of worker ownership. Automation does not create problems of ownership, nor can it resolve them. Ownership is created or destroyed by the actions of senior management. Worker ownership is enhanced and supported when employees are given the message that the organization is totally dependent upon their behavior, sense of commitment, and contribution to the decision-making process. This message must be communicated by management actions, not by statements of intentions.

Stated management intentions mean very little when their actions in implementing IT are poorly planned, underfunded, and understaffed. Technology implementations must be clearly directed toward the accepted goals and values of the company. No amount of talk about the need for technology alleviates the doubt which can spread throughout an organization. It is not true that actions speak louder than words. Actions are the only things that speak.

This would appear to contradict what has just been said about actions and words. How the two interrelate can be shown with an illustration.

An example: IRD Mechanalysis, a midwestern manufacturer of electronic control devices, has the following creed:

IRD Mechanalysis doesn't sell products, it establishes relationships.

Below this creed are the following derived behaviors.

This means that we provide:

Worldwide consulting services
Continuous customer training
Startup assistance with an extended warranty
Installation supervision and review
Predictive Maintenance Program (PMP) recommendations
Technical assistance

Followed by a goal statement:

"Helping turn maintenance into a profit center"

Note that the creedal statement, which is only words, leads to specific behaviors. The behaviors, in turn, lead to permanence in the relationship with clients and excellent word-of-mouth advertising. The reputation of this firm for service to its customers is unexcelled. So ingrained is this creed in IRD that every division is reputed to have its own version. The engineering staff says, "we don't sell a box, we establish relationships." This personalization of a senior management statement indicates the extent to which all employees have embraced the creed as their own. It also indicates how the phenomenon of employee ownership is supported by a group or team consensus.

A company that has propounded and supported such a creedal statement has provided its staff and employees with two things: a foundation on which to build and a future to create. The creed provides a value-oriented, ethical foundation for developing common expectations of behavior. The creed also provides a future vision to guide the company in data gathering, decision making, and evaluation of its efforts. Without such a statement, the enterprise is literally without a rudder. It is open to the vagaries of successive leaders and/or the changing pressures of the marketplace.

Without such a creed, an organization is also open to massive mistakes in the management of its computer department. An MIS department with no guiding vision from the organization also lacks its own internal guiding vision. Mistakes are made in technology purchases, software selection, and system implementation. But the worst feature is a lack of mission, direction, or purpose for the work.

Problem Solving: the Rational Response

America is a nation consumed by rationalism. This has led to an overuse of problem solving—commonly seen in the management of IT. Most technicians are excellent problem solvers. It's the nature of their work. When they begin their journey into the ranks of management, they take that skill along. But their journey requires that they learn generalized skills of management, including strategic management. They are not alone in this need. Many American managers are deficient in the skills of strategic management.

The creedal statement of IRD Mechanalysis clearly shows the nature of the journey they have started. It is not a rational statement. Neither is it irrational or nonrational. It is a foundational statement from which a host of conclusions and rational processes can flow. It is precisely this kind of creedal statement that is lacking in most organizations. And because it is lacking, their strategic management is in chaos.

Michael E. McGill (1988), in his book *American Business and the Quick Fix,* does an excellent job of debunking the myths that American businesses use in their attempts to solve their typical problems. We concur heartily with his analysis of the misplaced use of problem-solving techniques. However, his proposed solution is management by slogans rather than an identification of the root problem. The heart of the problem is the use of operational and tactical management skills to solve the strategic management problems of the organization. What is needed is strategic management. And strategic management must provide one all-powerful myth, one future vision, as the driving force of the organization.

The Elements of Strategic Management

In their book *In Search of Excellence* Peters and Waterman (1982) confessed that they had not anticipated that their search would lead them back to principles of leadership. They had expected some new finding or result rather than a repetition of old truths. It may be that they did both. They reaffirmed an old truth about leadership but clothed it in new and more effective detail. They noted that the outstanding leaders they studied focused their activities strongly on values. In addition, they found that the excellent companies had captured the truths and values of their founder and retained these even after the founder had left the organization.

We propose five steps to the development of this form of strategic leadership (Table 4-2). These will now be discussed.

Table 4-2
The Value Basis of Strategic Leadership

1. A stated mission for the organization
2. Behaviors that derive from that mission
3. The use of consensus in place of agreement
4. Control over the planning process
5. Development of knowledge from information

A Stated Mission for the Organization

When Wendy's International, Inc., was founded by R. David Thomas, he felt the taste of an old-fashioned hamburger in his mouth. Then he set about developing a company that would deliver that taste with as few accompanying menu items as necessary. He kept his vision of his business lean, and he worked hard to impart that vision to all who worked for him. His mission was to deliver that same taste, in that same hamburger, every time. He knew that the rest would follow. And it did.

The chronicles of successful business startups are replete with such instances of visionary perception. The founder, by sense or intuition, knows what the company should produce or provide. And the longer that person is in charge, the more deeply the vision is etched into the sinews of the organization. Time and changing circumstances may erode a company's success, the company does not collapse from internal weakness. The strength of such enterprises is not only in the founder's vision but in the fact that this vision includes a ready market for the product or service.

The founders of Precision Lenscrafters noted that consumers had to wait from 7 to 10 business days to get eyeglasses once their prescriptions were written. Lenscrafters had a better perception of service. Their goal was to provide quality eyeglasses, including prescription lenses, with incredible speed. They set out to do so in an hour and found that they could. Currently, their greatest risk is that someone will copy them. Their greatest strength is that they have transformed the vision into specific behaviors.

Behaviors Derived from the Mission

From their original vision the leaders of Lenscrafters developed a list of nine beliefs (Table 4-3). Later they added a tenth, upon which we will comment later. Eight of the nine beliefs use action verbs. They keep the focus on behaviors, not on concepts. The one belief that uses a verb of being tells each employee, "Your store is the most important part of our company."

Table 4-3
Precision Lenscrafters Creed

Nine mission-derived behaviors
- Nurture individuals
- Build on people's strengths
- Accept mistakes
- Focus on winning, not on individual scoring
- Push ideas
- Each store is a separate business
- Plan for the twenty-first century
- Demand the highest possible quality
- Constantly Improve

The eight action beliefs send value messages to each employee. They commit the organization to specific kinds of behaviors. They state norms for how to treat people. They encourage all employees to see themselves as valued by the company. They establish criteria for fairness in employee supervision and management. The first four beliefs, in particular, support each employee's perception of his or her uniqueness and ability to become a more responsible and valuable employee.

The last four beliefs stress the company's expectations of its employees. It expects ideas, future planning, high quality, and improvement. Each employee knows how to contribute to company success because these expectations are clearly stated. The belief that each store is a separate business sets a tone of responsibility and autonomy. It can, quite conceivably, make each store manager an entrepreneur. It certainly holds each store separately accountable for its performance. And it holds Lenscrafters accountable for the support of the behaviors its mission statement encourages.

The tenth belief emerged after Lenscrafters was in business for several years. The tenth belief is "have fun." One of the company's senior executives commented to us that it could be expressed better with the word "celebrate." The expectation behind this belief is that the company will continue to achieve and have reasons to celebrate. The expectation within this belief is that every employee should be part of that celebration. More than any of the other beliefs, this one tells each employee that he or she is a part owner of Lenscrafters.

Building on Consensus Rather Than Agreement

The problem with "yes" men is that they always agree on everything. The problem with those who encourage such behavior is that they believe that agreement is always needed. It isn't. But then, most of us already know that. What is often lacking is a way of handling disagreement. What is needed is a creative way of making decisions that allows for dissenting opinions without slowing down the process of decision making.

Typically, three methods are used for dealing with dissent. One is forced support from dissenters. This may be accomplished through the power of one's position or the weight of argument. The next two slow down the decision making. In the first, each participant in the decision is given time to review all the data and, hopefully, come to a common decision. An alternative is to allow everyone to contribute to the creation of a compromise solution. These methods assume that the right answer emerges when all parties are in agreement.

Consensus building isn't finding the right answer to a problem or situation. Consensus building assumes that there may be several equally effective decisions available. Data gathering may proceed in the same manner as in decision making but will be concluded with the presentation of several alternatives. Each of these alternatives will be weighted according to estimated advantages and disadvantages. Some of these advantages and disadvantages will clearly be based on data; others will be based on opinions. Agreement is essential on all data presented. Differences in opinions are left to stand. Each participant in the decision retains responsibility for his or her own opinions.

At this point, any number of decision techniques may be used. The goal is to select an option that has the support of the decision making group. Support for the accepted alternative may come in two ways. There is support for the alternative itself. There are others who support the group's choice for the sake of the organization. They may not agree with the decision, but they agree to support the group.

When employees participate in decision making, they require two levels of ownership for consensus building to take place: ownership of the organization and ownership of its decisions. They start with a sense of ownership of the organization. As long as this attitude is supported by management's actions, employees will be able to own management's decisions.

Two behaviors are required of management to support this transfer of ownership to employees. First, the company must allow employees to retain their opinions, including negative ones. Second, the company must show that it actively listens to and uses employees' information and opinions. The value of consensus building is that it allows employees to dissent from the decisions of management but not from the decision-making process.

As we define it, consensus building is not a proposal for massive employee involvement in company decisions. Many decisions can be made without the direct involvement of many employees. Consensus building is a plea for sensitivity toward the ownership issue in decision making. If a decision is to work, all those who will own that decision must be involved in some part of the process that leads to it. One of the weaknesses of the MIS systems development life cycle approach is that not enough emphasis is placed on ownership of the technical system. Ultimately, computer users are expected to own the systems they use. If they are to do this, they must be more intimately involved in the development and implementation of these systems.

Controlling the Planning Process

It is our experience that consensus building in the typical organization is not possible until management has gained control over the planning process. And no company controls planning until it can define it. Planning is the discovery and exploration of alternatives. It is not doing. Nor is it deciding. It is the necessary prelude to both of these activities. It involves divergent thinking. When it is managed well, it draws on the new, unusual, and radical ideas and concerns of employees, as well as on all the old knowledge and ways of work. And when it is managed well, it is done as a staff function, providing advice to line functions. Management control over planning is lost when staff members make line decisions.

Planning is also assimilative thinking. Having discovered and explored all alternatives, planners seek to assess whether any of these can be fitted to the enterprise's present purposes and goals. This filter does not seek to eliminate alternatives but rather to note whether the present mission and goals of the company can support each possible choice. If an alternative fits the enterprise, it can be considered for additional study and development. When an alternative does not fit the enterprise, either it must be rejected or the enterprise must be redefined.

3-M has been noted as a company that does an excellent job of this type of filtering. This model of planning is used whenever 3-M considers a new product. If the product fits the corporation, it is positioned in an existing division. If an existing division is not suitable, a new department or division may ultimately be created for it. If it does not fit, it may be rejected out of hand. Alternatively, 3-M may create a new company in an attempt to develop and market a new product. But the new product line will not be forced on the parent company if its doesn't fit the enterprise.

Note that planning serves as an advisory or staff function to management. It advises on the fit of each proposal to the organization's mission. It advises on alternative decisions and courses of action or inaction, including their potential impact. But the decision on assimilation remains with the organization's line management.

A similar process of planning should be followed when a change is planned in technology. The planning process for technology use and implementation must consider all possible alternatives and then must evaluate each according to its fit within the organization. The planning process is truncated when the technical planners ask the company to fit itself to their preferred choice of technology. In these instances, planning has changed the rules of management. It has changed itself into a management/line function.

Planning is kept in its proper role when management requires that it perform as a staff function. Staff functions are advisory. Line functions are decision making. Staff functions provide support for line functions and are evaluated in terms of the quality of support offered. Line functions are measured by performance and evaluated in terms of their productivity. The fact that staff functions have grown in most organizations, sometimes disproportionately to the overall company's growth, does not create a problem. The harm occurs when staff functions grow in power and are licensed to make decisions that belong to the line personnel.

There is one caveat that should be noted. As computer technology progresses, the technology increasingly invades line functions. For example, an automated teller machine (ATM) serves in a line function as much as a human teller does. Computer terminals at customer service desks are as much a part of the line function as the paper files are. The emergence of a totally integrated data base in a bank blurs the distinction between the line functions and staff functions of the computer and supporting MIS staff.

In this emerging partnership between MIS and company operations, care must be taken that the distinction between line and staff functions is maintained. Clarity in line and staff functions can be ensured by making sure that the product and/or service is the driving force behind all technological decisions. The following questions must be asked: First, what business are we in? Then, how did we agree to behave? And finally, how can the technology fit our organization?

A special caution is needed for governmental agencies. Many have planning departments which have been granted decision-making powers. Problems and proposals are referred to them for study and decision. In many instances, the preferences of line managers are overridden by those put in charge of planning. In some instances, the planners have strengthened their position through an alliance with the fiscal staff. Now they have double clout. Not only do they tell others how to do their work, they also tell them how to spend their money.

In the case of a previously cited state motor vehicles agency, it worked this way. The agency's director requested all departments to submit their requests for PCs. These requests were made part of departmental budget requests from the agency. The agency moneys available would accommodate about half of the PC requests. Enter the planning and fiscal staffs. They decided that the proper way to handle the situation was to award each department half of its requests.

The end result was chaos. No department received enough PCs to do the work for which they were needed. Now all of the agency's PCs are underutilized. If line managers had been brought into the decision-making process, they would have gladly delayed computerization of some departments in favor of those with the greater PC needs. Unfortunately, these managers were not permitted to be in charge of that decision.

It is our experience that effective line managers in state government have acquired control over their own decision-making process. They have recaptured control over their budgets from fiscal staff and over their planning from support staff. They have made it clear that as managers they are held accountable for their work and that they, therefore, exercise control over their own budgets and decisions. Because they are effective managers, they willingly accept support services from others. But they insist that these services remain advisory.

Developing Knowledge from Information

The planning process is directed toward two differing results: task-oriented decisions and goal-oriented decisions. Task-oriented decisions bring a project or task into being. It is decision making that tells us how goals are achieved. It involves the assignment of personnel, budget, and other resources. It requires statements of work and delegation and general empowerment of those assigned the task. This is information-based management.

At another level, the planning process results in goal-oriented decisions. A goal is simply a subset of an organization's future vision. It is a discrete and definable portion of that vision. When a goal decision is made, the organization is asking whether or not that goal belongs in the total vision of its future. Authors Peters and Waterman (1982) call this "stick to the knitting." Most companies will ask at least two questions about a new product or service. "Can it be done?" and "Will it make money?" Strategic planning asks a third, "Do we choose to do it?" Or, as we have previously stated, "Does it fit the organization?" This is knowledge-based management.

Knowledge-based management knows many things. It knows "who we are," "what we do," and "what we do well." It knows that other things may be doable, even profitable. But it knows that the company does not have to do all things or other things. In other words, the company chooses its "knitting."

Knowledge-based management also knows that IT technology is capable of much more than its current use. But it also knows that the organization does not have to have all of the things that the technology does or any one thing in particular.

Knowledge-based management is derived from management's sense of mission, its development of normative behaviors, and its compliance with its own ethical stance toward employees and clients. Data and information are insufficient for these purposes. Data can tell management when and how things work. Information can help management see the costs, the return on investment, and the other comparative values of its choices. Only knowledge can instruct management in whether the company ought to do something, whether a specific goal is part of its future vision.

Knowledge-based management does one more thing. It constantly seeks a better and clearer vision of what the future will be. It may be unique to human systems that those organizations which are most secure in their past successes can make the greatest accommodation to new circumstances. Those which are most secure in knowing what they are at the present time are most capable of the greatest change and new vision of what they might become in the future.

Human systems that have done their homework are best equipped to manage their futures. They do it more effectively because they have determined what they want to be and purposely plan in that direction. In the philosophical sense they exemplify the axiom "Cogito ergo sum," or "I think, therefore, I am." In the strategic management of business, they are examples of the axiom "I think, I plan, therefore, I will be."

Sensible Strategies for Implementation

Enterprises that lay the groundwork for strategic management throughout the organization can move on to the strategic management of technology implementation. There must first be a general framework of strategic thinking before strategic management of technology implementation is possible. Without this foundation, there is confusion between tactical and strategic planning. Too many managers assume that strategic thinking asks the question "how shall we go about doing the technology implementation?" This question is tactical in nature, not strategic.

The real strategic issue is, "what criteria shall we use as we plan our technology implementation?" This will be illustrated by three phases of the Technology Implementation Life Cycle: marketing the system, education, and human communications.

Marketing the System

Marketing has to do with selling the change that accompanies a new technology. Initially, one might think that the criterion for successful marketing is how well the employees accept the new system. Actually, the strategic criterion is how well the new technology promotes employee acceptance of the company. It is not the organization that must sell its use of technology. Rather, the technology must sell the company to its employees. When this marketing criterion is effectively used, employees accept almost any new technology that the company selects.

But loyalty must be given to the worker before it is expected from the worker. Loyalty is like trust; it is always earned. The company must have as one of its values that technology is used in order to enhance the worker, not to replace the worker. This does not eliminate the possibility that positions disappear and workers are displaced. It raises the issue of whether corporate values and actions provide the support the worker needs for transition to a new position.

To support this value, the organization must work with the avowed purpose of providing its workers the best tools for their work, including technical tools. As tools evolve and change, the organization must adjust and improve its work processes. Firms that wish to be competitive in their markets are well served by the integrated development of tools and employees. A healthy and effective management institutes a steady process of worker skills evolution and technological evolution. By maintaining this steady process of evolution, it avoids the traumas of technological change (see Appendix B).

Ideally then, technology should be placed in its proper perspective — as another part of the work processes. Within this context, the marketing of a new technology is viewed primarily as a step up to higher levels of employee effectiveness and efficiency. It is viewed as one of the primary employee benefits in the organization.

Education

Education involves the explanation of why technology is being installed or upgraded. Again, a mistaken criterion for effective technology implementation is how well has the company explained the need for and benefits of the new system. A more sufficient strategic criterion is how well the company has planned for continued development of the employees and the technology. It is true that each change in technology requires explanation. If it is not explained in some detail, employees will be forced to create their own explanations. Their explanations are inevitably the worst or wrong ones. But it should be clear that explaining any one change in technology is primarily a tactical matter.

The strategic issue focuses on the climate of the workplace in which technology is used. And the best climate for technological development is one that stresses employee development. Within this type of environment, employees are encouraged to seek advancement. First, they seek advancement based on their present skills and abilities. Later they may seek advancement to other positions within the company which build upon those skills and abilities. Given this situation, employees may safely assume that the company is providing them with the best possible tools to do their work. IT is seen as a challenge to growth and development, not as a threat to job security. In fact, the newer forms of technology are seen as their best allies in pursuit of advancement.

A company needs two policies to support the strategic management of technology implementations. First, it needs a policy that requires it to provide an explanation of all changes in technology. Consistent adherence to this policy builds employee trust and helps allay doubts in the midst of technical changes. Under this policy employees may still ask for explanations, but they are much more likely to give credence to adequate and rational replies. Not needing to make up their own explanations or having "positive thinking" thrown at them, the employees feel secure that the company knows what it is doing when adding or changing its technology.

Second, the company needs a policy that supports employee skills evolution. It needs to act in such a manner that it inscribes this policy deeply in the consciousness of each employee. To do so, it must recognize that there is a risk of skills extinction as technology advances and changes within the organization. The company must state that it views its employees as the most important part of its advances in productivity and efficiency. Finally, the organization must offer and support training and other skills development opportunities that improve employees' skills as the technology improves.

Human Communications

Human communications involves those actions that the organization takes to institute ongoing communications between technicians and users of technology. A mistaken criterion is the forms of communication that the company has established between technicians and users. Responding to this criterion, organizations have established newsletters, hot lines, and other devices. These are laudable efforts, but they are tactical endeavors which respond to tactical questions.

The strategic criterion for effective technology implementation has to do with how well the company gives *and receives* communication about technology. This criterion requires more than the development of technology "house organs." It requires the development of a feed-forward process of sharing information about the organization's technology. It involves a broad-based sharing of information and knowledge within the company, including a flow from the company to employees, from employees to the company, and from employee to employee.

This feedback process may also be seen as feed forward. It is an expression of the organization's concern for enlisting all employees in the improved use of technology. It encourages employees to propose new technological uses and applications. It opens the channels of communication so that all can send messages, as well as receive them. Within this forum, all employees perceive that their messages are honored and used in the organization's planning and decision making.

This form of open communication and shared ownership of decision making raises employees' expectations about corporate communications. Company newsletters, suggestion systems, announcements, and so on are expected and respected. Because the company is willing to listen, the employees listen when the company speaks — including when it speaks about technology.

A Reprise: Strategic Planning for Implementation

Just as there is frequent confusion between strategic and tactical planning, so there is a lack of clarity about the stages of strategic planning. There is a tendency to jump to the last stage. For example, many organizations move too quickly to a consideration of the benefits of automation. For them strategic planning has to do with questions such as these:

Will IT make us more competitive?

Will we have better data and better decisions?

Will our managers have more time for other work?

Will we provide better service to our customers?

Will the planning function operate better?

Will IT aid in the development and growth of our organization?

The scenario that emerges is that the benefits of technology are most impressive, especially when backed by vendor advertisements and demonstrations. It is then assumed that since the benefits are so obvious, everyone pitches in to make the implementation fly. If this script had a subtitle, it would be: "Since we need the technology so badly, we'll have to learn how to use it." But this process omits the necessary first step in strategic planning: the examination of present resources.

The resources of any organization are easy to identify when tangibles alone are counted. It is relatively simple to list assets, whether liquid or fixed. It becomes more difficult when nontangibles such as employee skills are considered. There are means by which employee skills can be ascertained and recorded for use in strategic planning. Employee skills are among the present resources of the organization which must be considered when planning a technology implementation. Even the process of employee skills evolution becomes a resource to the company. If skills evolution is ongoing, there will be a base of constantly expanding resources.

However, the most significant nontangible resource that an organization can develop for technology implementation is a value-oriented, ethical foundation for employee relations. The most effective way to do this is through shared ownership of the company.

The most basic element of ownership is that all employees have a common sense and a common understanding of the business they are in and the values they share. They must have a common answer to the question "What business are we in?" They must have a common understanding of how they behave when carrying out this vision. And they must see how technology fits into the vision.

Technological change will come more easily to some organizations than others, depending on their business environment and culture. Some are more technologically driven or dependent than others. They require constant technological improvements. In these cases, technological changes occur with greater ease, since the employees expect regular changes. Such changes are viewed as "part of the scene around here."

For most organizations, however, there must be a conscientious effort to anticipate the ownership issue and to plan for its inclusion in technology implementations. Strategically, this will involve the development of, or references to, the company's mission statement. Tactically, this will involve management behaviors that reinforce the organizational value that people are more important than technology. Operationally, it will involve the use of integrated methods and procedures for technology implementation.

Technology implementations work when each level of management makes its own unique contribution to the effort. Then, and only then, can the Technology Implementation Life Cycle be used most effectively in an organization.

5

The Technology Implementation Life Cycle: Part One

When you don't know where you are going, any road will get you there just as fast.

—The Cheshire Cat

A Note to the Executive Reader

Chapters 5 and 6 present the eight phases of the Technology Implementation Life Cycle. Each contains a great amount of detail. If you wish, you can read only the executive summary that introduces each life cycle phase.*

By now we hope it is evident that the problems of technology are not technological problems. They are management problems requiring management solutions. What follows is the detailed explanation of the fully integrated process of implementation that we call the "Technology Implementation Life Cycle." This cycle has three characteristics: (1) It is a sequence of activities presented in chronological order; (2) it is a true process, moving in cyclical fashion back to its original starting point; (3) it provides an integrated methodology for implementing technical systems into the human systems of businesses and organizations.

---

*Executive summaries are on pages 95-102, 107-110, 115-116 and 123-125.

Implementation Avoidance

We believe that there is a need for a more finely controlled and detailed approach to the implementation of IT. Even though technology implementation problems have been observed and documented, organizations continue to implement technical systems incorrectly. Even when a systematic process of computer implementation such as The McConnell Method (Appendix B) is explained, management avoids using it. We wondered why. Then a consultant friend gave us some sound advice: "Never assume that you know what motivates others. Learn to listen for what is motivating them." So we listened, and we noted that many senior executives avoid planning technology implementations. Their reasons are listed in Table 5-1.

Theory X True Believers

There are some managers who still believe in theory X management. Not just some of the time—all of the time. They assert the logic and evidence of their belief without ever realizing what it is that they really believe. Their basic assumption is that the problem belongs to someone else. They refuse to deal with technology implementation problems because of their own need to absolve themselves of responsibility. When someone talks to these managers about planned implementations, they make comments like the following:

"I have all kinds of problems with my users. I'm never sure what I ought to do."

"If I give too much information to the users, I will be turning the asylum over to the inmates."

"If I am not careful, I will stir the users up."

Quite frankly, it is very difficult to change such people. In some circumstances, they must be ordered to plan IT implementations. In other situations, they may have to be moved out of the way. If they are to participate in a properly planned implementation, they must first be converted to a new management style and attitude. Without this transformation, they will inevitably subvert or sabotage the effort.

Table 5-1
Reasons for Avoiding Planned Technology Implementation

1. Theory X true believers
2. "Let George do it"
3. The resource poor
4. Business questions

"Let George Do It"

These managers believe that they have identified the implementation problems and the people who can solve them. Close examination of their opinions reveals that they have a very narrow view of the nature of the problems. They also have a narrow view of what steps must be taken to ensure adequate implementation. Most generally, they do not even think of going beyond barely adequate efforts. They make statements such as these:

> "Our systems analysts support our end users. They take care of system implementation."

> "The vendor provides implementation support. I don't have to do anything."

This management group believes in "letting George do it." They also believe that the final responsibility for implementation rests with the technology user. Those who express this view are often very competent in using their own computers. Their experience in developing their PC skills has been almost exclusively positive. They may sincerely believe that everyone else can have the same positive experience. They offer these comments:

> "The end users can manage their own implementation."

> "Our computer users are very experienced; they do not need any more support."

> "The implementation problem is self-resolving. People know how to use computers, especially PCs."

Admittedly, computer hype has contributed to this deficient insight. The phrase "user friendly" has convinced some people that the computer truly is friendly. But, user friendly is a marketing slogan and in no way reflects the true relationship between technology and users. It is human gullibility that causes us to believe such slogans. The problems of implementation are not solved by user-friendly technology. A careful survey of past implementation efforts and of present user support needs provides a devastating insight: In most instances, it shows serious deficiencies in implementation planning, strategies, and tactics. But be prepared—not everyone wants to hear the truth, the whole truth, the unvarnished truth.

The Resource Poor

There are those who claim that the pressure to produce and support systems does not permit them the "luxury" of attending to implementation needs. They continue to use their resources to design, produce, and install new technologies. They assume that their design decisions justify the systems they create. Oddly enough, at this very time, many people are bemoaning the lack of accountability in the computerization of American business. The criticism points to an insufficient cost-to-benefit analysis or a lack of cost-to-benefit comparisons of all alternative technological solutions. Although there will always be some who bemoan a lack of resources, it appears that the real problem is a lack of planning. Meanwhile, those who think that they are resource poor continue to say the following:

"I don't have enough time to get requested systems up and running. How will I ever have time to plan implementation?"

"I can't meet systems installation deadlines now. Don't ask me to add more steps to the process."

"I don't have enough budget to add the personnel I would need to do a planned implementation."

Such managers may be victims rather than guilty parties. They may have fallen into the trap of American businesses—fascination with and belief in technology as a solution to business problems. Highly skilled in using technological systems yet poorly informed about human systems, they readily accept their role as purveyors of the latest, best technology. This difficulty will be resolved when management begins planning the development of technology while keeping in mind the vital role of people in its successful use.

Business Questions

Some of the business questions we hear about implementations sound negative at first. For example, people question planned implementations thus:

"How much will this cost me?"

"How long will this take?"

If taken at face value, there is nothing wrong with these questions. They are good business questions. Their problem is that they are seldom accompanied by other necessary inquiries, such as these:

"What will it cost me if I don't do a planned implementation?"

"How long will it take to get the system running correctly if we don't have a planned implementation?"

In business, questions are like numbers. No one question (number) has meaning apart from its comparison to another question (number). It is our belief that the cost of unplanned implementation is *always greater* than the cost of planned implementation.

We also believe that the time needed to achieve effective system use is *always greater* without planned implementation.

What we believe is that management needs a detailed description of a planned implementation. That is what we have provided in this and the next chapter.

Planned Implementation

The implementation of IT requires attention to eight sequential phases. We call these the Technology Implementation Life Cycle (Fig. 5-1). The eight phases are:

1. Preimplementation
2. Human design*
3. Marketing*
4. Education*
5. Training*
6. Documentation*
7. Human communications*
8. Postimplementation

The phases are sequential but often overlap during use. However, they are sequential because each builds on the successful completion of the preceding one. For this reason, each phase must be evaluated separately upon its completion to determine its effectiveness. That is why the last step of each phase states that the Technology Implementation Life Cycle user should "note those steps (in this phase) which need improvement."

The Technology Implementation Life Cycle is divided into two parts. The first part is the leadership function. The second part is the administration function. Fig. 5-2 shows the two halves of the cycle. Pre and postimplementation are joined together to show their foundational role in the entire cycle.

The leadership function flows out of preimplementation and consists of three phases: human design, marketing, and education. This function is the subject of this chapter. In it we show that leadership is the groundwork for what follows. Its phases are components of the preparatory stage which readies the human system to accept, absorb, and use technology. We also show that inattention to these phases of technology implementation greatly undercuts the success of the effort.

---

*These six phases were initially developed as The McConnell Method™** by co-author Vicki McConnell (see Appendix B for more detail).

**Trademark application pending in the name of The McConnell Group, 2900 Craig's Way, Columbus, Ohio 43221.

	ACTIVITY	GOAL
1. Preimplementation		
	Gather Data on Workplace, Personnel Work, Tasks, etc.	Determine Planning Alternatives, Needed Resources, and Possible Roadblocks
2. Human Design		
	Study Automated Workplace and Establish Criteria for Its Human Design	Eliminate Deterrents and Establish Incentives for Productivity, Human Physiology, and Psychology
3. Marketing		
	Develop and Implement a Strategy for "Selling" Technical Systems and the Changes They Cause	Introduce Technology So That Worker "Buys" the System and "Owns" the System
4. Education		
	Educate Workers About the Demands New Technology Will Make on Them and the Benefits It Will Provide	Reduce Worker Stress Concerning Technology and Increase Confidence in The Ability to Use It Productively
5. Training		
	Develop and Implement a Sequential, Natural Program of Skill Growth	Develop Workers Who Are Minimally Computer Competent and Primed for Additional Computer Skills Evolution
6. Documentation		
	Compose and Distribute Documents That Explain How the System Works	Provide Easy Access to and Effective Assistance from Reference Materials So That Workers Can Complete Automated Tasks
7. Human Communications		
	Establish and Maintain Continuing Means of Communication with Workers	Create Opportunities for Dialogue Between Workers and Information Technology, Technicians, and Management
8. Postimplementation		
	Compile Evaluation of Each Phase Into One Document and Review Entire Implementation Process	Feed Forward Evaluation Results to Improve the Next Technology Implementation

FIG. 5-1   The Technology Implementation Life Cycle, Based on The McConnell Method

Chapter 6 presents three phases of the administration function which focus on the organization's work: training, documentation, and human communications. These phases are administrative because they bring the technical and human systems together into a common process of work that is both integrated and efficient. The administration function produces those products or services which define the organization's purpose. Chapter 6 concludes with the postimplementation phase which lays the groundwork for an organization's next use of the Technology Implementation Life Cycle.

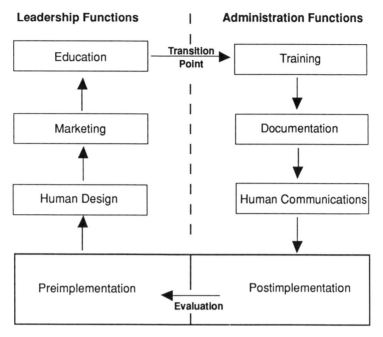

FIG. 5-2   Major Functional Components of the Technology Implementation Life Cycle

This is a true cycle of activity, but it is divided into two important functions, leadership and administration. Leadership is the function of preparing the organization and its members to accept new technologies. Administration is the function of preparing users for the productive use of new technology.

Phase 1: Preimplementation

The major goal of the preimplementation phase (Fig. 5-3) is the development of openness and honesty about the real costs and benefits of implementation. The preimplementation phase is designed to shift the focus away from getting the technical system up and running to getting the user up and running. Without this type of preplanning, the process of implementation will suffer two major defects. First, it will be fragmented. Second, it will lack criteria for evaluating its effectiveness.

The steps in the preimplementation phase are:*

1. Define the scope of the system and its implementation.

2. Identify, profile, and select an implementation task force.

---

*Each phase of the Technology Implementation Life Cycle is broken into a series of detailed and explicit steps (see Appendix A). The authors recognize that not all of these steps are applicable in every technology implementation. They will be content to leave that judgment to the person in charge of technology implementation. The process for making these judgments is explained in Chapter 7.

3. Identify required implementation resources.
4. Prepare a preliminary implementation plan for senior management approval.
5. Assign tasks and deadlines to the implementation task force.
6. Establish times of periodic review and evaluation of the implementation process.
7. Note those steps which need improvement.

Define the Scope of the System and Its Implementation

The comments which follow use the installation of a new mainframe application as an example. From this example, one can extrapolate to more complex implementations, multiple applications, and different hardware. The use of a mainframe example is not meant to ignore the increasing use of PCs. Examples will be given of other situations using PCs to show how the principles and tasks of the Technology Implementation Life Cycle can be applied to them.

We have stated that technology exists to serve the human system of an organization. If this is true, then it is the employees who will ultimately judge whether a system has been effectively implemented. Their evaluation will be done in one of two ways. If it is done according to stated written criteria (Table 5-2) it will be done well. If it is done by unstated and unwritten criteria, it will be done poorly.

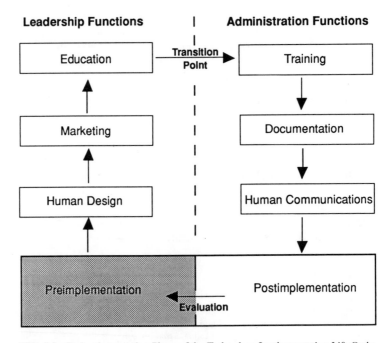

FIG. 5-3 Preimplementation Phase of the Technology Implementation Life Cycle

Table 5-2
Stated and Written Criteria for Evaluation

1. Parameters of a software application
   a. All it is capable of doing
   b. Immediate cost justification
2. General goals/achievements of implementation
3. Measures used to demonstrate achievement

The stated written criteria for an implementation evaluation must be prepared by end user management and must cover three areas. The first area encompasses a software application's parameters. Each application has two parameters. The first consists of all those capabilities that the application offers the user. The second is narrower. It refers to those tasks which users must initially be capable of performing in order to justify the cost of the application.

One immediate goal of a technology implementation should be a cost justification of the installed system. For most line managers, this occurs when their staff can do the tasks they are supposed to be doing. If this goal is effectively achieved, these managers are prepared to have their staff move on to other technical skills and uses.

Keep the focus on immediate results; then move on to higher application uses. Take a clue from the PC users who train themselves. That's how they do it.

The second criterion looks at what the implementation process itself should accomplish. It focuses on what users are learning about technology and how that learning contributes to the greater development of the organization. This requires the use of "before" and after" measures of users' technical understanding and skill. User profiles, which gather such data, are explained in detail in phase 3, marketing.

It is likely that most managers misstate their implementation support needs because they do not know the technical skill level of their staff. Developing the general employee skills in technology use aids implementation. But this effort must be planned and measured. And it must be done in close cooperation with user management if it is to succeed.

The final preimplementation criterion, setting measures of achievement, brings out the best in end user managers. They must answer the question "How will we know that we have met our stated goals in this implementation?" These criteria must be end user performance related. From them the implementation task force can work backward in an if, then manner: If this criterion will evaluate our success, then we must be sure to do the following during an implementation. The implementation task force must work out this "if, then" process with user managers.

Identify, Profile, and Select an Implementation Task Force

An effective implementation requires a task force. The task force's size should reflect the size of the technical system being implemented. It should be multidisciplinary. Most recognize the need for interdisciplinary skills, particularly technical and management abilities. However, effective implementation is achieved when other cross-disciplines are represented in such a group.

A task force with the customary mix of technical and management skills is necessary. However, the task force should also be made up of two other groups. A second invaluable mix is a cross section of employees who represent the different workers using the system, including their supervisors and managers. A third mix brings critical expertise and skills to the implementation process. It includes, but is not limited to, professional trainers, educators, communicators, and writers.

Perhaps the key ingredient in any task force is a senior management representative who fully participates. This person should not serve as the task force's chairperson, but as a unique resource to it. Specifically, a senior executive can provide advice as the task force assesses the level of support and the resources needed for an implementation. If top management does not provide the resources asked for by the task force, the senior executive becomes a firsthand observer who can see the consequences of such executive decisions and their direct impact on effective implementations.

Care should be taken that this senior executive does not intervene too frequently on behalf of the task force. That executive's basic role is that of a participant and observer/recorder. This person's function is to provide direct senior management input into the implementation process and personal observation of the impact that resource allocation has on effectiveness.

Identify Required Implementation Resources

At this point, it is too early in the implementation effort to construct a final resource budget. However, it is possible to construct a resource estimate. The evaluation criteria and task force members' experience should be adequate for the task. An inexperienced task force may be advised to gather as much data as possible. Each of the eight phases of the Technology Implementation Life Cycle has data-gathering steps. The task force should review all of these steps and construct a plan for data gathering that combines as many steps as possible in one effort. Using this plan as a guide, the task force can construct a sampling procedure to determine an estimate of the time, money, and personnel needed for an implementation.

One thing a task force must do is to connect the expenditure of funds to the achievement of specific goals derived from the *use* of the system to be implemented. It is the "if, then" script described previously (in the step, "Define the Scope of the System and Its Implementation") which clarifies implementation goals. But now resources are assigned to each goal in the following fashion: "If" we wish to achieve the following, "then" we must do the following, "and" at this cost to us. The logical connection between these factors must be clearly demonstrated so that the reverse is self-evident to senior management: If we do not expend these resources, we will not do the necessary implementation steps which ensure that employees can use a new system.

There is a tendency to underestimate the resources needed to implement ITs. When this happens, systems are poorly installed and users often do not use all of their capabilities. This results in expensive systems functioning far below their potential levels of effectiveness. Most organizations are not well informed on these costs. As a consequence, the cost of proper implementation often seems very large the first time the Technology Implementation Life Cycle is used. For this reason, we recommend that the cycle be applied initially to reasonably sized applications, with careful cost justification of all expenditures, or that smaller portions of a large application be used.

Three benefits will accrue. First, the initial attempts at planned implementation will avoid the risk of overexpenditure. Second, the business will establish a pattern of reasonable implementation procedures with required cost justification. And third, it will develop the attitude that technology implementation is a natural process, an ongoing cycle of organizational activity.

Prepare a Preliminary Implementation Plan for Senior Management Approval

The task force should prepare an initial implementation plan which includes the following:

> Parameters of the application
>
> Required goals of the implementation
>
> Resources needed to meet these goals
>
> Timetable of expected activities
>
> Evaluation criteria

This plan should be concise. It can consist of an outline with limited supporting text. It should include a list of major implementation milestones, noting the dates when the task force will provide senior management further reports and required approvals. This initial plan should be formally presented by the task force to top management for review and approval.

This is a critical step. Many senior managers are woefully ignorant of the technology and the steps required to bring it to full and effective operation. Technology will not be fully integrated into the business until this deficiency is corrected. Executive commitment to technology is enhanced by their involvement in the implementation process.

Care should be taken to explain to senior management that this preliminary blueprint is a general outline and not a detailed plan. However, this preliminary plan should challenge them to approve the necessary resources and support needed to ensure effective implementation. As system installation progresses, the task force should expand on its first implementation plan, developing it in greater detail.

Assign Tasks and Deadlines to the Implementation Task Force

The task force is a working body, with one member serving as the chairperson. The chairperson should have line accountability to the executive to whom the task force reports. The chairperson should have line authority over task force members who are assigned to specific implementation responsibilities.

Some tasks may require special expertise not found among the members. For example, the person who writes documentation for users may not be a member of the implementation task force. In such a case, a task force member should be assigned to coordinate with the documentation writer regarding this task. It is vital that all steps affecting documentation be coordinated with the documentation writer. Likewise, all documentation activities affecting the success of the implementation should be coordinated with the task force.

Now is the time to search through the personnel of the firm for those with skills needed during an implementation. For example, professionals who work in training, public relations/information, marketing, or advertising are expert in areas that relate to the phases of marketing the system, educating the users, and maintaining user-technician communications. Their use for temporary task force assignments is invaluable, if not critical, to an implementation.

Once implementation responsibilities have been assigned, a timetable should be established. A process similar to pert charting can be used. This allows all individuals to determine whether the schedule is realistic so that they can complete their assigned tasks on time. The task force chairperson manages the timetable for the entire implementation and decides where coordination is needed. This pert chart approach asks "Who needs to have what done in order for another to begin a specific task?" or "In what sequence must tasks be completed to maintain progress?" or "What tasks must be coordinated for this phase to be completed?"

Once the timetable is established, the task force's reporting and tracking mechanisms can be set up. It should be noted that these reports and meetings are for the internal management of the task force. They do not constitute, or contribute directly to, any reports to senior management. Reports to senior management flow out of the next step.

Establish Times of Periodic Review and Evaluation of the Implementation Process

There are several things that senior management needs to know about an implementation. It needs to know that the process is on schedule. It needs to know that resources are being used within tolerable time and money limits. And it needs to know that evaluation criteria are being met. These are the essential elements of strategic management: time, resources, and evaluation criteria.

We recommend that top management receive a report upon the completion of each of the eight phases of the life cycle. The task force will need to develop its own evaluation criteria for each phase as it relates to the general goals of the implementation. Its reports to senior management should focus on what the task force has accomplished and what goals it has met. Senior management reports should avoid extensive implementation activity lists.

We recommend that the task force chairperson consider reviewing these reports during a meeting with the senior executive to whom he or she reports. This encourages discussion, allows for midcourse corrections, and assists in maintaining top management involvement and approval.

Note Those Steps Which Need Improvement

Given the increasing complexity of IT, a controlled, iterative process seems best suited to implementation. The process needs to be iterative because complex systems require time and thought. Those responsible for implementation need the opportunity to constantly examine their decisions and plans. It needs to be a controlled process because no organization can be stuck in the iterative loop forever. Each implementation needs to have a beginning and an end. Each of the phases of the Technology Implementation Life Cycle ends with the suggestion to go back and make improvements. This is our gentle reminder to constantly evaluate and improve the Technology Implementation Life Cycle process.

Phase 2: Human Design

Living with IT is like sleeping with an elephant. It is best to keep one eye open at all times lest the beast roll over on you. And roll over it does. In the compendium "Computer Culture," Annals of The New York Academy of Sciences, Alphonse Chapanis (1984) notes how computerization has led to poorly designed work stations. This, in turn, has led to higher rates of illness among video display terminal (VDT) users. It has also led to impoverishment of job tasks, which, in turn, has led to high levels of worker dissatisfaction. The author's conclusion? "Computers should enrich human lives, not dehumanize them."

It does little good to claim that this result occurs by accident rather than by design. "I didn't mean to hurt you" is the cry of a child disclaiming responsibility for his or her actions. "I'm sorry, it won't happen again" is the responsible adult's response. Confronting human design issues is an implementation step that is long overdue. Too often these issues have been ignored and people have been hurt. When properly done, human design includes the study of automation's impact on the workplace, how people work, how they relate to their work, and how they relate to one another at work (Fig. 5-4).

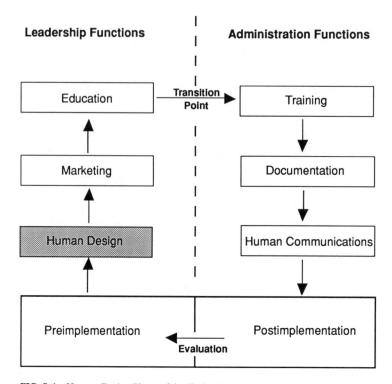

FIG. 5-4 Human Design Phase of the Technology Implementation Life Cycle

Previously in this chapter we used a mainframe computer software application as an example. However, at this point we also need to consider the impact of changing computer hardware. Some readers may note that the term "ergonomics"* is not used in this phase. That is intentional because we believe that it has a more limited meaning than the term "human design." The term "human design" also has the advantage of providing an immediately clear interpretation. Of course, automation should be "designed for humans"; who else?

The steps in the human design phase of implementation are as follows:

1. Conduct a workplace impact study.

2. Gather user demographics.

3. Review the organization's criteria/standards for human design.

---

*Ergonomics, according to Dennis Longley and Michael Shain (1989), "is the study of people in relation to their working environment. It is concerned with the design of man-machine interfaces to improve factors affecting health, efficiency, comfort and safety." Common usage often limits its scope to the interface between computer hardware/software and the user.

4. Review the procedures for human design evaluation.
   a. Hardware procedures.
   b. Software procedures.

5. Consult with the human design review committee.

6. Design user screens and reports.

7. Pilot test screens and reports.

8. Periodically review screens and reports.

9. Note those steps which need improvement.

Conduct a Workplace Impact Study

The overall question which a workplace impact study addresses is whether the workplace is prepared for the technological changes to be introduced. Answering this question assumes two kinds of knowledge. The first is an awareness of the kind of change that is proposed. The second is an ability to assess impacts. Major changes occur when an office or other workplace changes from manual to automated systems. Less severe changes may occur in the transition from one level of automation to another. Keep this point clearly in mind: The technicians will not know the severity of the impact. Only the users will be able to define the extent and severity of the change involved.

What management is often not aware of is the impact on workers who must now use VDTs to do their work. VDTs lessen employee mobility. They often confine workers for longer periods of time to their work areas. They reduce social interactions. VDTs can create the need to change office furnishings, lighting, and floor plans. And finally, there are some health risks to employees who use VDTs. But what is really overlooked is that all of these changes create costs for every organization that automates.

Costs are not intrinsically bad. They are the first necessary step in the conduct of any business. Unplanned costs are intrinsically bad because they are uncontrolled. The only way that costs can be controlled is when they are anticipated, identified, and managed by choice. When I choose my costs, I am in control. When they occur accidentally, the costs are in control.

The costs of a technology implementation include the planned and unplanned impacts that the system has on its users. The first step in controlling these costs is to identify where they occur. Nothing is of greater assistance in this initial step than historical data—knowing where technological impacts have arisen in the past and where they are present today. These data should also include any current problems that users are experiencing. Care should be taken to include in this data gathering any human design problems which were corrected and how they were corrected.

Note that workers are affected by technology through both direct and indirect contact with it. Direct effects are a result of the use of the technology, for example, the actual work done while at a computer. Indirect effects include all changes in the work environment, such as changes in associations, supervision, and status in the work force. Once noted, a record of these effects is an important and primary resource for all subsequent implementations. That record must be kept current and must be related to specific instances of technological change so that cause and effect relationships can at least be inferred.

After historical data are reviewed, work areas targeted for new systems installation can be evaluated. At this stage, the objective is to determine where human design impacts will occur. The primary question is whether the work area is well designed for technology use. This is not a simple yes/no proposition. Organizations must establish their own human design criteria for the automated workplace. Without such criteria, it is impossible to assess properly the impact of any new system on the workers and their work area.

These impacts go beyond the physical to the organizational and social. IT influences how people work and how they relate to one another as they work. Automation of a workplace changes the style of work and, therefore, the attitude employees have about work. These impacts must be anticipated in order to be controlled. Automation changes how employees interact socially with one another. From this they develop their emotional reactions to being at work.

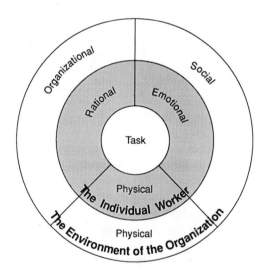

FIG. 5-5 Human Design Factors

Six factors of human design are noted; three apply to the individual worker and three apply to the organizational environment. The relationship of each factor to the task of work is shown by placing the task in the central position.

It is common for workers to comment after an automation that "it feels different at work." They see the old work patterns disappear and with them the loss of contact with other employees—some of whom may be good friends. They feel deprived, sometimes emotionally starved. These impacts create real costs for a company, though they may not be directly or immediately measurable. Nonetheless, if they are to be controlled, they must be anticipated (Fig. 5-5).

Gather User Demographics

No one group of users will react to a change exactly the same way as another group. There are typical responses, average responses, and even common responses, but not the same responses. Many of these differences depend upon demographic variables such as age, gender, job position, work performed, length of service with a company, and education. The work of the implementation task force is simplified when there is a historical account of how employees responded to past technology changes. If historical data are analyzed by demographic variables, they assist the task force in anticipating probable employee responses to new implementations. For example, it is more likely that older employees who have experienced or observed computers displacing fellow workers harbor very negative attitudes toward automation.

Some companies have found it helpful to survey workers periodically concerning their reactions to systems. This information, broken out demographically, provides an implementation task force with specific cautions and advice. It also provides a basis for individual or group interviews which can provide detail concerning employees' reactions to poor installations and employees' ideas on how to improve the implementation process.

It should be noted that the task force can combine this data-gathering task with the data-gathering tasks of other phases of the implementation. Later in this chapter, we will comment on such data needs when we discuss profiling technology users before planning the education and training phases of an implementation. All such data needs can be gathered through one instrument or one interviewing process.

Review the Organization's Criteria/Standards for Human Design

Every organization that uses IT needs human design criteria and standards concerning hardware, software, and the user's workplace. Tables 5-3, 5-4, and 5-5 provide examples of human design criteria. As an organization develops its own criteria, it probably will discover that these lists need to be much longer and more detailed.

All human design criteria should be approved by senior management, reviewed annually, and upgraded as the technology changes and advances. These standards must also be accompanied by procedures explaining how they are to be applied, with

Table 5-3
Human Design Hardware Concerns

Movable VDT screens
Detachable keyboards
Glare guards for VDT screens
General flexibility in positioning VDT equipment

Table 5-4
Human Design Software Concerns

Computer screens and reports
    Compatibility
    Reliability
    Standardization
    Ease of use
    Ease of learning
    Security

Table 5-5
Human Design Concerns About the Workplace

Physical needs of the worker
Organizational needs of the worker
Social needs of the worker

policies citing how they will be enforced. In the latter case, we recommend that a multidisciplinary human design review committee (see the subsequent step "Consult with the Human Design Review Committee" for further explanation) be appointed for their review and enforcement.

If an organization has no human design standards, it is imperative to establish them. For the first implementation, it may be more realistic for a task force to establish human design standards for that implementation alone. However, this should be only a temporary expedient. Every organization using IT should eventually develop human design standards. Several governmental bodies have already legislated or mandated human design standards for VDT use. If organizations do not handle the matter for themselves, how long will it be before the government steps in and does it for them?

Lastly, it is vital that executive management approve these standards. Their endorsement is critical to the success of the human design phase. Without executive endorsement it is difficult, if not impossible, for a task force to enforce companywide human design standards.

Review the Procedures for Human Design Evaluation

The implementation task force should use human design criteria to develop the evaluation of the company's technology. Any deviations from established criteria should be reviewed and corrected, with subsequent approval by the users and by top management.

The human design committee should establish the criteria for hardware purchases. The following three steps indicate how an organization can handle old and new purchases of hardware. The first step is to review and evaluate existing hardware to determine if it complies with human design criteria. If it does not, it should at least be gradually replaced through a plan of attrition.

The second step is to establish procedures for continual review and improvement of the human design hardware criteria. Computer hardware is constantly evolving. Each new release contains features not found in previous models. The organization must, therefore, constantly update its criteria on human design just to stay current with the existing hardware.

The third step is to establish procedures for the purchase of computer hardware. These procedures should include a report and a review of all hardware purchases to ensure their compliance with the company's standards. There should be appropriate penalties for the violation of human design standards, including an appeal procedure for requested hardware purchases that do not meet company criteria.

Our recommended approach to software human design also includes a three-step procedure. Step 1 is to design screens and reports according to predetermined human design criteria. Once developed, the screens and reports should be reviewed and approved by the workers who will use them. This review and approval should also include user management, even if they do not work directly with the screens and reports.

Step 2 is to pilot test all applications software and to obtain user sign-off before the system is released for general use.

Step 3 is a periodic review and evaluation of the system to determine if it does what the users expected it to do. The results of these evaluations should be reviewed by the technology implementation task force and filed with the human design review committee.

Consult with the Human Design Review Committee

We recommend that all organizations which use IT establish a human design review committee with representation from the corporate medical staff, executive management, the legal department, union(s), the health insurance staff, and the purchasing and facilities management. This should be a standing committee meeting at stated intervals, but no less than once a year. It should be responsible for establishing and reviewing the organization's criteria, procedures, and activities in the human design of its technology.

The technology implementation task force should consult directly with this committee, or its members, as required. The task force should file all required reports concerning human design with this committee. The human design committee should guide and advise the task force in all human design areas, and may be given the authority to approve task force actions.

Design User Screens and Reports

Using organizationally accepted human design standards, system reports and screens are designed, reviewed for compliance, and given a first approval. Reports and screens should be evaluated for their effectiveness and efficiency during use. The true efficiency of screen and report design is not concerned with how long it takes to design them, but rather with how easy they are for the user to learn and use.

Pilot Test Screens and Reports

All computer screens and reports should be subjected to a "reality test." This is more commonly called a "pilot test." A pilot test is usually administered to determine if a technical system works as it should. A reality test is administered to ascertain if the computer screens and reports correspond reasonably well to the way a user works while using them. A reality test can be conducted as a "walkthrough," with selected users working with the screens and/or reports to perform typical system tasks. When they have finished "test driving" the system, they are interviewed. Their reactions, comments, and suggestions are recorded.

These records note how the users feel about the system's ability to perform as expected, including their comfort and satisfaction with the system; their ability to learn and use the system easily; their opinion of the system's ability to support them in their work; and their recommendations for system improvements and enhancements. These recommendations are used for final system redesign. Once redesign is completed, assuming that some changes are needed, the screens and reports are given final approval and sign-off by the users.

Periodically Review Screens and Reports

The task force should set a date by which all computer screens and reports will be evaluated. Once this final review is completed, necessary revisions are made. Then the task force establishes dates and procedures for periodic review of reports and screens by user management.

This is seldom done. Most changes in reports and screens occur when an entire system is changed. In our opinion, this accounts for the many poor screen and report designs in use today. Screens need periodic review to determine their continuing effectiveness and efficiency. Likewise, reports need regular evaluation to ascertain their continued usefulness, timeliness, and relevance.

A word of caution: Computer screen and report review is also an important step in the analysis of any software package under consideration for purchase. However, it must be recognized that the review and evaluation of reports and screens is and remains a management issue, not a technological one. The frequency of review and of changes should be decided by the operational managers who use the screens and reports.

Note Those Steps Which Need Improvement

Two things influence the progressive improvement in the human design of a company's hardware and software and the users' workplace. First, any organization that uses the Technology Implementation Life Cycle discovers its own areas for improvement. Second, improvements in technology design may occur in areas that affect human use. The implementation task force should keep thorough records of all improvements in human design areas and all difficulties encountered. This information should be shared with the organization's human design committee.

Phase 3: Marketing

When we first talk to people about marketing, they usually state that "marketing plans are developed when you have a product to sell, not when you're implementing a computer system." Then we ask, "Who in the organization is the owner of the new system?" At first, they may assert that it is the organization. Then we ask, "Who uses the new system?" Now our point is made because the user is always the owner of the new system — no one else. Getting a system from the its developer to its user requires a change of ownership. Planning how a change of ownership happens is "marketing" (Fig. 5-6).

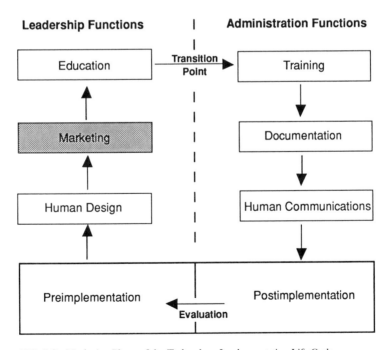

FIG. 5-6   Marketing Phase of the Technology Implementation Life Cycle

Sometimes the "sale" of a new system never takes place, and therefore, the system is never fully owned by the user. There are organizations with unused software applications sitting on the shelf. These are classic cases of systems that were never "sold" to their intended users. And because the users didn't "buy" them, they were never installed. What a waste, and often all for lack of a marketing plan.

The first question that a good marketer asks is, "What is it that we are selling?" In the case of IT the sell has consistently been the "sizzle." That is, most selling has centered on the advantages of technical systems. As a marketing pitch, advantages have limited value to their users. Computer users must be sold on the new work style inherent in automation. For them, this is the steak.

Selling a new work style to a nontechnical user is difficult for technicians for two reasons. First, technicians don't work where the users work (although PCs are rapidly changing this situation). Second, technicians don't do the user's work. They often don't understand the buyer. And understanding the buyer is the key to selling and to developing a marketing plan. One has to start by asking what the buyer is buying.

If the user of IT is to buy the next implementation, this means finding out what the users want to improve about their work. It means finding out how they personally want to grow and develop. In sales language, don't try to sell them what you're selling, sell them what they're buying. The steps in this process are given below. Note the heavy emphasis placed on data gathering in step 1. We believe that these data are critical to marketing and vital to many successive phases of the implementation.

The steps in the marketing phase of implementation are as follows:

1. Gather data on potential technology impacts.
   a. Review and assess previous implementations.
   b. Identify impacts unique to the technology implementation.
   c. Measure and study preimplementation productivity and work styles.
   d. Profile users.
   e. Conduct a reality pretest of the users.
   f. Conduct an IT attitude survey.
   g. Identify the corporate culture and subcultures of user groups.
   h. Form user focus groups.

2. Verify system delivery and installation date.

3. Prepare a marketing plan.

4. Identify required marketing resources.

5. Assign marketing plan tasks.

6. Execute the marketing plan.

7. Evaluate the marketing plan's results.

8. Prepare a marketing report for management.

9. Note those steps which need improvement.

Gather Data on Potential Technology Impacts

There are three stages to user acceptance of information technology. The first is an initial buy-in, much like the process that occurs when you see a car you really want. This buy-in is completed when you purchase the car. The second stage leads to ownership and ultimately to pride of ownership. This occurs after regular, effective use of a new system. This is the point at which the employee wants to show off his or her skill at using the technology and the application. The final stage is fine tuning, where the worker finds a way of personalizing the use of an application, as is possible with a PC spreadsheet. At this point, the system is almost the worker's own creation and no longer something provided by others.

Each of these three stages is supported by the three phases of the Technology Implementation Life Cycle which follow the marketing phase. Phase 4, education, provides a reasoned approach to the need for technology. This promotes the user's initial buy-in. Phase 5, training, supports the user's desire to perform well using the system. This fuels the desire to be a proud owner. Phase 7, human communications, facilitates two-way communication between technicians and users. This process aids users in personalizing their use of the technology through the suggestions and recommendations they provide to the technical staff.

Since these three implementation phases cover the various facets of user acceptance, why is marketing needed? It is required to shift the focus from the technology to the user. Marketing lays the groundwork for the phases of education, training, and human communications which follow. But success in marketing depends on gathering and effectively using data about the users.

Review and Assess Previous Implementations

The time-saving characteristics of computers have been oversold. As a result, there has been a strong future focus to implementations. The technology is oversold on the basis of what it will do for us in the future. But users do not live on future promises. They live in the present. And that present is based on the reality of how well past technology implementations were done. If previous implementations were done well, they created "credits" which can be spent on future implementations. If they were botched, they created problems for all future implementations.

The only people who can honestly report on the success or failure of past implementations are the users who were involved. They are the people who must be consulted to help determine if a new implementation will be welcomed or feared. They are also the best people to describe for the implementation task force what worked during past implementations and what did not.

Identify Impacts Unique to the Technology Implementation

No two ITs affect a human system the same way. Each screen, report, and function sends a unique set of ripples throughout the organization. At a minimum three groups should be involved in assessing the potential impacts of a new IT: technicians, users, and user managers. The technicians who developed the application should be required to prepare a formal report on the changes in work styles and procedures that are designed into the IT. Users and their managers should independently examine this report to provide their assessment of the impact of the new IT.

Measure and Study Preimplementation Productivity and Work Styles

Information on current employee productivity and work styles is essential to developing the education and training phases of an implementation. It is also necessary for the design of an effective marketing plan. A marketing plan links the old work style to the new one. It also starts a flow of activity that continues on through education, training, and human communications. Good marketing is more than a one-shot effort. It is aimed at providing total satisfaction with the new system of work and repeat "sales" of new technology.

Much of the information on work styles should be gathered during the initial analysis and design phases of the traditional systems development life cycle. The overlap of this life cycle with the Technology Implementation Life Cycle is discussed in Chapter 7. Economy of effort suggests that these two life cycles are highly coordinated in order to control costs and to increase the efficiency and effectiveness of each.

One reason for gathering data on past employee work styles is to discover what marketing approaches work with the users. Sometimes it appears that previous implementations have worked because of a key member of the user group. For example, there may be one user whose opinions are trusted by others in the work group. This person can assist in the promotion of an implementation. There may be a user who has had positive experiences with a similar application. This person can speak out in support of it. The aim is to look for individuals in the user group who support an implementation in some way.

Sometimes a supervisor can provide access to a group of users. Supervisors who have good working relations with their staff can serve as a liaison between the MIS staff and themselves. The good will and acceptance of a supervisor facilitate the acceptance of any new system. One rule must be followed when working through supervisors: Always keep them fully informed so that they can address all staff questions and concerns. If you expect to have their trust, you must gain their confidence.

Information about current work styles can be used to "qualify" the users. Qualifying users (like qualifying customers) means finding their "hot button." For example, if part of their present work is onerous and the new system lightens that burden, that benefit may be used to sell the system's features and benefits. In this manner, the new system gains immediate value in the users' minds. It represents something they already want to buy.

Profile Users

Every firm that uses IT should develop a profile of its users and their system experience and skills. This information should be stored as a data base so that the implementation task force can retrieve it in a number of ways. The data retrieval system may be arranged according to job category (manager, professional, clerical), type of technology use (data input, inquiry only, report use), type of system (mainframe, minicomputer, PC), type of application (word processing, spreadsheet, inventory, personnel, accounting), or general demographics (age, gender, length of present employment).

Conduct a Reality Pretest of the Users

Product loyalty is built around product expectations. The person who loyally returns to the same product does so out of an expectation regarding that product. End users have expectations about new technologies. Some are true, some are false, but all are real to the users. And these users are disappointed if the product (an IT) does not meet their expectations. One of the critical steps in marketing any technology is ensuring that all customers (users) hold common expectations about the product (the technical system).

To do this, one must know what the users already believe that a new system is going to do. Do they think that it will change their work styles? Do they believe that people will be moved to new jobs? Do they anticipate that people will lose their jobs? The key to effective data gathering is to ask them what changes they think automation will cause. Do not try to change any of their opinions, with the possible exception of the one regarding loss of jobs. Be sure that management is informed immediately regarding any opinions that employees will be losing jobs. Once started, the rumor of job losses is most difficult to stop, and it can destroy the anticipated benefits of automation.

Conduct an IT Attitude Survey

Does management know what opinions and feelings employees have about automation? This is important information that every firm needs if it expects to use technology successfully. For example, some people do not trust computer-generated numbers. They want to see whether the computer is right and will check the results against an adding machine tape every time. Some people work with a system only because they must. Others love the machine.

This range of attitudes is not new to the reader. What may be new is the knowledge of how many people hold which opinions and attitudes. What may be new information is the personal experiences that formed their attitudes. And what may shock is how resistant their attitudes make users to new technologies.

It is our experience that most workers have positive attitudes about work and want to do the job right. Many are willing to adjust to new technology. But many don't know how to get past their own negative experiences and attitudes. The fact that someone has asked about these experiences and attitudes alerts them to management's readiness to support them during the transition to a new technology.

We have also found that personality factors contribute significantly to the manner in which people interpret their experiences with automation and develop their attitudes. We use the Personal Profile System and the Myers/Briggs Type Indicator (see Appendix C for further explanation) to assist MIS personnel when planning marketing programs so that the diversity of personalities are considered and satisfied.

Identify the Corporate Culture and Subcultures of User Groups

Every organization has a dominant culture. Even its subunits can develop their unique culture or personality, which may agree or disagree with the primary culture. Effective implementation planning will consider the culture of the users affected. Their culture provides the values, customs, rites, and rituals through which the group accepts or rejects all change (Deal and Kennedy 1982). There is a general rule that connects culture to technology implementations. You cannot sell a technology change if you do not understand the corporate culture.

Form User Focus Groups

Focus groups are a technique used by many companies to learn from customers how to improve their business. They consist of selected customers who are invited to a meeting where they share opinions and suggestions about a company's products, customer service, and so on. Focus groups are usually informal because the emphasis is on keeping the customers talking. The hosts and hostesses do not try to explain or justify criticisms. Rather, they "focus" on asking questions, collecting information, and listening to what the customers have to say.

MIS staffs, which provide services, can make effective use of the focus group technique to enhance their image and value. If created early in the implementation process, focus groups can assist in implementation planning. If drawn together repeatedly, users who participate in the implementation can also assist in monitoring the implementation as it happens. If established on a permanent basis, focus groups can be used to reveal system difficulties after installation, to share tips and tricks on system use, and to recommend system enhancements or improvements.

Verify System Delivery and Installation Date

Take heed of Murphy's law at this point: If anything can delay the installation of the system, it will, and it will happen at the worst possible moment. The best experiences with technology implementation occur when the task force is able to set the date, time, and place of a system installation. However, before an installation proceeds, all hardware and applications software must be checked to guarantee that they are operating properly. Nothing, repeat, nothing will "unsell" a system more quickly and completely than a failed or delayed installation.

Prepare a Marketing Plan

A technology implementation plan describes the sequence of activities that occur from the time the system is brought into the user's work area until it becomes the old way of doing work. A marketing plan describes those elements of the implementation plan which focus on the user's attitudes toward and acceptance of new technology.

Because the marketing plan relates to the entire sequence of user acceptance, it covers all of the following steps:

Observing and studying the user's environment

Qualifying the user

Justifying the change in work styles

Developing the user's skills for system use

Installing and using the system

Assisting the user until the system is a normal part of the work routine

Providing ongoing communication between technician and user

The marketing plan is developed so that it supports all of the phases of the technology implementation that follow it. It identifies and develops a general marketing approach. It anticipates potential implementation roadblocks. It designates the different marketing tasks most likely to keep the implementation moving to completion.

Identify Required Marketing Resources

The major difficulty in allocating resources to marketing is management attitude's that users have no choice about automation. That attitude reflects only half of the situation. It is true with regard to the initial decision by senior management to proceed with the development or purchase of a new system. It is false with regard to the implementation. In the implementation, the only people who have decision-making power are the users. In our experience, most failed implementations misfired because the employees did not support them. That is the major reason why marketing must be a part of the implementation process with sufficient resources. But what kinds of resources?

The major resource needed in marketing is the time of employees. It is time needed for data gathering. It is time needed to consult users. It is time needed to plan the follow-up steps of education, training, documentation, and human communications. In fact, the marketing plan sets the criteria for the time needed to integrate the new technology into the work of the users. Time and people are needed. These are the primary costs to the organization.

Assign Marketing Plan Tasks

The design and coordination of the marketing plan should be the responsibility of one person on the task force, designated perhaps as the marketing coordinator or manager. Data gathering and development of a marketing plan's basic concepts are this person's responsibility. The execution of the marketing plan is assigned to those who are charged with the implementation's education, training, documentation, and human communications. The marketing manager is responsible for coordination, review, and evaluation of marketing as it carries over to the other phases of the implementation.

Execute the Marketing Plan

Execution of a marketing plan is difficult in part because marketing is done by everyone involved in the implementation, while the primary responsibility belongs to the marketing coordinator. This person works closely with the task force chairperson, the human design committee head, and other key implementation personnel. When a system is installed, it can "spill over" to other phases of the process. For this reason, and because the marketing coordinator is a key task force member, he or she should be involved in each phase of the implementation.

Evaluate the Marketing Plan's Results

A constant review of marketing as implementation proceeds is recommended. Each previously mentioned step is evaluated and included in a review report. These steps are listed under the step "Prepare a Marketing Plan." When the entire implementation process is completed, these reports are combined into one document with recommendations for subsequent marketing efforts and suggested improvements.

Prepare a Marketing Report for Management

A special condensed report on marketing is prepared for senior management. This report includes the following items:

The status of employees' readiness before implementation

The marketing plan

Use of the marketing plan during the implementation process

Anticipated problems with employee acceptance of a technology and how these problems are addressed by marketing and/or the Technology Implementation Life Cycle

Benefits of the marketing plan

Present status of employees using the new system and their readiness for additional changes in technology

Recommendations for future implementations

This report is reviewed and approved by the senior executive to whom the task force reports. The plan and the marketing evaluation constitute part of the system's historical record. This record is used by subsequent task forces for the benefit and improvement of new implementations.

Note Those Steps Which Need Improvement

Marketing is an acquired skill. It is acquired in the doing, not in the design. Marketing insights are gained by task force members as they move through successive technology implementations. The marketing techniques that work during a system's installation, as well as those that do not, should be carefully noted. If an organization intends to improve in this phase, it must risk constant experimentation to discover during each unique system installation what sells the technology.

Phase 4: Education

In Western society, there is no longer any agreement about what education is. At one time, to be educated meant that one had acquired the tools needed to think. While there were cultural biases about which tools to select, there was little doubt that learning to think was the essence of education. This concept soon developed into learning to think in specific terms for specific professions. Now society is at the point where education is so broad, offering so many majors, that college graduates don't seem to fit in anywhere. American businesses have begun to notice this educational defect in their new employees. Businesses often complain that they must educate college graduates because they are no longer equipped to think in ways that make them immediately useful in their jobs.

While the difficulties of American higher education are much broader than the scope of this book, they do point to the basic concern of this phase: Organizations now have the additional burden of educating employees to use IT. This situation will continue because of the increasing amount and impact of IT on all areas of work. Some believe that academia will not be able to stay abreast of the changing technology.

An organization's general automation needs are too broad to be covered adequately by colleges and universities. They simply cannot be expected to teach every student every IT skill that may be needed in a future job.

The education phase of the Technology Implementation Life Cycle is both general and specific (Fig. 5-7). It is general in that it teaches employees how to think about technology. It is specific in that it relates to individual technology implementations. It informs employees about an implementation, including its goals and value. It also explains the role of users in the implementation.

The education phase of the Technology Implementation does not end when an implementation is completed. It has initiated an educational process that should continue throughout a person's employment. There will be no graduation; no point at which education ends. The educational phase will explain each new implementation. But it will always start with answering the question, "why do we automate?"

It is said of some mountain climbers that they climb the mountain because it is there. That is a bit of romantic self-deception for which they may be forgiven. In truth, they climb the mountain because they decide to do so. And they do it for their own unique reasons. Similarly, firms automate not because the technology is available, but because they decide to do so. And each company decides for its own unique reasons.

But the questions can be raised, "Why must automation be explained? There was no need to explain past technological changes." That is not true. Employees have always had a need to understand, but management has not always comprehended or

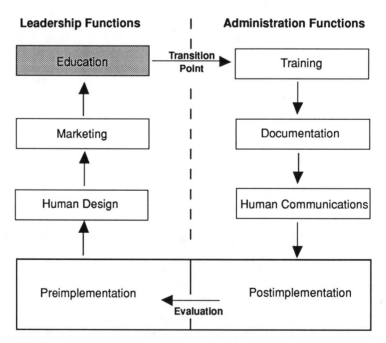

FIG. 5-7 Education Phase of the Technology Implementation Life Cycle

honored that need. Explaining management decisions is a natural and necessary part of running any enterprise.

We believe that in the past, American companies gained an advantage because of the physical resources and technological advantage of our country. That advantage is rapidly declining and is unlikely to return. It seems increasingly true that all the world shares the same resources and the same technology. The emerging advantage for any nation or enterprise is in the manner in which it uses its human resources. We believe that the lasting competitive advantage lies with those organizations that are able to combine their human resources, physical resources, and technology into a winning combination. To do this, their employees must be well educated about the technology used by the organization.

Two forms of technology education are included in the education phase. The first is general knowledge about possible technology uses. The second is specific information about a particular IT being implemented. Both are referenced in the education steps described.

The steps in the education phase of implementation are as follows:

1. Identify user learners.
2. Establish user education criteria.
3. Identify required user education.
4. Conduct user focus groups.
5. Prepare user education objectives.
6. Develop a user education syllabus.
7. Select user education methods.
8. Choose user education media.
9. Develop a user education curriculum.
10. Develop a user education course catalogue.
11. Promote user education courses.
12. Conduct user education.
13. Evaluate user education and courses.
14. Prepare a report for management on user education.
15. Revise user education and courses.
16. Note those steps which need improvement.

Identify User Learners

There is a temptation to say that all employees should be learners. While this is true, it is not the best starting point. Education should start first with those IT users who are directly affected by an implementation. They deserve and need an explanation of the new system. If education doesn't start with them, these front-line employees will invent their own explanation. Either the organization explains the technology change or employees invent their own explanations. Be assured that if they do it themselves, they will have the wrong explanation, possibly the worst one.

Computers, of one sort or another, are often the first wave or IT in the company. As the organization learns how to introduce computerization effectively, it can develop educational standards that guide all of its efforts at technological change. The following statement could serve an organization's computer education goal:

> The goal of computer education is to provide a basis for developing, introducing, and using technology in the most effective and efficient manner.

A general goal statement such as this one reinforces the need to educate employees at all levels of the organization about computerization. Some education is common to all. Some is targeted to specific users because of their specialized work. Regardless of the type of user education, its purpose is to equip employees to think about, be involved in, and anticipate the computerization process.

Establish User Education Criteria

Two kinds of user education criteria are required. The first is based on the company's general automation needs. To develop these criteria, the organization must examine the nature of its operation, the business environment, and the competition. This information either dictates or suggests the need or opportunity for automation. It helps the organization answer the following question:

> What do we, as an organization need to know, in order to think about, plan, and create our own IT future?

The second type of user education criteria is required to evaluate the implementation of a specific technology. To develop these criteria, the organization must ask what information its employees need in order to make an effective and smooth transition to the new technology. In more common terms, these criteria answer the following question:

> What do employees need to know in order to accept technology and to acquire skill in its effective use?

Identify Required User Education

The key to effective user education is the organization's ability to make two different assessments. The first is an analysis of all the directions in which relevant technology is moving. A second is a projection of the organization's future uses of this technology. This research is usually conducted by the top MIS staff.

The nature of this futures research has been changed by the PC. Research and study on future PC developments is now conducted by a broad spectrum of employees, including non-technical users. In this circumstance, the MIS staff's role has become that of coordinating and listening, in addition to researching and advising. But whether the MIS staff is doing the primary research or coordinating a broader research effort, the goal is to define user education needs based on an estimate of the technology the business will use.

Conduct User Focus Groups

We believe in the value of the focus group as a vital and dynamic information gathering tool. Employees can join together to express their concerns, ideas, and suggestions about automation. Properly used, focus groups can uncover data that might otherwise be left unexpressed. The common expression "There is safety in numbers" comes to mind. Actually, the operating principle here is "There is power in numbers." That is, since there are more of "us" present saying the same thing, maybe management will really listen to what we have to say. Maybe what we say will make a difference.

In the case of a mainframe computer system, gathering individual users into a group and asking for their comments and suggestions has a more profound impact than scattered, individual comments. In the PC world, individual users meeting and identifying common problems also demonstrates that there is power in the group.

Prepare User Education Objectives

Education or learning objectives are clear, concise statements which structure an education course. To be effective, they must be developed and written down *before* any further course development is done. If this is not done, the education itself can be unclear. A sample objective for general technology education might be: "Without the aid of any reference material, all employees will be able to list and define the four basic functions of a computer system."

The same process of writing down learning objectives occurs in the training phase (see Chapter 6, phase 5, the step entitled "Prepare User Training Objectives") of an implementation. When written for training, learning objectives focus on a particular task that the user is expected to do once the training is complete. When written for education, the objectives focus on attitudes and knowledge that are often critical to a motivated, successful technology user.

Education provides information and knowledge about the "why" of technology. Training provides some of that but focuses more on developing a user's skill; it is the "how" of technology.

However, both education and training objectives answer three questions: (1) What is the technology user's expected *terminal behavior*? That is, what will the learner be able to do as a result of the education? (2) What are the *conditions* associated with that terminal behavior? An example of this is, will the user have to perform with or without aids, reference materials, and so on? (3) What will be the user's *minimum level of performance*? That is, at what speed, in what quantity, and/or with what quality will the learner be expected to complete the terminal behavior?

These objectives are the criteria from which user education evaluations should be developed (see the step of this phase entitled "Evaluate User Education and Courses"). Evaluations must be based on some type of measurement. Baseline data and end data must be available so that results can be quantified. Only then can the results of technology education be linked to the original objectives to determine whether they have been met.

Develop a User Education Syllabus

A syllabus is an outline or road map of a user education course. It is based minimally upon a clear understanding of the users' education needs, their previous technology education, and the nature and demands of the systems being taught. Since the syllabus is designed to communicate to the user, it should be composed in a simple and direct style.

Select User Education Methods

A wide variety of education methods exist. Good user education employs an effective combination of these. Different methods allow for the differences in the way people learn. Variety also makes learning more interesting to all. Examples include classroom lectures with discussions, guest lecturers/speakers, demonstrations, tours or field trips, and computer-based training (CBT).

Choose User Education Media

Educational media support the various learning methods. These media include textbooks, workbooks, slides or overhead transparencies, computer simulations, individual computers, videotapes, and films. An employee also may learn using a textbook with self-tests or a workbook accompanied by audio tapes or CBT courseware.

Develop a User Education Curriculum

If employees are to keep abreast of changing technology, they must be constantly educated and trained. Continual IT evolution also drives the need to constantly develop a relevant user educational curriculum. After all users are confronted by: (1) the steady advance of all technology, and (2) the consistent progression of their organization's technology. Either circumstance is sufficient to justify the need for ongoing user education. Taken together, they make it mandatory.

To be effective, the user education curriculum should differentiate between two types of courses. Foundational courses (i.e., a basic introduction to computer terms and concepts) prepare the user for workplace automation. The next higher level of courses prepare the user for specific applications (e.g., the basics of computer-aided design).

Develop a User Education Course Catalogue

A user education course catalogue, periodically updated, is a way of notifying employees about current education offerings. However, it is better not to presume that the catalogue can do the whole job. The catalogue is basically a reference document. The key to selling user education is supervisor and manager support. Employees should not have to beg or fight with their management for the opportunity to attend user education courses. Those who manage user education should assume the need to work closely with the supervisors and managers of those employees who need or want user education.

Promote User Education Courses

One insurance company has developed as broad a range of CBT courses as any we have seen. It publishes a catalogue listing these courses. The success of such a program depends on the attitude of the company's executives toward computer education. In this company, senior and junior executives are expected to be primary CBT learners. Because the CBT offerings are professional and executives use them, they know how valuable these courses are to their subordinates. It is the executives in this company who promote and facilitate employee education.

Conduct User Education

Formal user education is offered before a system's installation. The classroom, however, is not the only place to educate users. Less structured, informal opportunities to learn occur when users are informed about new systems through newsletters and other company publications (more about that in Chapter 6, phase 7, human communications). User focus groups, mentioned under phase 3, Marketing, are also educational opportunities. The key to effective technology education is to realize that it is a constant process that occurs both inside and outside of the classroom. It is a process essential to moving a user on to the next phase, training. It is vital to maintaining employee and organizational viability in an increasingly technical, competitive world.

Evaluate User Education and Courses

When evaluating user education look at (1) the user education process and (2) the final results or utility of the education. The first determines if the predetermined education objectives have been met. This is ascertained by asking participants to complete evaluation forms which ask objective and subjective questions. These questions begin to measure learning and solicit participant comments and suggestions about user education.

The second evaluation criteria is gathered from the learner's manager. Once a user has completed an education course, his or her manager is asked to complete an education evaluation form. In this case, they are asked to rate the utility and value of the education to the user's job performance. We also recommend conducting a final evaluation three to six months after a course has been concluded. Both the learner and his or her manager should complete this later evaluation. Waiting for several months allows the user to return to work and apply what has been learned. An evaluation from this longer perspective may be the most valuable of all.

When evaluating user education, three elements need to be kept in balance: personnel development, technological development, and business development. We strongly believe that the interrelationship and balance of these three elements make organizations more viable in this technological age. More is said about this concern in Chapter 8.

Prepare a User Education Report for Management

Those responsible for user education should prepare regular reports for senior management. These reports should include the three areas listed in Table 5-6.

The preparation of this report requires the cooperation of educators, MIS staff, and user management. It includes future planned goals for the organization's user education and the process for top management's review and approval.

Revise User Education and Courses

The annual report and review of user education is used in meetings with senior management to assist in the revision, development, and enhancement of the com-

Table 5-6
User Education Evaluation

1. Educational learnings
   a. Subjects covered
   b. Individual participants
2. New level of knowledge about technology in the organization
3. Impacts of user education
   a. In support of present work and tasks
   b. In support of future technology use

pany's general education. Whenever a user education change is made, it is important to determine whether former students need to attend revised courses in order to stay current.

Note Those Steps Which Need Improvement

There is a sense of employee development when a process of user education is in place. There is a perception that employees are changing, that they are making things happen. At this point, it is important for management to keep a clear, stated goal for employee development. It should not drift in any direction it wants. Flexibility can be provided, but there must be a general framework for the organization's educational efforts and programs. Management must move the organization in the direction they choose to go, toward the technological future they have chosen.

Comment: Halfway Home

The completion of these four phases should lead to the preparation of employees for new technology. The human system is ready to accept, own, and effectively use systems. Negative deterrents and attitudes have been eliminated or controlled; positive possibilities and attitudes have been developed. Only after this has been accomplished is an effort made to combine human and technical systems to produce the organization's products and/or services.

6

The Technology Implementation Life Cycle: Part Two

Employers now are a fussy lot
Who demand a skill I haven't got;
They make me feel so out of place
To confess, I cannot interface!

—*Nathanial Pastir*

In Chapter 5 we explained how the Technology Implementation Life Cycle is divided into two functions. The first, leadership, prepares the organization for the process of technology implementation. The second, administration, is described in this chapter. It consists of the last four phases of the Technology Implementation Life Cycle: training, documentation, human communications, and postimplementation (Fig. 6-1).*

Throughout this chapter we focus on combining the technology, the worker, and the human system into an integrated and efficient process of work.

Phase 5: Training

Most managers understand the importance of training; very few understand its complexity. In Table 6-1 we have identified three issues that should help the typical manager grasp the intricacies of effective and efficient training.

---

*Executive summaries are on pages 133–136, 143–145, 151–152, and 157–158.

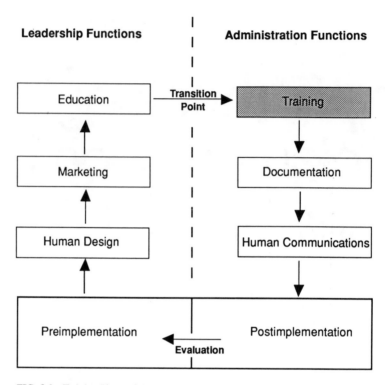

Leadership Functions   **Administration Functions**

FIG. 6-1   Training Phase of the Technology Implementation Life Cycle

In his classic work *Human Competence* (1978), Thomas Gilbert chides managers for not understanding when training is needed and when training alternatives are required. Gilbert observes that unnecessary training can have a negative impact on workers. This is especially true when the workers are not performing well because of their managers' failure to supervise or delegate properly. In this case, using training as a solution destroys confidence. It can impute ignorance to those being trained when, in fact, they know how to do their job.

Even when knowledge is the issue, training is not always the answer. Gilbert suggests that job aids are often more productive and effective in creating positive employee attitudes than training. Although not all of Gilbert's comments are concerned with IT changes, his words of caution should be heeded. He reminds us that

Table 6-1
IT Training Issues

1. Know when training is needed
2. Know why training is needed
3. Know the circumstances under which training occurs

the first question that must be asked when implementing technical systems is whether training is the proper method of employee skill development.

We concede that most technology implementations require some form of user training since, the emerging ITs are so new and different. But there must be a careful consideration and use of alternative skill development methods. A range of options are presented in this chapter as adjuncts to traditional classroom training. We also advise those responsible to review constantly the effectiveness of present IT training methods.

Lastly, IT training is complex because it deals with more complicated subject matter than is often foreseen. When technology is implemented two types of changes occur. First, employees now do their work differently. This may mean that they associate with people they have not worked with before. They may report to new bosses. They may be responsible for new products or services. They may move to a new work area. All of these changes create a need for support during their transition to new work styles.

Second, the changes imposed by IT implementation often affect work groups, departments, and even the organization itself. IT training programs must anticipate and account for this possible result. For this reason, we have included the larger concern of organizational change in our description of the training steps recommended during technology implementations.

The steps in the training phase of implementation are as follows:

1. Identify user trainees.
2. Identify user backup personnel.
3. Establish user training criteria.
4. Prepare user training objectives.
5. Select user training approach(es).
6. Identify user training resources.
7. Develop user training lesson plan.
8. Identify user training media.
9. Compare the user training lesson plan to the companion documentation.
10. Develop user training materials and documentation.
11. Pilot test user training.
12. Evaluate and revise user training.
13. Develop a user training course catalogue.
14. Promote user training.
15. Conduct user training.
16. Provide user training and documentation.
17. Evaluate user training and documentation.

(continued on page 136)

18. Revise user training and documentation.

19. Prepare a user training report for management.

20. Note those steps which need improvement.

Identify User Trainees

This step is far more specific than its counterpart in phase 3, education. In that phase there was a concern for identifying the overall IT educational needs of the organization, as well as those of its employees. In this phase, training, there is a stronger concern to emulate the traditional "needs analysis" of the training process. This step, and several that follow it, are elements of a training needs analysis, though we have named them differently.

This step focuses on the user's needs. Two cautions are important. First, user training must be neither too comprehensively nor too narrowly defined. We know of no simple criteria by which to distinguish between the two. Our experience shows that careful monitoring of the user training pilot test allows the evaluator to determine if the training is balanced.

The other caution concerns the critical need for user management's involvement in training. These managers need to understand the skill development process, as well as the training outcomes. This may mean designing special IT management training to complement user training. After all, managers and supervisors cannot oversee the work of others if they do not understand how employees acquire competence in that work. Untrained managers are prone to make inordinate demands on their staff. The staff may attribute this to a lack of care and concern. Most often it occurs because the managers simply do not understand the day-to-day details of the work and how workers learn that work.

We can recommend two steps. First, provide introductory sessions with user managers. Explain the training goals, the process to be used, and the follow-up procedures; in short, give them a comprehensive overview of what is involved in training their personnel. Once this is completed, train the user managers and their staff together. There may be some awkwardness in this situation, but it can be resolved. For example, we have worked with a PC training company that places learners in semiprivate carrels at their own machines. Managers and staff are trained together, and the risk of embarrassing less IT skilled managers is removed by the physical layout of the training room.

Identify User Backup Personnel

Employee illnesses, vacations, promotions, and terminations can lead to severe disruptions in systems use—especially when there are no trained replacements. Well-planned training includes identifying and training those employees who will step in to continue a system's operation when the designated user is not at work. Every manager should be certain that there is always trained backup personnel.

Establish User Training Criteria

For user training to be effective, an organization's managers, in consultation with its IT trainers, must set the criteria by which training is developed, conducted, and evaluated. Note what is stated—managers must set the criteria. We do not believe that trainers are the proper people to establish the criteria for effective training. The effectiveness of training is determined by the workers' performance once they have returned to work and their manager has observed them using what they have learned.

The manager's role is to state what knowledge, skills, and attitudes must be learned in the training process. The trainer's role is that of training expert. The manager must defer to the trainer in all matters relating to how the learning shall occur. This process of setting training criteria is very similar to the process of setting the criteria for changes in technology. The role of managers must be central to the decision to implement new technology. IT specialists can describe the technology, including its uses and its advantages. However, it is the manager of the work process who can best describe, plan, and manage its practical uses.

One factor must not be lost in determining who does what. The process of setting user training criteria must combine the best efforts of trainers and managers, with each contributing his or her unique perspective and knowledge.

There is a need for one final comment. User training criteria must relate to the organization's overall plan for technology use, as well as individual skill development. This means that the training criteria must be application or technology specific, yet broad enough to relate to the general pattern of organizational technology use and development.

Prepare User Training Objectives

One of the most difficult tasks is the writing of specific and measurable training objectives. Yet this task must be done. User training, because it is focused on skill development, must produce observable results. Training objectives should be written before any training is developed or presented. Writing training objectives is the trainers' way of stating what they intend to do, holding themselves to these criteria, and then measuring what they have done. These objectives deal with the observable and measurable behaviors of those trained.

Select User Training Approach(es)

We have identified five basic approaches to effective IT user training (Table 6-2): one-on-one, group, lecture, liaison, and programmed learning. With one-on-one and group training, the trainer leads a learner (one-on-one) or learners (group) through a sequence of hands-on training. With the lecture approach, trainers present information in a lecture format. In liaison training, a member of the user department acts as an adjunct trainer, assisting in user training of fellow employees. Programmed learn-

Table 6-2
Five IT Training Approaches

1. One-on-one
2. Group
3. Lecture
4. Liaison
5. Programmed learning

ing provides users with independent learning situations. Typical programmed learning include CBT, interactive video discs, and video or audio tapes with a workbook.

The most effective user training uses a combination of these approaches. The choice of approaches is determined by several factors, such as user training learning objectives, users' availability, users' previous skill levels, number of users to be trained, and number of user trainers.

Identify User Training Resources

Far too often, management acts as though they think that trainers can shake training out of their sleeves. But then, far too seldom has management integrated its training programs into the overall objective of developing its people, organization, and business. Training resources, such as time, money, people, facilities, and equipment, will always be scarce until this integration is achieved. The integration of training into a corporate wide process of development automatically includes the justification of adequate resources.

Apart from integration, the indispensable requirement for the cost justification of training is that it relate to management requirements. If these requirements are the basis of user training objectives, there is a line of logic available to justify the necessary resources. This conclusion is tied directly to our earlier comment on the need for managers to be involved in setting the criteria for training.

User trainers can make this assertion: Management has certain needs and we meet them in this manner. Therefore, training costs must be justified as follows: Trainers must be prepared to show (through a formal report to management, for example) that the approaches and resources selected are the most effective and reasonable for meeting training objectives and satisfying management needs. The commitment to effective user training must come from top management. If it doesn't, each successive budget year poses a threat to its funding.

Develop User Training Lesson Plan

Little need be said about developing training lesson plans. This procedure is fairly standard and generally well known among professional trainers. While each trainer develops a unique approach, their concerns are remarkably alike. Each strives to present logical, properly sequenced learnings which facilitate employee skill development. Lesson plans serve as the trainer's road map. That is, they provide a detailed plan of exactly how training is conducted. Lesson plans cannot be fully developed until the trainer knows who the learners are, what the training objectives are, and what training approaches and resources exist.

Identify User Training Media

User training media should be selected which support the training approaches chosen. In our experience, the most effective training uses a combination that is neither too lean nor too rich. Common examples of training media include, but are not limited to, workbooks, videos, audio tapes, interactive video discs, CBT courseware, and the computer itself.

Compare the User Training Lesson Plan to the Companion Documentation

Whether purchased from a vendor or developed by company professionals, all software applications require user documentation. Before instructing users, the trainer needs to compare the user documentation to the training lesson plan. This comparison serves several useful purposes. It may uncover ways in which the documentation can be used during training. It may point up additional areas of training need. And it may suggest areas where changing or upgrading user documentation is necessary to meet the end user's needs.

Most documentation is designed to tell the users how the system operates. What the users want is documentation that tells them how to use a system. Therefore, good user documentation needs to be more job or task specific. If it isn't, supplemental or alternative documentation should be provided. In our experience, some of the most effective and productive user documentation is created by training professionals, not MIS professionals.

Develop User Training Materials and Documentation

We recommend that the development of training materials and user documentation be done as parallel activities. The information that trainers gather as they learn a system can serve as the basis for developing both user training materials and documentation. But it must be kept in mind that these two products are designed for different purposes and should not be used interchangeably. Training materials are used to transfer skills to the user. Their use may be continued as on-the-job aids once training is completed. Documentation, on the other hand, is a reference tool that provides ready, timely access to bits of information that help the user to use the system. For these reasons, training aids and user documentation are often quite different in style and content.

Training materials are more likely to be sequential in nature, designed for the training process. Documentation is usually encyclopedic in style because it is designed as reference material to be searched quickly. Once users have been trained to use a system, they can use the documentation to gradually increase the breadth of their understanding and competence. However, documentation by nature is unsuitable as the basis of a training program. In fact, we believe that user documentation should *never* be substituted for a training program.

Pilot Test User Training

Like new computer software, new user training should be debugged. This pilot test draws on a representative group of future system users. The pilot test group should reflect the variety of existing skills, the range of ages, and the assortment of general work experience. Where possible, there should be at least one supervisor or manager in the test group.

The pilot test of the training should consume 150% of the time envisioned for the final training program. The additional time is needed for periodic evaluation. For example, evaluation times for a day-long training program should occur at least once every morning and once every afternoon. A week or so later, an overall debriefing should be held at the conclusion of the pilot test. This debriefing should focus on the applicability and usefulness of the training to the users once they return to work and use the system.

Evaluate and Revise User Training

Any weaknesses in the training program discovered during the pilot test can now be corrected by the trainer. Once revisions are completed, the trainer presents the product for a final quick review to the pilot test participants. This is done using a briefing format. User and MIS attendance at this briefing allows them to observe the trainer's presentation and to observe the reactions of the pilot test trainees. It is also a strong demonstration of their approval and support to this training effort.

Develop a User Training Course Catalogue

The development of a user training course catalogue and other promotional materials is strongly recommended. The circulation of this information stimulates greater employee interest and participation in user training. Support for user training programs also can be indicated by a letter or memo of endorsement from executive management which appears as an introduction to a user training course catalogue.

Senior management support is vital. In its absence, managers will decide on their own whether training is important or needed. Some managers will always try to get by with the least amount of training possible. Open support from senior management sends a message to all that the change in technology is needed and supported—together with the training for that technology.

Promote User Training

Beyond conventional user training advertising, we recommend that senior management require all managers to attend periodic management briefings conducted by the training staff. In these briefings, the training staff presents a manager's overview of a new IT application and its subsequent training. This type of information sharing keeps management involved in employees' training and creates realistic expectations of what IT training requires and delivers.

Conduct User Training

The key to effective IT user training, particularly during an implementation process, is advance planning. A timetable of training support should be established according to the following criteria: First, the beginning of training should coincide with the installation of the equipment or application.

Second, this date must be determined jointly with user managers to ensure the availability of personnel for the training sessions.

Third, those being trained on the same application should be trained at approximately the same time.

Fourth, transition planning has a significant impact on the success of the training effort. When trainees return to their regular work, time must be allocated for continued use and development of their new skills. Their managers will have to coordinated their continuing work demands so that learnings can be transitioned from the classroom to the workplace. Productivity is expected to decline in the initial period of transition. But with advance planning, the transition process can be smooth and the expected benefits achieved.

Provide User Training and Documentation

Documentation, including job aids, are given to the user upon completion of training. Once trainees have completed the sequence of training, they can move on to the encyclopedic content of user documentation. But this is a difficult transition to make.

Training time should be set aside to acquaint trainees with the content of the user documentation. They need to learn how the material is organized, how to locate required information, and whom to call for help.

Evaluate User Training and Documentation

The training staff should contact trainees one week, three weeks, and six months following their initial training. The one- and three-week follow-ups ensure that the user is making a smooth transition from the old work system to the new one. During these early contacts, trainers should ask users if they are experiencing any difficulties in using the new system, the job aids, or the documentation. Trainers should be looking for users who need more training or assistance. Perhaps a user didn't learn the material the first time but was too embarrassed to say so. Perhaps a user thought that he or she understood the training but realized, upon returning to work, that this was not so. Or perhaps a user has moved beyond what has been taught and is ready to learn more. A caution: Users usually will not take the initiative in the above situations. It is always the job of the user trainer to follow up and make certain that the training has been done completely and correctly.

The six-month follow-up should be used to determine whether users have successfully transferred the new skills to their daily work. We recommend that user managers be included in all follow-ups. This may be done in a number of ways: through written evaluations, scheduled meetings, or impromptu visits to a manager's office. If managers are expected to support the transition to the new IT, they must be supported when their staffs return from training.

Revise User Training and Documentation

The six-month follow-up provides the most comprehensive data for evaluation of an IT user training program. By then the trainees will have the perspective of distance. They will be able to provide more detailed comments on how the training helped and how it might be improved. Managers are also better equipped to comment on employee productivity. This is also an excellent opportunity to review user documentation for possible revision and/or updating.

Prepare a User Training Report for Management

Many reports on training simply list the number of people trained and the subjects offered. More than statistics are needed if management is to understand and support user training. To be effective, training functions should be integrated into management functions. The management report on user training must show how it supports (1) the plans for IT technology upgrades, (2) specific IT implementations, (3) management plans for staff education and training, and (4) impacts on employee productivity levels.

A management report provides one important opportunity to confirm the benefits an organization receives for the training dollars spent. The training function cannot be taken on faith. This has been proved during times of budget reduction, when training is always one of the first areas to experience cutbacks. The IT value and benefit of IT user training must be demonstrated.

Note Those Steps Which Need Improvement

The best trainers constantly seek ways to improve their work. This means doing many of the customary things, such as maintaining well-organized written records, including all learner suggestions, critiques, and evaluations. But in the case of new ITs it also involves close liaison and coordination with user managers. Their advice and suggestions can provide trainers with a needed overview of training strengths and weaknesses as they affect the workplace.

A Note to Senior Managers

In order to demonstrate their value to the organization, effective IT user trainers identify what training must achieve. First, they define what management expects of them. These initial expectations have three qualities: They are minimal, necessary, and measurable. From these expectations, trainers can demonstrate the effective use of their time and resources.

Next, the trainers can plot a succession of improvements in training that demonstrate value-added benefits to senior management. These are measured benefits, not just assertions. They are benefits specific to the organization, not just generalizations about training. And they are part of an integrated approach to the development of the organization's technology.

This effort to prove the value of training supports the continued improvement and integrity of the training function. But the ultimate form of support comes when management realizes the need for continued improvement of its employees in their work-related tasks. Given this view, management may integrate training into a broad, comprehensive program of development of its employees, organization, and business.

Phase 6: Documentation

It seems that the only thing that exceeds the quantity of computer software is the quantity of user documentation written to explain it. And the only thing that exceeds the range of computer software quality (poor to good) is the range in quality of its documentation (incomprehensible to esoteric).

One benefit of the PC revolution is the pressure that it placed on PC vendors to produce easy-to-use software. Part of that pressure has spilled over into the accompanying user reference material, better known as "user documentation." If the vendor's documentation is awkward, jargon laden, and generally of little value, the word soon spreads from PC users to potential buyers. Because the PC market is more user driven than other IT markets, many PC software vendors have developed more usable documentation for the average person.

Unfortunately, not all user documentation follows this pattern. Much of it consists of highly technical explanations characterized by burdensome and incomprehensible jargon. It often does not help the user in need of a quick explanation. To be truly useful, the documentation must fit the user and his or her work. It must be informative and practical. Writing this kind of documentation requires a shift in focus, from explaining the technology to supporting the process of work (Fig. 6-2).

The steps in the documentation phase of implementation are as follows:

1. Identify required user documentation.
2. Identify user documentation resources.
3. Establish user documentation standards.
4. Outline preliminary user documentation.
5. Determine the user documentation style.
6. Prepare user documentation.
7. Measure the reading and interest levels of user documentation.
8. Pilot test user documentation.
9. Evaluate the user documentation pilot test.
10. Revise/edit user documentation.
11. Package user documentation.
12. Provide user documentation.
13. Train users to use documentation.
14. Evaluate user documentation.
15. Revise user documentation.
16. Maintain a current user documentation roster.
17. Prepare and distribute user documentation updates.
18. Note those steps which need improvement.

Identify Required User Documentation

A user often has a greater need for a variety of documentation aids than for an awkwardly written, cumbersome user manual. A user's reference manual will be

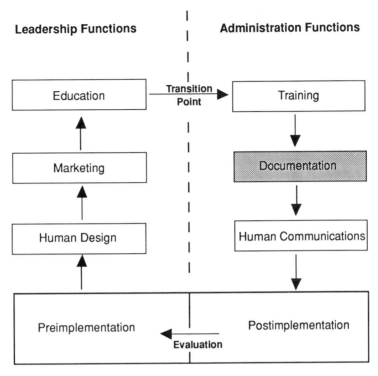

FIG. 6-2 Documentation Phase of the Technology Implementation Life Cycle

needed. But in addition, there will often be a need for job aids, prompter cards, cheat sheets, and other miniaturized forms of assistance. The range of options available is as great as the trainer's inventiveness. The effective range of options depends on understanding the user's workplace, tasks, and preferences in work styles. The goal is to find what formats best explain a particular system to the types of users who will be using the system.

Other elements that influence format choices include the type of work being done (whether repetitive or not), the frequency with which tasks are changed, the support available from co-workers, and the availability of a hot line or a help desk.

Identify User Documentation Resources

Three critical resources are needed for the creation of effective documentation: skilled writers, time for the research and study of user documentation needs, and a budget to pay for the creation of the required documentation. Skilled writers have the ability to link technical terminology to the language of the user and to write in a variety of styles which maintain the reader's interest and attention.

The study of user needs was described in the preceding step. Since it is a cost factor, it must be identified, quantified, and written as a budget item. The potential costs of a variety of user support documents also needs to be determined and budgeted. For example, prompter cards provide longer and better service if plastic laminated.

The process of developing a variety of effective documentation aids is a long-range task. It requires close cooperation of writers, trainers, users, and supervisors. The justification for this close and extended cooperation is that it increases the productivity of the users. This effort produces gradual improvements, but only over time. For this reason, care should be taken to measure and demonstrate the effect of good user documentation and job aids.

Establish User Documentation Standards

The nice thing about dictionaries is that they all use the same alphabet. Sounds ridiculous, doesn't it? This is such a customary fact of life that it escapes our notice. What is missed is that someone, sometime, had to establish a standard that said, "This is the order. It will be done this way." And ever since then, it has been a lot easier for all of us to find words.

For the same reason, each firm should establish user documentation standards. These standards make it much easier for everyone to use the documentation. But they provide much more than ease of use. They dictate such document characteristics as scope, format, and writing style. They determine such procedures as review, updating and distribution of documents. Such standards can be used for the creation of all user documentation.

This is critical, because the standards provide consistency to the computer user. This consistency is especially helpful to those users who must work with multiple systems and, therefore, multiple documentation. If the standards are adhered to, the user can find the needed information more readily, and use it more easily. Now reality impinges and tells us that this dream will be shattered by the inconsistencies of PC documentation.

There is no ready solution to this problem. It would be impossible to force all software producers to adopt one standard, particularly since that standard would most likely vary from the one each company has already created. It would be far too expensive for every organization to rewrite all of its PC documentation to adhere to its own internal standards. However, by establishing standards and developing the skills to write documentation that meets them, organizations are well prepared to evaluate PC documentation before they buy a PC package. Once PC documentation is evaluated, the firm can issue its own supplemental materials to aid its PC users.

Outline Preliminary User Documentation

The outlining of user documentation accomplishes two things. It provides a road map for the development of the document and indicates the size of the final product.

This can be helpful in deciding whether all the information should be provided in one or several books. The size of the projected documentation also gives the trainer an indication of how complex the training should be.

The complexity of the training depends on the interaction of the system to be used and the work requirements. This would not be so if all users were systems analysts or programmers. Clearly, they are not. The development of a detailed outline flushes out the hidden problems of bringing a complex application and an equally complex work situation into an effective working relationship.

Determine the User Documentation Style

There are at least four styles of documentation: text, sequential, cookbook, and playscript. Some user documentation is a combination of these formats. We recommend that user documentation standards stipulate acceptable documentation styles. Stipulating the styles aids writers in maintaining consistency in their work. The result is that users will move more easily between the documentation for different systems.

Prepare User Documentation

As with all writing, several drafts are needed before a final copy is approved. The first draft is used to test the general content for its reading grade and interest levels. The second draft is a working document for review and evaluation by trainers, users, and others involved in the pilot testing of training and documentation materials. The third draft is the final product for distribution to users.

Measure the Reading and Interest Levels of User Documentation

The first draft of user documentation is reviewed in two ways: for its reading grade level and its reader interest. The Gunning Fog Index is suitable for determining the grade level of the material. User documentation should be written at the general reading grade level of its intended readers. User profile data can provide this information by asking the user to state the highest grade level of formal education he or she has completed.

Another literacy instrument, the Rudy Flesch Human Interest Test, is suitable for determining the documentation's interest level. We realize that a documentation writer cannot become carried away with this concern. While a writer wishes to maintain the reader's full interest, user documentation is not the type of reading material upon which one dwells at length. It does not, cannot, and should not read like a novel. It is reference material and should avoid becoming familiar in tone or chatty in style. Having entered that caveat, we hasten to add that neither should it be as dry as a technical tome.

Pilot Test User Documentation

The second draft of the documentation is used at the end of the pilot test of the training program. It is distributed to the trainees during the pilot test. Once they have had a chance to test use it, they can provide valuable feedback on its usability, clarity, and other factors. This process has the advantage of reducing training and documentation pilot test costs, because both can be tested by the same group at roughly the same time.

Evaluate the User Documentation Pilot Test

Tracking user performance in the use of a new technology can provide a "sort" on the impact of training versus the impact and utility of documentation. Effective training brings users to a level of competence in the new application. Good documentation aids them during the time of transition. It supports them in maintaining and improving their level of performance from the time of training. It is the amount of improvement after training which measures the documentation's effectiveness. Users who participate in the pilot test may also be requested to keep a learning journal during and after training. They can record pertinent observations about the training and the documentation in their journals to be shared later with trainers and documentation writers. These observations are important in revising, updating, and constantly improving any user documentation.

Revise/Edit User Documentation

User documentation is revised and/or edited upon completion of its evaluation. When the final document is completed, with all aids and supplemental materials, it should be reviewed once more by the pilot test group.

Package User Documentation

The manner in which the document is packaged should reflect its use. For example, if there are expected to be frequent updates and revisions, the most suitable binding is a three-ring binder. If the documentation is for a single application, with limited uses and not likely to be changed, the most suitable package is a spiral binder or a perfect glued spine. If a one-page job aid, such as a prompter card, is prepared and used for constant reference, it can be laminated. The appearance of the job aid should also be suitable to the organization. Most not-for-profit agencies choose inexpensive packaging. Computer vendors, by contrast, tend to produce slicker, more expensive reference materials.

However, the key to successful packaging is the documentation's use. The work environment, the tasks to be done, and the customary work style of the users dictate the packaging selected. These should be the top three criteria used to decide what the final product looks like, thus ensuring its value and benefits.

Provide User Documentation

Documentation should always be distributed in a controlled manner. The organization must have the assurance that all employees who need these materials have them. Initially, all documentation and job aids are distributed during or following training, while updates are distributed on an as-needed basis.

Train Users to Use Documentation

At times there is a temptation to assume that the user can understand how to use the documentation without any briefing or instruction. We believe that such instances are rare. Besides, the real issue is how effectively users can use a system once they return to work. For this reason, we believe that documentation should be distributed as an immediate follow-up to training. By the same token, updates and changes in the documentation need to be distributed in a controlled manner.

As an example, in some companies users are expected to come to a central location to turn in old documentation and to receive new documentation. At that time, they can read through the document, ask questions concerning its contents, and participate in a mini training session on its use. This procedure supports and trains users in the use of documentation while controlling its distribution.

Evaluate User Documentation

The documentation phase does not end once the user documentation has been distributed. It is essential that all documentation be evaluated for effectiveness and usability. Once this evaluation is completed, it can be determined if revisions are needed. This evaluation should be done three to six months following the documentation's initial distribution and use. By this time, any important difficulties in using it will have been experienced by the user.

Revise User Documentation

Revisions can be managed in several ways. New pages can be inserted which provide updated explanations for hard-bound books. Entirely new documentation manuals can be substituted for old ones. Three-hole punched pages can be distributed for manuals in ring binders whose contents change frequently. This allows the users to change the pages of their manual where system changes have been noted. Some revisions may be so extensive that pilot testing is recommended to ensure the continued usefulness of the document. This decision also depends on the document's importance to and impact on user productivity.

Trainers should spot check the accuracy and thoroughness of documentation revision. We have encountered situations where users were working with hopelessly out-of-date documentation. Vicki's preference, where possible, is to hand deliver the revisions and request the return of the old manual or the out-of-date pages. This is more time-consuming and sometimes logistically difficult. However, it aids the user who continues to operate a system with outdated documentation and keeps complaining that the system "just doesn't work right anymore."

Maintain a Current User Documentation Roster

If an organization is to receive maximum value from its investment in documentation, a current roster of documentation users is critical. This roster is an inventory of all user documentation and those who have received them. It is often helpful to maintain such a roster in two forms. One is an alphabetical listing of all users, noting what documentation they have received. The other is a list of all forms of documentation, noting who their users are. The first style provides a handy reference for planning and promoting additional education and training programs. It may be cross-referenced with the user's profile (recommended early in the Technology Implementation Life Cycle). The second style makes the distribution of updates and revisions easier.

Prepare and Distribute User Documentation Updates

We have described our recommendation for the distribution of documentation revisions. The same methods are advocated for the distribution of documentation updates. Regardless of the method, we strongly recommend that it be stated as a part of user documentation standards. The critical need is to establish an adequate tracking system of documentation distribution, ensuring that outdated material is returned and new material is distributed.

Note Those Steps Which Need Improvement

The last step in user documentation consists of talking with, visiting, and/or surveying the user. That is the only way documentation writers will know how their product assists users', where they can make changes, and how they can improve future user reference material.

Phase 7: Human Communications

Occasionally in the course of our consulting, a very poignant thing happens. We encounter bright, talented technicians who are so absorbed in technology that they find it easier to talk to machines than to people. They often comment that they are mildly distressed about their behavior and wonder what to do about it. Obviously, there are many things that each of them can do about the tendency to withdraw from others. What may be less obvious is that this personal tendency is nourished by numerous corporate behaviors.

Many of the communication problems in American organizations arise from the tendency to develop a one-dimensional work force. In work situations, each individual is encouraged to develop a specialty and to use that specialty for advancement. The broad-based generalist is discouraged. This trend, in turn, has the effect of discouraging sharing across skill areas. Now enters the IT specialist, highly skilled in all areas of technology but unskilled in communication with others. It should be no surprise that these people tend to withdraw from human communication to their world of technology.

In today's business environment, there is a growing awareness that human communication is essential to the success, and even survival, of the company. Effective communication has three characteristics: (1) it crosses disciplines or skill areas, (2) it is ongoing, and (3) it results in clearer, higher levels of understanding between those involved (Table 6-3).

These three criteria apply to IT implementations (Fig. 6-3). There must be a communication system or network between technicians and users which promotes sharing of ideas and knowledge. Ongoing sharing helps each understand the other's attitudes, perspectives, and work. This is not an occasion-specific activity, such as requirements gathering. It involves a continuing commitment to speak and listen to one another. Communication leads to new information and new understanding for both parties.

The steps in the human communications phase of implementation are as follows:

1. Identify the internal impacts of IT.
2. Identify the external impacts of IT.
3. Identify and design human communications strategies.
4. Identify the human communications resources required.
5. Develop the human communications plan.
6. Execute the human communications plan.
7. Evaluate the human communications plan.
8. Revise the human communications plan.
9. Prepare a human communications report for management.
10. Note the steps which need improvement.

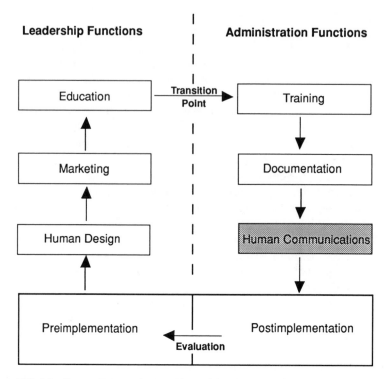

FIG. 6-3   Human Communications Phase of the Technology Implementation Life Cycle

Identify the Internal Impacts of IT

Every technician needs to know both the internal and external users of an organization's IT. The planning and management of effective IT implementations requires that all users be identified and supported. The first step is to identify all areas within the business that are affected by technology. These impacts will vary according to the technology and the user's work.

For example, the PC impact is distributed in terms of both hardware and software. PC users generally expect to use a wide range of software applications. Secretarial and other support staff, on the other hand, are expected to use certain

Table 6-3
Effective Communication in Organizations

1. Crosses disciplines and skill areas
2. Is ongoing
3. Creates new levels of understanding for both parties

standard programs. However, there are significant differences between some of these applications, such as between word processing and spreadsheet software. Data entry functions are even more restricted in terms of the worker's tasks. Data entry clerks use a limited number of features to perform a small range of tasks.

The three examples show that each level of IT use requires different forms of communication. The content varies with each group of users and the type of application. But all types of technology users need an appropriate form of human communications to aid them in their work.

Identify the External Impacts of IT

The same need for human communications applies to the relationship between the technician and the external user of the company's technology. Each time an organization exposes its customers to its technology, whether it is a bank automatic teller machine, ATM, a grocery store scanner, or a department store point-of-sale system, it faces the risk of communicating a negative image of the company through a failure in human communications. In our experience, the negative impression occurs when there is no effective means of human intervention between customer and machine. When the machine is in control, the transaction is dehumanized. If the transaction breaks down, the customers are also dehumanized. Ask them!

A friend of ours, waiting in line at his local bank's ATM, noticed that the line was not moving. He walked to the front of the line and observed an elderly man standing at the ATM, trying to finish his transaction. Finally, our friend moved closer to watch. The gentleman was attempting to withdraw money. Each time he came to the ATM's instruction "Please enter your personal identification number: _____" he tried to write his number on the ATM screen with his ballpoint pen. The computer-literate person might find this mistake humorous. The human communications expert will tell you that it is melancholy—and the ATM's fault. The machine failed to communicate with the customer. Worse, it failed to provide a means for the customer to communicate with it.

We are not proposing that organizations reduce their customers' uses of technology. What we are proposing is a management study of the interactions between customers and technology. There are solutions to the problems we have cited, but the solutions cannot be developed until the problems are identified. And the problems are not noticed unless the impacts of the technology are studied and identified.

Identify and Design Human Communications Strategies

Every case of human-technology interaction needs a corresponding human communications strategy developed for it. Karl vividly recalls the care his local Kroger grocery store took to introduce its computerized item/price scanning system. The benefits to the customer were clearly stated in materials distributed to customers and on signs in the store. Shelf pricing was retained for the benefit of the comparison shopper. The store continued to offer the merchandise for free if the scanner provided an incorrect price.

This grocery chain recognized that the technology interacts as much with the customer as with the checkout clerk and acted accordingly. Management assessed each customer-scanner encounter and its possible risks. Then they designed and implemented a series of communications strategies designed to minimize those risks. Their behavior was a classic example of an effective IT human communications strategy designed to minimize risks.

The goal of management should be the development of a human communications system designed to exploit the creative and innovative potential of users and technology. It may be granted that the technician knows the technology better than the user. However, the user knows the uses of the technology better than the technician. The customary flow of information about technology is from the technician to the user. This does half of the job. The other half of the job is a flow of information about the uses of the technology from the user to the technician.

Human communications strategies include such things as monthly newsletters, new system "rollout" ceremonies, new system demonstrations, bulletin board flyers, "name-the-new-system" contests, computer center tours and/or open houses, and an MIS annual report for users. All of these are designed to get attention, communicate excitement, generate understanding, and create acceptance of new ITs.

Identify the Human Communications Resources Required

The resources needed for an effective, ongoing human communications program are determined by the communications strategy that is selected. Many IT implementations call for a combination of strategies and resources. Once the strategy is set, the corporate resources of marketing, advertising, public relations, internal publications, and human resource development may be drawn upon to assist the MIS department in its human communications efforts.

Human communications planning sessions with implementation task force members, users, and other corporate resource people can be helpful in identifying what resources are needed and which ones are available. This includes the type and number of personnel required, the amount of staff time needed, the media chosen, and the costs of production and distribution.

Develop the Human Communications Plan

A human communications plan focuses on the negative and positive impacts of IT. It controls the risks of new technology and expands its potential uses. It accounts for the varying needs of different users. It recognizes the differences in the way people communicate.

The plan also provides stability and regularity to communication efforts. To achieve this, the plan should focus on the gradual building of communication efforts. Sequencing and timing are the keys. Care should be taken to select the sequence in which each communications strategy is added to the program. For example, start with a technology newsletter targeted to a principal department or set of system users, such as everyone who uses spreadsheets. Once the value and utility of that newsletter has been established, move on to another group of users, departments, and so on. Once this form of communications has taken root, it is possible to move on to the next strategy.

Execute the Human Communications Plan

Execution is always a matter of timing. Timing can mean several things. Timing asks what people are most excited about "at this moment." The successful start of a human communications plan may hinge on whether the audience is excited about its subject matter. Timing asks what resources are available for existing efforts and for the next steps. The successful continuation of a human communications plan requires that the effort not outrun its resources.

A human communications plan can begin with one implementation. For example, a special newsletter about a new word processing system can be developed to provide information during the implementation. This may be a simple one page communication which informs the user in nontechnical language about the new technology. It may highlight installation dates, system features and benefits, and new terms and concepts. This type of publication could be simple and temporary, being published only during the installation and transition to the technology. When it is no longer needed, the publication can be terminated. If it is useful as ongoing communication, it can continue.

Evaluate the Human Communications Plan

The evaluation of a human communications plan begins with the question "What did we do?" This can be a simple chronicle of publications and events. However, if it is limited to this information, it misses a major point. A record of activities also consists of how users have responded to the communication effort. The second question is "What did we accomplish?" This must be answered by surveying the users to determine their perception of the impact that human communications had on their IT use. The third question is "What is the payoff to the organization?" The users and their managers should answer this one. The technical staff also should provide some data based on their continuing interaction with users. A carefully constructed survey followed up with selected personal interviews is a good way to collect this type of information.

Revise the Human Communications Plan

The revision of an IT human communications plan is an important step toward improving future communications efforts. We find the focus group technique a constructive means for reviewing what has been done and what can be done to improve future communications. Revisions should also be done cautiously, using the principles of sequencing and timing discussed above.

Prepare a Human Communications Report for Management

Reports on human communications are given to management at the conclusion of each technology implementation. These reports include the perceptions of three groups: users, technicians, and communications specialists. Each group notes its perceptions of how the communications plan played a role in an implementation.

A truly interactive communications program reveals a variety of information about technology implementation and use. This information includes (1) problem areas in implementation, (2) problem areas in use, (3) implementation techniques and approaches that were effective, (4) technology uses that went well, (5) enhancements in technology use that were achieved, and (6) enhancements and improvements that are recommended.

Comment on Management and Human Communications

None of the above will happen until MIS has assigned responsibility for human communications to a specific staff member and is committed to that person's involvement in the process of building better communications between MIS and users. In the authors' experience, this is the hardest sale of all. Today's standard wisdom seems to be that MIS professionals are not supposed to be communicators; they're supposed to be analysts, coders, and technicians. But the times they are a'changing.

The new technologies are driving the technicians into the workplace. Human communications skills are rising in priority on the list of things managers expect of their technical staff. There is a growing recognition that technology can no longer be installed. It must be implemented. And implementation always involves human communications.

Note Those Steps Which Need Improvement

We should simply add a word of caution: In human communications especially, if something isn't broken, don't fix it. In this area, people appreciate simplicity and traditions. Keep the focus on finding what works—and stay with it.

Phase 8: Postimplementation

Some IT implementations come to an end. For them there is a discrete point at which all the significant steps of a new system startup are concluded. These are planned implementations. Other implementations never end. They dribble on endlessly, with mounting costs, insignificant returns on investment and continuing frustration among users. These are the unplanned or poorly executed implementations. The only way to determine which type of implementation an organization is experiencing is to assess an implementation for its achievements (Fig. 6-4).

The steps in the postimplementation phase of implementation are as follows:

1. Administer a user reality posttest.
2. Administer a user postimplementation attitude survey.
3. Conduct a performance measurement study.
4. Develop recommendations to improve the Technology Implementation Life Cycle.
5. Prepare a postimplementation report for management.
6. Revise the Technology Implementation Life Cycle.

Administer a User Reality Posttest

An information system is a product purchased by its users. This statement has nothing to do with who spent the money to buy it. It is an assertion that the users are always the owners of new technology. Satisfied owners use the technology more effectively and more productively than unsatisfied ones. Previously satisfied buyers will also return to buy other new technology. One of the basics of effective salesmanship is to always point to the "sale after the sale." Meeting the expectations of the client in the present sale is the key to all future sales.

In order to measure user expectations, we recommend that an IT reality test be administered to users at the conclusion of an implementation. This test should ask open ended questions such as these:

1. How does the new technology meet your expectations?
2. How well did the implementation go for you?
3. How did the implementation assist you to overcome any fears or concerns you had about the technology?
4. How comfortable do you feel with the new technology?
5. Were there any pleasant or unpleasant surprises in the new technology?
6. How would you describe this new technology to someone considering its use?

Remember, the purpose of the reality test is to ascertain users' perceptions of a specific information technology.

Administer a User Postimplementation Attitude Survey

The purpose of this survey is to determine any general attitude changes of users toward IT and its use. At this point, the survey should be similar to or the same as the one used in marketing (phase 2, the step entitled "Conduct an IT Attitude Survey"). It is administered following all major IT implementations.

While the user reality test measures workers' expectations of a specific application, the attitude survey measures their general feelings about IT. Each of these plays a role in defining the needs and success of all subsequent implementations.

Conduct a Performance Measurement Study

The implementation task force does not conduct the performance measurement study. User management does. This study is based on the criteria set down by user

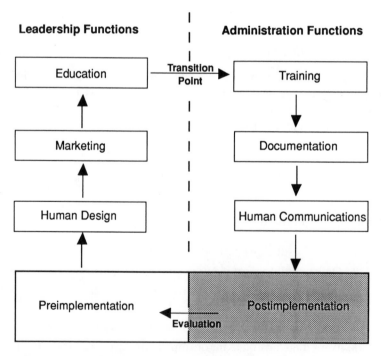

FIG. 6-4 Postimplementation Phase of the Technology Implementation Life Cycle

management during the preimplementation phase. To recapitulate, these are the stated and written criteria for evaluation.

1. Parameters of a software application
   a. All it is capable of doing
   b. Immediate cost justification
2. General goals/achievements of implementation
3. Measures used to demonstrate achievement

At this point, user managers and the implementation task force must decide whether the implementation is concluded or additional work is needed. Remember, it is not whether you did what you said you would do that counts. What counts is whether you accomplished what you set out to accomplish.

Develop Recommendations to Improve the Technology Implementation Life Cycle

As with any other organizational activity, there is a need for stated, periodic evaluation and improvement. The recommendations that flow out of each Technology Implementation Life Cycle may be used immediately or they may be delayed for management review. However, they must be recorded. We recommend that any organization that regularly changes its IT develop a corporate policy for the review of its implementation procedures. This should be the responsibility of the executive who supervises the implementation task force.

Prepare a Postimplementation Report for Management

At this point, a report for senior management is written which summarizes the implementation just completed. It evaluates the effectiveness of the Technology Implementation Life Cycle and proposes any changes needed for the next implementation.

This report is conveyed to senior management by the senior executive who works with the implementation task force and is responsible for implementing life cycle policies and procedures. Courtesy copies should be sent to appropriate user managers.

Revise the Technology Implementation Life Cycle

After receiving comments and reactions from senior management, the executive responsible for the organization's Technology Implementation Life Cycle meets with the implementation task force to review the report and their achievements. This executive is responsible for deciding, with the consent of the task force, where to make appropriate changes.

Concluding Comments

The cost of quality studies shows that quality control costs less in the long run than substandard worker performance. That is why quality is worth the effort. These studies also show that it takes a concentrated, controlled, and determined effort to achieve quality performance. That is often why management does not seek quality.

The answer to this dilemma is to institute a gradual process of technology implementation which provides rewards and benefits each time it is used. We provide an example of this process in the next chapter.

7

The Power Is in the Process

People whose lives are affected by a decision must be a part of the process of arriving at that decision.

—John Naisbitt

This chapter begins with three assumptions that are necessary for the effective use of the Technology Implementation Life Cycle (Table 7-1).

The first assumption is stated in the title of this chapter: The real power to get things done rests in the processes used, not in the systems. There is a tendency to think that immediate and substantive changes can be made in organizations through the adoption of new systems. One of these is IT systems. Often there is surprise when a new system does not produce the expected changes. Changes do occur, but they are generally not the changes that were anticipated.

The reality is that systems can only introduce the elements of change. The institutionalization of change takes time. And it is processes that manage change, not systems. A new system can influence, restrict, and often direct the nature of change. Most new systems are initiated by changes in technology. New computer systems, and

Table 7-1
Three Assumptions

1. The power to get things done rests in processes, not systems.
2. Organizations must have more precise and realistic expectations concerning IT.
3. There is an urgent need to use technology.

the change they bring, are a constant factor in every organization's future activities. But change itself is carried out by the processes within the host organization.

The second assumption is a concern for the development of more precise, realistic, and optimistic expectations about IT. This technology, we assert, is both finite and infinite. That is, it will constantly fail its users because of its limits, but it will also constantly amaze them with its unlimited capabilities. They must prepare for that fact. Simplistic attitudes, whether positive or negative, will not serve organizational needs. Management must be prepared for honest and open appraisals. Management must learn to govern its expectations, being neither too optimistic nor too pessimistic about the outcomes of automation.

The final assumption concerns the urgent need for action. In an increasingly global marketplace, the technological advances and the resources of business are increasingly available to all competitors. Typical comments on competitive advantage suggest that the only variable in technological advantage is the company's human resources. We support this contention but add several thoughts. The ultimate advantage will come to those competitors who devise an interactive relationship between technology and people. In this way they will use their technology to enhance their workers' abilities, skills, and knowledge. For those who do not, bankruptcy will become easier every year.

The subjects of realistic expectations and the urgency to automate are covered in Chapter 8. The remainder of this chapter examines the process of change management. We begin the study of processes by examining the characteristics of "change masters," so named by Rosabeth Moss Kanter (1983) in her book of the same name. Change masters are individuals who can successfully bring organizations through periods of development and change—or, as she defines them, "those people and organizations adept at the art of anticipating the need for, and of leading, productive change." The definitions and explanations of change masters given below are ours.

The Change Masters (Table 7-2)

One of the major problems in computer implementations is that American organizations tend to focus on technical systems to make the organizational processes work. In truth, technical systems will never reach their potential until the problems within the organizational processes have been solved. But solving the problems within these

Table 7-2
Rule 1 for Change Masters

Effective change masters understand the difference between a process and a system. They know what each contributes to the success of the organization. Because they know this they strive to keep their focus on the human, or organizational, processes in order to make technical systems work.

processes will not be as easy as anticipated. There is a tendency to dismiss human processes rather than to understand them. This may occur for very personal reasons.

Each of us has had some negative experiences with certain kinds of bureaucratic processes. These experiences have taught us to believe that processes are used to stop things from happening, to slow down things that should be done. When this perspective is broadened to include all processes, managers may institute one of three solutions to handle their perceived problem with the processes of the organization (Table 7-3).

Managers who view the process as "not working" will sidestep it. They will find an alternative method to solve their problem or manage their concern. Managers who view the process as "clogged up" will use the process by pushing their agenda through it or by using their political clout. Managers who view the process as being controlled by "key movers" will use their influence to get things done.

The conclusion drawn from such experiences is that processes are inherently dysfunctional. We contend that dysfunctional processes occur because of problems in human behavior, not because of problems inherent in processes. Not every process prevents things from getting done. There are processes that push the work forward. If our comments are to carry any weight, each person will have to overcome his or her own personal bias based on previous experience with dysfunctional processes. There is, however, another problem that blocks our understanding of processes (Table 7-4).

One of the greatest difficulties in the use of processes is that they never stand still. This is particularly true of human processes. They are always "caught in mid-flight." Understanding them is difficult because they are always doing things when they are being examined. To "see" a process is to look at something in action, not something shut down.

On the other hand, both technical and human systems, can be made to stand still. They can be shut down while they are examined. For this reason, the components of systems are open to discovery and examination. The development of their taxonomy is easier. With processes there is always the "black box" phenomenon. The inputs can be seen. The outputs can be observed. But inside the process, there is often a feeling of helplessness which best expressed by the statement, "Darned if we know how it happened."

Table 7-3
Three Nonsolutions to Process Problems

1. Sidestep them
2. Push them through the process
3. Use personal influence

Table 7-4
Rule 2 for Change Masters

Effective change masters know that processes are always harder to understand and master than systems because they never stand still.

Table 7-5
Rule 3 for Change Masters

Effective change masters understand that systems and processes are always interwoven with one another.

For example, most computer users refer to their documentation when they have a problem with the system. Typically, the problem they experience in using the documentation is that it is encyclopedic in style. The writing style used for user reference documentation is best suited to describing the application as a *system*. The user, however, is operating the application as a *process* of work. The style of documentation writing is often ill-suited to describing a process. This mismatch is evidenced by two frequently voiced complaints of documentation users: (1) they spend too much time finding the help they need, and (2) they often have to look in several different places to find the pieces of the answer, which they then assemble into the complete answer.

The difference between systems and processes is highlighted by the diagrams used to describe them. Most diagrams of systems, though often complex, are reasonable and understandable. Many diagrams of processes appear incoherent, extremely complicated, yet insufficient to describe all that happens. It is generally easier to identify and understand a system than a process. Similarly, many of our readers will easily understand that the Technology Implementation Life Cycle is a system, or, more properly, a systematic way of implementing technology. Yet it is not that alone. As we shall see, it is also a process (Table 7-5).

The Technology Implementation Life Cycle is both a system and a process. Understanding this fact is essential to its correct use and application. At times it is difficult to separate and distinguish the different elements of system and process in the Technology Implementation Life Cycle. In order to use this implementation method properly, it must first be viewed as a process. It must also be introduced to others as a process, and it must be linked to the social and work processes of the organization. How that is done is the subject of this chapter.

Process and System: a Definitional Concern

Definitions of process and system are given below. The definition of a process is our creation and combines elements of other definitions we have seen. The definition of a system includes several options, in the general order of their use, taken directly from commonly used dictionaries. The differences between a process and a system can be readily seen in these definitions. For emphasis, the statements in Table 7-6 should be noted.

Table 7-6
Differences: Process vs. System

A process is most often described as an activity. A system is most often described as a condition.

A process has an end product distinct from the process itself. A process is generally valued because of the end product it provides.

A system serves a process. It is valued because of the way it facilitates the process to which it connects. The end product of a system is the manner in which it does its work. For example, computer systems are often extolled for their speed.

Process Definition

A "process" can be defined as follows: "An interrelated set of activities, generally sequential, which tend to accomplish a purpose." In business and government, they provide either a product or a service.

System Definitions

A "system" can be defined as follows:

"A group of interacting, interrelated, or interdependent elements forming a complex whole."

"A set of interrelated ideas or principles" or, in a more tangible use, "a group of interacting mechanical or electrical operations."

As these definitions indicate an effective and valuable IT, including hardware and software, will combine the properties of both a process and a system. For example, the computer system may provide a framework within which a new or improved work process can operate. The system may be a new way of interrelating financial data so that senior management can project alternative futures in doing strategic planning. In this last example, the computer system will change both the data employed by the organization and the planning process.

Given their dual nature, computer systems inevitably change the systems and processes of work. Problems in implementation occur whenever there is a failure to recognize that both the system and the process of work have been changed as the result of computerization. With the recognition of both of these changes comes the need to manage both. Generally, the ability to manage both types of changes is not found among those responsible for implementations.

For example, computer technicians are often highly skilled at managing systems changes. They recognize that it is standard practice to allow the old and new systems to run in parallel for a time. For most technicians, this is primarily a safety measure. For many, there is also a recognition that differences between systems dictate some

Table 7-7
Characteristics of the Process of Change

1. It is cyclical and iterative
2. It is incremental
3. It is planned
4. It is maintained as an open system

time for transition. The insights of technicians are linked most closely to their understanding of computers, not of work processes.

A change in a work process requires attention to a different set of data and problems. It requires one to go beyond the needs of the technical system to the needs of the human system. A change in work processes can be handled only by a method of change management. It requires management of the changes in human processes and systems of work that accompany technology implementation. This method of change management is itself a process and has the characteristics listed in Table 7-7.

Effective use of the Technology Implementation Life Cycle requires the management of change in work systems and processes. It requires that the above characteristics be part of the process of implementation.

A Cyclical and Iterative Process

When developing a project plan, most people think in a straight line. There is a beginning point, an end point, and a line of activities between the two. Sometimes there is a feedback loop to indicate evaluation or additional information. The feedback loop is used to redesign the plan or to make sure that it works according to established criteria. But the general plan is still a straight line with a neat beginning and end.

Three employees of Procter and Gamble challenged this straight-line assumption. They developed a general project plan using a model of individual learning. What emerged was a four-step, repetitive cycle of activities (Fig. 7-1) that has broad applications to technology implementations. Their research findings were originally published in the *Sloan Management Review (SMR)*, (Spring, 1976). SMR's editors made the following comment at the beginning of the article: "The R&D process has been the source of considerable interest in recent years to managers, and the Procter & Gamble Company has long been recognized for its outstanding success in this area." The editors continued: "In this article, the authors describe how they developed a better understanding of the R&D process at Procter & Gamble by applying the David Kolb model of experiential learning (Kolb 1984) to the organizational learning process. The model, which postulates a four-step repetitive cycle, was validated through a number of experiments *and the authors suggest ways in which the*

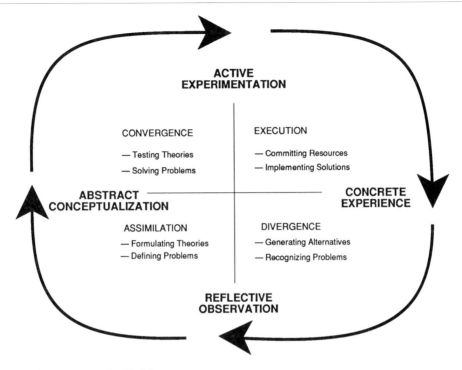

FIG. 7-1 The Learning Model

The Learning Model is based on right-sided and left-sided brain functions as applied to learning and education. Its use has been extended to general development and management of change. The Procter and Gamble researchers applied it to group activities and learning.

model might be used to improve the production of new knowledge in organizations" (emphasis added).*

The Procter and Gamble research is remarkably similar to a number of theoretical frameworks which attempt to explain organizational behavior. The cycle begins with the known, concrete experience of an organization or individual. It postulates that the next step is some form of assessment, observation, or reflection which affirms the past but suggests alternatives as well. The ability to bring together past continuities and new divergences into one interrelated whole requires theorizing and the review of alternatives, impacts, and options. Once a general theoretical framework has been established and supported, the next step is to select from among alternatives and to focus one's individual or organizational efforts. The final step is to

*Reprinted and quoted from "R&D Organizations as Learning Systems," by Barbara Carlsson, Peter Keane, and J. Bruce Martin, *Sloan Management Review* (17, 3, 1976), pp. 1–16, by permission of the publisher. Copyright © 1976 by the Sloan Management Review Association. All rights reserved.

take action, to test one's theories and decisions in the crucible of real life. This, in turn, brings the cycle back to concrete experience.

In the discussion of their findings, the Procter and Gamble researchers point to several significant observations that they culled from their study. One is that the deficiencies of a research team can be predicted based on their level of competence in each of the four stages of research. For example, a research team strong in theorizing but weak in execution will be creative, but lacking in focus and in the testing of its hypothesis. While this seems elemental, it is only deceptively simple. It mimics a problem of computer implementations. Many computer system development teams are rich in technical and creative skills but lack the execution skills for effective implementation.

As we examined and studied the article and the learning model, it became apparent to us that the traditional systems development life cycle accomplishes about half of the job of technology implementation. It explores the full range of options, theorizes from these, and can lead to excellent decisions on the kinds of systems that are needed. But it does little to link the systems to the operational world of the end user. We, therefore, propose a dynamic integration of the traditional systems development life cycle and the Technology Implementation Life Cycle to meet the full range of worker needs during a technology implementation. This is shown in Fig. 7-2.

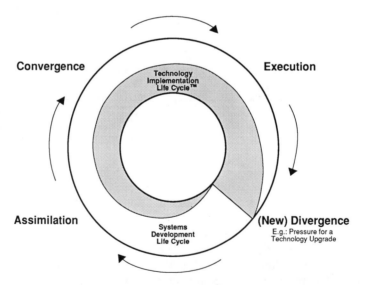

FIG. 7-2   Process: The Need to Integrate the Systems Development Life Cycle and the Technology Implementation Life Cycle

The system development life cycle is the standard method for managing the development of computer applications. We developed the Technology Implementation Life Cycle as its complement. When the two are integrated, the interests of the technician and the end user are both served.

The process of implementation begins during the first stages of systems development, where the focus is primarily on data gathering and planning. As the activities of the systems development life cycle decline in number and intensity, the activities associated with the Technology Implementation Life Cycle gradually increase. This should be viewed as a natural phenomenon, not as an imposed rule. It is natural because there are natural differences and natural links between the two life cycles.

The systems development life cycle is concerned with delivering the very best system it can create. The Technology Implementation Life Cycle is designed to make the most effective and efficient use of that system. Once it is understood that developing and implementing computer systems is a process, the differences between these two life cycles can be understood. They have different roles and different levels of activity, depending upon where in the cycle an organization is.

A second observation of the Procter and Gamble researchers is that effective project teams tend to move through the learning cycle in an iterative fashion. That is, one time through the cycle does not get the job done. The project teams seem to know that only so much data can be handled in one pass through the cycle. John Carroll, in an article in *Datamation* magazine (Carroll 1984), touches on a similar concern when he writes on the need to use minimalist principles in developing computer user training.

The problems he identifies are related in part to the user's tendency to see the computer training program as it relates to work and as a long-term learning process. In contrast, the technical trainer views training primarily as the imparting of information regarding a system. The technical trainer may think that the whole job can be done in one sitting. The user views the matter more as an iterative and gradual process of skill development, as with the learning model.

An equally interesting article appeared in the professional magazine *Computer Practices* (Mantei and Teorey 1988), titled "Cost/Benefit Analysis for Incorporating Human Factors in the Software Life Cycle." The article intends simply to cost justify additional data gathering and testing of software by the computer user so that better software can be developed. It does that, but it also supports the view that development and implementation must be integrated with one another in a more dynamic manner. It also confirms that the development/implementation process should be much more cyclical and iterative than those previously designed and managed.

The process of software selection and use in the PC environment is similar to this cyclical and iterative process, particularly when the computer user is in charge. Picture a PC with four or five different word processing packages installed and available to the user. The typical user would approach such a situation by experimenting with the use of each package. The user would seek the word processing package which most closely mimics his or her old style of working or the one which is easiest to follow.

Once the selection is made, learning the new way of working will proceed much as follows: The user will try a small and easy sample of regular work. When this is mastered, the user will move on to another work task that is a little more sophisticated.

The user will proceed in this fashion until all work tasks are mastered, not until the software is mastered. After all, the user is paid for the work produced, not for the extent of his or her knowledge of a computer system.

An Incremental Process

Effective leaders go about their work in an incremental fashion. To most of us, this may mean that they do things in small steps or stages. Although they do things in steps, there is more to it than that. Effective use of an incremental process requires a great deal of insight into human behavior. It requires knowledge of the manner in which people tolerate change. Developing an incremental process involves more than just taking a big change and moving people through it in bits and pieces. An effective incremental process has the features described in Table 7-8.

A Strategic Goal

A strategic goal provides clarity of purpose as people are led through a process of incremental change. In effect, it builds morale for the lengthy process of introducing the Technology Implementation Life Cycle. Morale is not something that can be imposed on people. It is not increased through pep talks or rallies. Morale arises from a sense of common purpose, self direction, and shared coordination of work activities—all of which arise from a strategic goal.

The best strategic goals develop from a combination of the directive efforts of a leader and the participation and data of employees. When an organization seeks to use IT, there is a need for a leader who can set a standard of excellence and who can state this standard in a way that leads to the support of others. Effective strategic leaders keep their goal statements purposely open, or vague in detail, so that employees at all levels can contribute to the form and intent of the goal.

For example, some banks and other financial institutions are moving toward a more common computerized data base that is accessible to all departments. This development cries out for a strategic statement that sets a direction, a purpose, and a mission for sharing common data. "We are a team!" would be an adequate goal statement in this context. It would let all the participants know that they are to act as a team. It would tell them that customers must experience teamwork in their

Table 7-8

Features of an Effective Incremental Process of Technology Implementation

1. It has a strategic goal.
2. It focuses on the needs of an organization's employees and work groups.
3. It recognizes the cognitive limits of learners and organizations.
4. It legitimizes and supports the users' need for psychological comfort in the use of technological systems.
5. It has long-range payoffs as major goals.

association with bank employees. It would tell employees to share customers with one another through the common data base. A great amount of detailed work must follow from this statement, but the statement itself can provide focus and direction for all such efforts.

In recent years, much has been said about the need for a chief information officer (CIO) who can provide a sense of direction to the organization's automation. Whether such a position is needed is a moot point. There is a need, however, for someone to provide strategic leadership for automation of the workplace.

Work Group Needs

An effective incremental process focuses on employee and work groups needs. Part of the problem of technology implementation lies in the difficulty of defining users' needs easily and comprehensively. Some user requirements are missed through inattention to detail or because of the personal bias of the technician. Sometimes there is simply not enough time for users to describe all of their needs for system designers. But it is not that "we" or "they" are the problem. Some things just take time. Finding and meeting users' needs is one of them.

We have already suggested that work groups may be located in operational, tactical, or strategic areas of the organization. Thus, users needs will vary according to the responsibilities associated with each level of work. They will also vary according to the particular work a person does within each level. And they will differ according to the skills a system demands of its users.

The work group's needs also differ according to the stage of automation that the organization has reached. Work groups are affected differently during each phase. In the initial stage of big systems development, work groups will be affected either very much, as people are replaced or work is drastically changed, or very little, because the technical system has not yet touched their group. The impact on work groups will broaden as the technology moves more to information sharing. At this stage, each worker will be forced to develop new skills for using technology and handling the subsequent new work relationships. In the final stage of this socioeconomic change, each work group will be confronted with changes in work goals, work styles, and organizational power structures.

Cognitive Limits

An effective incremental process will recognize the cognitive limits of the participants. The previously cited article by Carroll on minimalist training affirms this principle and is a profitable addition to our comments. In addition to what it says, we wish to note three principles: timing, sequencing, and processing. Timing recognizes that there are optimum times of readiness for new things. Employees should be scheduled through the implementation process at times of maximum readiness to learn.

Sequencing assumes that people learn and gain skills best in a proper sequence. Learning and skill development need to be set into a natural sequence, both for the sake of the subject matter and for the sake of the learners. The best sequence of learning may vary according to the work group's tasks. Processing recognizes that people need time to absorb one type of learning before continuing on to the next. This absorption phenomenon must account for both the level of content which can be absorbed and the degree of comfort achieved with what has been learned.

Psychological Comfort

An effective incremental process will focus on the psychological comfort levels of users before it moves on to the next stage of IT. The absorption of new technology requires several stages of learner adjustment. The first stage is content adjustment. This need is more easily defined and detected than psychological adjustment. There are numerous ways to measure this need. People can be tested for content retention and recall. There are ways to measure the impact of new skills on productivity levels. However, the psychological adjustment to a new work system is not as easily measured.

Psychological comfort levels are more often observed and measured indirectly. They are noted in the comments workers make about a system, such as "I'll never go back to a typewriter again." They are noted in the manner in which workers assist one another in using the new technology. They can be measured through general attitudinal surveys of user comfort with computers. Keep this principle in mind: The psychological comfort level of one computer implementation automatically becomes a primary motivational factor for the next computer implementation.

Long-Range Payoff

All of the preceding leads to the final factor in an effective incremental process: It develops its own built-in payoff. This will take years to do, but an effective Technology Implementation Life Cycle program can develop a flexible and adaptable attitude toward the implementation and use of ITs. The ultimate long-term payoff will be an increase in the organization's ability to absorb and profit from ever-advancing forms of technology.

A Planned Process

The Technology Implementation Life Cycle will not be introduced by verbiage, or logic, or even by this book. There must be a planned process for its introduction. And it must be a management-introduced, planned, and approved process. A haphazard introduction of this implementation methodology will fail. Its values and benefits will not be perceived. Done poorly, it may be considered simply as an additional expense without any commensurate return on investment. A series of steps must be followed to introduce and use the Technology Implementation Life Cycle (Table 7-9).

Table 7-9
Steps in Developing a Planned Process for Introducing the Technology Implementation Life Cycle

1. Assess existing organizational strengths in technology implementation.
2. Select an IT of appropriate complexity for implementation.
3. Select essential elements of the Technology Implementation Life Cycle for introduction.
4. Determine and acquire necessary resources.
5. Plan and execute selected elements of the Technology Implementation Life Cycle.

Assess the Existing Organizational Strengths in Technology Implementation

Every effort should be made to identify the present level of effectiveness in implementing ITs. One must be careful that this does not become an overassessment. For too long, people have told us that "we already do that" when in fact they do not. Strengths in technology implementation must be judged according to the criteria stated in the Technology Implementation Life Cycle.

Do not try to expand or rely too heavily on known strengths. Just be sure that no diminution of effort occurs in areas of strength while promoting development in areas of weakness. Keep existing strengths of technology implementation controlled and at their present and customary level.

Select an IT of Appropriate Complexity for Implementation

Select an IT of manageable size, yet of sufficient importance to the organization that its effective implementation will be noted and appreciated. The system should be related to a work group or department in which the intended users have shown support for change. They need not be technology users at the present time, but they must be a progressive group that is adaptable to new technology. It is very important to do an extensive profile of the intended users. No matter what other shortcuts may be used this first time through the Technology Implementation Life Cycle, do not cut back on the user profile.

Select the Essential Phases or Steps of the Technology Implementation Life Cycle for Introduction

We recommend that all eight phases of the Technology Implementation Life Cycle be employed every time an IT is implemented. However, as the methodology is being introduced, the implementation task force needs to assess how complex and thorough a task it can manage as it gradually acquires skills in using the various parts of the methodology. Just as technology users need to make incremental progress toward higher levels, so do those who use the Technology Implementation Life Cycle.

The decision on which components to stress and use requires three types of information: (1) the characteristics of IT, (2) the profile of the intended users, and (3) the criteria for measuring effectiveness and productivity when the implementation is completed. An examination of these should demonstrate the need for this decision making to be a cooperative effort between the MIS manager and the user manager. This cooperation will ensure the choice of the implementation phases or steps most essential and most necessary for judging the implementation to be a success.

Determine and Acquire Necessary Resources

The continued cooperation of MIS manager and user manager will often be needed to gain approval for necessary resources. Senior managers in operational work units often have readier access to the full resources of the firm than do senior managers in MIS. Their support of resource acquisition may be vital to the success of an implementation, particularly when certain necessary skills are not available among MIS personnel. Care must be taken, however, whenever borrowed staff are used in technology implementations. Their use needs to be carefully justified both in advance and at the conclusion of the implementation. Wherever possible, each resource request should be linked to specific, measurable outcomes of value to the end user and to the company.

Resources may be borrowed from other divisions or units. For example, marketing personnel can assist in the development of the second phase, marketing. The public information/relations staff can assist in the development of phase 7, human communications. Training and human resource development professionals can help in phases 4 and 5, education and training, respectively. When other corporate personnel are used, care should be taken that their expected duties are stated in writing, carefully limited, approved by their manager, and carefully scheduled. They must be held accountable for their work and their timetable. If they aren't, the implementation will flounder.

The use of borrowed staff has grave negative possibilities unless they are carefully managed. There must be time for loaned personnel to be incorporated into a project. They will need sufficient briefing on the nature and goals of the project—particularly to understand its values and benefits to the organization. Their potential contribution to the success of the project should be emphasized. Remember, borrowed staff will have only a limited personal investment in a project unless steps are taken to increase their commitment to it. One way to reinforce their value to a project is to provide suitable recognition and rewards upon the completion of their tasks. This can be done by writing a personal letter of appreciation to their manager with a request that it be made part of their personnel file.

Plan and Execute the Selected Phases or Steps of the Technology Implementation Life Cycle

Planning and executing the Technology Implementation Life Cycle has already been detailed in Chapters 5 and 6. Here we stress that careful attention should be paid to advance planning, to close administration, and to regular reports to senior management. It is not the number of phases or steps from the Technology Implementation Life Cycle that are used that will sell this process in its first introduction. The effort will be sold by its quality and by how effectively its results are communicated to senior management.

Close reporting relationships with senior management should be maintained throughout every phase and use of the Technology Implementation Life Cycle. The implementation task force should prepare for oral or written briefings on its major decisions. These should be presented to senior management at stated intervals. The relationship between the implementation task force and senior management should be clearly stated. These meetings are designed for review purposes, advice, and comments, rather than for approval.

Management must remember that the implementation task force must have free rein to experiment with this process, to learn it, and to adapt it to their circumstances. The task force must remember to honor that freedom by exercising control over its own actions. It must maintain close supervision over all phases and steps of the process. It must assume responsibility for any mistakes or errors in judgment and report them immediately when corrections are completed. In particular, it must work closely with the management of user departments in order to assess how productive this new program is in its immediate impact and what future gains it promises.

A word of caution is in order. During presentations of the Technology Implementation Life Cycle or its predecessor, The McConnell Method, we are frequently asked, "What will this cost?" This question can lead to grave consequences unless the implementation task force has done its research. In order to answer this question, the task force must research the cost of previous implementation attempts. When the cost of an effective implementation is raised, they can then point to the costs of past ineffective efforts. They may list lost worker time, unused ITs, lost advantages in the marketplace, and dozens of other hidden costs that every organization has absorbed for far too long.

This procedure is needed because the costs of effective technology implementation are known and observed. The costs of ineffective implementations are often hidden and ignored. Every organization in which we have consulted has had higher hidden costs due to poor technology implementations than the open costs associated with quality implementations. We are always pleased to assist an organization to anticipate the costs of the Technology Implementation Life Cycle, provided that they review the costs of previous implementations. The situation is analogous to the cost of quality control.

Every study we have seen on the cost of quality shows that a lack of quality control leads to higher losses. Quality may be costly, but it is measurable, capable of control, and can be used to create profit. A lack of quality is seldom measured, is itself a lack of control, and is always a cost center. Unfortunately, too few organizations have studied the costs they suffer due to a lack of quality control. Without this information there can be no evaluation of the cost of quality. Numbers by themselves have no meaning. They must have other numbers for comparison. And when the numbers for comparison are available, quality always wins.

A final capstone to this discussion is to point out to senior management that the only costs that can be controlled are those that are known. Hidden costs are beyond control. But this is a two-edged sword, for it requires the advance planning for an effective technology implementation to include the costs of ineffective implementation in one's own organization.

An effective first use of the Technology Implementation Life Cycle will achieve the following: First, skills will be gained in applying selected steps of this cycle to the process of implementation. Second, some of the advantages of this process will have been demonstrated to senior management. Finally, a beginning will have been made in understanding that technology implementations must always be an open system process. That is, there will always be something new to learn or do in order to maintain this process at its highest level of effectiveness.

Effective Processes Require an Open System

In order to energize their systems, organizations must remain open to new ideas, new leaders, new developments, and new technologies. CEOs who want to reenergize a failing business will add new personnel selectively. Entrepreneurs flourish in an open market that allows the free flow of new ideas and the emergence of new businesses. Many entrepreneurs leave the safe haven of a large firm to strike out on their own because a new idea becomes the driving force in their lives. Innovative large businesses will often set up a program of "intrapreneurship" to encourage the development of new products and service ideas within their companies. Special steps will be taken to keep the intrapreneurs fresh and open to new ideas and to protect them from the stultifying effect of old organizational patterns and concepts.

The new way of doing business, the new product or service, or the new and innovative concept requires an open system. Similarly, the process of the Technology Implementation Life Cycle requires an open system. An open system is one in which energy can be absorbed, converted, organized, and used. It is open to external energies, whether these be food, air, ideas, or even technology. Businesses operate most effectively when they retain an openness to external energy. Henceforth, we shall use the term "energy" to refer to all environmental resources available for the use of the organization. This can include raw materials, funds, research, ideas, technology, and whatever else can be used by the organization to build itself and to achieve its goals.

John R. Sherwood, founder of Management Design, Inc., and Evaluation Services of Cincinnati, Ohio, has developed a model of systems/processes that shows how new energy enters old organizations. He calls it a "Structural Dynamics Model™,"* thus capturing the concepts of both systems theory and process models. He often uses biological analogies in explaining his model.

---

*"Structural Dynamics Analysis"™ is used by permission of John R. Sherwood, Evaluation Services, 5572 East Galbraith Road, Cincinnati, OH 45236; (513) 791-1957.

First, all human systems have two basic phases, an "anabolic" phase of preparation to do their work, and a "catabolic" phase in which they actually perform their work. Second, there are at least two key points in the cycle of a human system's life. Each of these is a transition point. One occurs when there is a transition from preparation to implementation, the other when there is a transition from implementation to preparation.

Third, all human systems must discard waste elements. Sometimes entire systems are gradually discarded and replaced by newer systems. This discarding of waste constitutes an energy drain on the system, energy that must be replaced. Our skin is an example of this process. It constantly grows and moves slowly to the surface. As it reaches the surface, each successive layer dies, providing us with a protective shield. It is then sloughed off—discarded—to be replaced by the next layer. This creates an energy drain on our bodily system. The development of new skin requires new energy expenditures. Because this bodily process is constant, we may not notice it.

Most of us also fail to notice the amount of energy that is needed to replace old systems with new ones in the largest human system—the organization. When an old system wears out, it needs to be replaced. It needs new parts. It needs new structures. And it needs the energy to put them all together. Even the simple act of acquiring one new function and placing it within the existing system requires new energy. All human systems need energy from outside sources. This energy need is just as vital to large organizational systems as it is to the individual who needs food, light, and other forms of energy (Fig. 7-3).

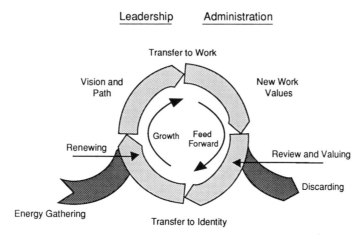

FIG. 7-3   The Human Organization: An Open Systems Model (An Adaptation of the Structural Dynamics Analysis Model™ of John Sherwood)

This figure provides the basis for the discussion that follows. Three key points should be kept in mind. All human systems need to organize and need to do their work. All human systems need a cyclical process to maintain their activity. All human systems discard waste and seek new energy to survive.

Table 7-10
Phases in the Technology Implementation Process

1. Energy gathering: Each organization must gather the right kind of energy.
2. Vision and path: Energy use is directed toward the real needs and purposes of the organization.
3. Doing human work: All work is viewed as human work; all accomplishment as human accomplishment.
4. Feed forward: The only way to preserve the past is to plan the future.
   Stage 1 of feed forward: new values
   Stage 2 of feed forward: reviewing and valuing
   Stage 3 of feed forward: discarding and renewing

Models such as this are valuable not because they prove anything, but because they reinforce and visualize what we know to be true. This model reinforces common truths about the commonsense way that things get done. This model also reinforces the way the Technology Implementation Life Cycle fits into the phases of an organization's life cycle. It shows the correct manner in which management must introduce the Technology Implementation Life Cycle in its organization (Table 7-10).

Introducing the Technology Implementation Life Cycle Into the Organization

Phase 1: Energy Gathering

THEOREM

As a living human system, each organization must
gather the right kind of energy.

The energy needs of living systems differ according to their biology. The energy needs of social systems differ as well. This is an accepted fact, though seldom noted. Technology is a source of energy and differs according to the energy needs of each user. The technology of a manufacturing company that provides a product differs from that of an enterprise which offers a service. The many different types and sizes of IT are more than an indication of human inventiveness and competitiveness. They are a sign of the differing needs of technology users. Technology, as a source of energy for the organization, must be matched to its needs.

In a very real sense, technology vendors do not need to find their place in the market. They need to find a user's needs in the market and meet those needs. It is the

IT user's identity that must determine how vendors relate to their market. Or perhaps the responsibility should be placed clearly on the users. They need to clarify and understand their identity as an organization and then move toward those energy sources (and ITs) that will meet their needs.

In the initial phase of introducing IT, the most essential energy elements must be identified. That is, the organization must answer this question: "According to the identity, the purposes, and the driving forces of our enterprise, what are our IT needs?" The question addresses the issue of how the technology will support the users' accepted ways of living and working together. This tradition of living and working safeguards the underlying values that hold the people of the organization together. The initial phases of technology implementation and use must support this aspect of the organization's identity.

Phase 2: Vision and Path

THEOREM

Energy use must be directed toward the real needs and purposes of the organization.

There are two energy sources that contribute to the development of an organization's vision or sense of direction. One is the traditional identity; the other is the outside wisdom—the new energy brought into the organization. If the internal, traditional energy source predominates, there will be a tendency to do things the way they have always been done. If the external energy source predominates, there will be a tendency to throw everything out and start over again. Somewhere between these extremes lies the most dynamic solution, an interaction between old and new wisdom. That interaction must be value based, asking questions about "who we are," "what we do," and "how we behave."

In this manner, a dynamic tension will be introduced as the old base is stretched to accommodate a new goal while maintaining a common direction and purpose. This tension is essential to the continued vitality of the enterprise. It is the basis for energy absorption into the system. It is the basis for the maintenance of a continual process of improvement and accommodation to the environment. In its absence, there will be a decline of energy. Internal competition for power will increase. There will be a gradual decline from dynamic and vital goals to maintenance goals to survival goals.

Having a vision, the organization now needs a path to travel towards that vision. The values of the organization will provide this path. For example, if someone is overheard complaining about a computer training program and says, "That's not the way we treat people around here," a distinct value message is being conveyed. Such messages speak to the concern for responsible management of the organization.

Policies reside in the written codes and oral traditions of the organization. They tell individual members how to behave as they move toward goal accomplishment. They inform them how to make decisions on the implementation of technical systems. They tell leaders how to behave. They provide guidance for leaders as they direct, motivate, and control the behaviors of their followers. They instruct leaders on how to build a consensus among followers on contemplated courses of action.

If technology implementations are done without reference to the policies of the organization, they will create chaos in the human system at the same time that they bring order to the technical system. They will inevitably cause the two systems to war with one another. Let the technical expert listen.

We support the highest levels of technology use, the greatest expansion of technological discovery, and the strongest backing for implementation of IT. We believe in technology. But we believe in it in a particular way—as a support system for human systems. We do not believe in it in any other way. The only way that technology can be used safely is when it is integrated into the human system in a way that prepares it to support the work of that system. That is the objective of the first two phases.

Phase 3: Doing Human Work

THEOREM

All work must be viewed as human work, all accomplishment as human accomplishment.

In his description of this phase, John Sherwood says, "while culture and identity deal with the fundamental nature and purpose of the company, implementation deals with its capacity to produce." In many ways, this statement parallels our concerns about technology implementation. It must also be concerned with the capacity to produce. In order to achieve this, the Technology Implementation Life Cycle must pass through a crucial transitional point.

In biology this is called the "liminal point." It is an identifiable time during which the organism ceases its preparation to work and begins to implement its working processes. We have observed organizations in which this transition is avoided during technology implementations. Instead, having organized one new system for use, the technicians pass it along to users as a formal project and move on to the next technical project. They develop a pattern of recycling through development stages, either delegating or neglecting the implementation stages.

Wherever this happens, there is a similar pattern among those who work with technology. Their tendency is to stay in the implementation cycle and to reject new systems, new ways of work. To be sure, employees can be coerced, but their hearts will not be in it, nor will they achieve the peak efficiencies projected for them by the technical expert.

None of us will ever achieve peak efficiency in the use of technology until we can pass through this organizational liminal point. To achieve this, there must be a tacit acceptance of the equal value of development and implementation and of their mutual dependence on one another. Development must be seen as a necessary prelude to implementation. It must be evaluated, in part, on how well it leads to implementation. Implementation must be seen as having a major role in feeding information forward to the next round of development. It too must be evaluated, in part, on how well it supports development.

Phase 4: Feed Forward

THEOREM

The only way to preserve the past is to plan the future.

The term "feedback" is more familiar, yet "feed forward" is rapidly gaining recognition. Feedback is more appropriate for describing the need for systems to return to equilibrium. In human systems, this often means the return to the old way of doing things. Equilibrium is a state in which things are getting done as they should be. It is not a bad state of affairs unless the environment is changing.

For an organization, equilibrium presents a future risk unless there is equilibrium in its environment. If the environment is changing, the organization must feed forward in order to survive. And that is exactly the present situation. Our environment is changing, and it is changing rapidly and drastically. A great deal of the change is technologically driven. We believe that technological change, more than any other kind of change, requires that organizations use feed forward.

We use the term "feed forward" to mean the development of a system, given its environmental possibilities, to a new and natural stage of existence and activity. Feed forward is a process that engenders new possibilities within old systems. It is a process that makes new things possible, acceptable, and achievable. It consists of several stages, none of which can be eliminated without endangering the emergence of new organizational forms and activities.

Stage 1 of Feed Forward: New Values

When a new form of work is introduced and effectively implemented, it produces new values in the workplace. These values are attached (1) to the thing produced, (2) to the achievement in producing it, (3) to the new skills used, and (4) to the new work relationships. These values become the source of strength and continuity for the organization. They also become a repository of "markers" on which management can draw in subsequent computer implementations. In sociological terms, these are called "innovative credits." Technology implementation leaders will know that they have earned innovative credits when the next set of users are ready and eager to follow a new implementation.

Stage 2 of Feed Forward: Reviewing and Valuing

The next stage involves reviewing the new work forms for their strength and valuing these new forms for their utility. Reviewing is an examination of the work-related behaviors of employees. It asks the question "What did we do?" The reference is purposely plural to include all workers. The answer will be a log of activities and a record of resource use. It will note the contribution of every person. It will be a journal of commitment and relationships. It is best accomplished as a team effort, with every worker adding his or her insights to the list of activities.

Valuing raises the issue of whether the new forms of work have utility to the organization. Utility can be examined in two ways. One way is to ask whether the activities of work produced the desired products or services. In effect, this inquiry asks, "Did we accomplish what we said we would?" Additionally, the issue should be raised whether the new form of work is a more effective way of providing products or services and, therefore, a more effective way of supporting the organization. The second concern of utility is whether these products and services benefit the organization. New forms of work, including IT, should produce some additional benefit to the organization. In valuing there is always a comparison of two things. The valuing questions are raised so that workers will understand that the commitments they make are important to the health of the organization.

Stage 3 of Feed Forward: Discarding and Renewing

Eventually, all old things are discarded. In human organizations, it is best when systems of work are discarded by those who own them. The owners know the value of the old way of work and can test the value of the new system before the old one is discarded. People feel ownership of the technology associated with their work. It is not right to make them give it up in favor of a new technology. This is exactly where some managers cause problems. They try to force the discarding of an old system before users have tested the new system. Users need the opportunity to do their own review and valuing and to make their own decision to discard the old system.

There is a truth that is hard to acknowledge, but it is a part of human reality: We all have our security blankets. And we never discard them without first acquiring a substitute. The substitute may require that the user adjust. The user will need time to develop new internal attitudes and a sense of security in the new system.

In the workplace, the old way of doing things is a security blanket. No one takes a security blanket away from someone else. It can only be discarded by its owner—when the owner is ready. Why fight it? Examine the difference made in marketing an IT if it is first introduced with a pilot test. A pilot test gives the users a chance to prepare to discard the old way. The process of running parallel systems is often extolled for the practice it provides users. It also gives them a security blanket by having the old system available as a backup. Its greatest benefit is that it places the decision to discard the old system in the hands of the users and in its proper position in the cycle of implementation.

If new systems are imposed on users without their consent, the users will not transfer their old system of values to the new system of work. When the old way of doing things is discarded at the proper place in the process, users will be comfortable with transferring their old values to the new system. When the process of change is followed, users will combine their old work values with new values and fit them to the new style of work. The newly combined values, as part of the new way of working, will provide new energy for the organization. The users themselves will aid the organization to feed forward into another cycle of the process. The users will provide the organization with the necessary internal dynamics to adjust continually to its environment.

Summary: Growing the Organization

Growth occurs in human systems when two sources of energy come together. One is internal. It is the potential that the living system has for growth. The second is external. It comes through the growth nutrients, the new wisdom and technologies, that are absorbed by the system. From their very beginning, human social systems do have internal potential for growth and change. But this potential is often stifled by the constraints imposed on these systems.

Recent articles on entrepreneurship comment on this phenomenon, showing how the original potential of an enterprise was gradually stifled by management behavior. Two rules need to be affirmed. Organizations cannot be force fed into growth if their internal potential has been diminished, crippled, or destroyed. And organizations cannot realize their potential for growth and change without acquiring some form of external energy.

The application to IT is this: ITs are external energy sources that can be fed into the human social system. But in order for the new energy to do its work effectively, the human system must have a potential for growth. The opposite is equally true. In order for a dynamic living human system to expand and grow, it must acquire necessary outside sources of energy, including ITs. But this process must always have the guidance of managers, who are responsible for the human organization and its technology.

The involvement of the human factor is not always recognized. We are intrigued by popular accounts in the press about factories in which everyone goes home at night, and when the last person turns off all the lights, the machines keep working at their jobs. These articles often give the impression that no humans are involved. That is a gross misrepresentation of the truth, even if it is a factual statement. The process of doing work is always a human task. It must always be guided by human hands, human hearts, and human minds.

The factory cited above exists because a human system built it and allows it to continue in operation. Its products are sent forth to serve other human systems. Its workers go home to their private human systems and return to work in the factory's organizational human system. The factory will always need the firm guidance of a human hand. A self-evident principle, you say? Yes, but not always understood and not often applied.

We will have achieved a significant breakthrough in computerizing the corporation when we understand that all technical systems need human guidance in order to serve human needs. When we achieve this insight, management will be prepared to bring new forms of technology into our places of work. Then our organizations will be able to go back through the loop of technology implementation effectively. And we will be prepared to evaluate each of these implementations by the only criterion that has any validity—whether they serve the human system.

Winning or Losing the Future

The problem with the future is that it isn't what it used to be.

—Paul Valery

George Beeler Revisited

We began this book with the story of George Beeler as portrayed in *Inc.* magazine. For several generations his family has worked in the auto industry. Now George finds his world changing more radically and rapidly than he cares to think about. As the author of the *Inc.* magazine article commented, "This is not the world George Beeler expected to live in."

It is equally important to listen to George's words. "We're all under the ax right now. You drop that ax on these (automobile) companies and you're dropping the ax on a . . . whole damn world. That's the world of my father and my son. That's my world."

And with that plea, George Beeler makes the point: When the future is lost, the past is lost as well. That is the reality behind the George Beeler story. The future and the past are always lost together. One day we look back and ask ourselves, "What happened? How did we get into such a mess?" A typical reaction to such a predicament is to look for a path back to the way things used to be. That is an approach called "problem solving."

Unfortunately, you cannot go back to the future. Problem solving applies correctives, that is, solutions which try to re-create a past condition. However, the use of correctives may apply an incorrect solution because the right problems were not identified. Correctives inevitably put the focus on symptoms rather than problems. Their use leads to nostalgia, the feelings we had when things were good. There is an avoidance of the causes, behaviors, and/or environment that made it possible for good things to happen. Correctives are similar to feedback mechanisms. They return an organization to a state of equilibrium. But using correctives will not generate the new behaviors that are needed to create the future.

The solution is to realize that the future is always won in the present, by those who say, "We're going to make it happen." This is a feed-forward process. As a process, feed forward requires more of its human users. It asks them to retain effective pieces of the past but always to drive forward to the future. It expects them to work to create the future they seek. It expects them to do so with a realistic awareness of environmental forces that will constrain or encourage their efforts. And it does so by allowing them to make choices, many of which involve IT.

In this book, we have placed a wide range of choices in the hands of managers. We have asked them to decide how they intend to recognize employees for their achievements. We have alerted them to their employees' need for assurance through management consistency and for involvement in the organization through ownership. We have prodded management to choose the most effective methods of implementing new technologies using the Technology Implementation Life Cycle. We have proposed a working model for processing technology changes in an organization. Now we must express a final caution about the real complexities faced by all of us as we move together into a new age of automation.

Making choices about technology will never be as simple, or as direct, or as uncomplicated as it was in the past. All past and present choices are now subject to the constant evaluation of quickly emerging, new technologies. Every choice made in one moment of time is subject to the scrutiny of the future moment when the technology has advanced, making the old choice obsolete.

The need to choose our technological future will not go away. Either the technology advances without our participation, thereby being thrust upon us, or we take control of our technological future. To maintain control, we must do the things listed in Table 8-1.

Table 8-1

Requirements for Control of an Advancing Technology

1. Set common expectations regarding technology
2. Control technology through people management
3. Recognize the trends in technology development, particularly as they relate to the business
4. Recognize the need to organize the entire business to control its technology

Setting Common Expectations
Regarding Technology

The simpler the tool, the easier it is to have common expectations about its use and value. An analogy may be helpful. As tools go, there is a great distance between the hammer and the computer. A hammer is much easier to understand. Look at a hammer, and you know its use. It drives nails in and pulls them out. To the expert carpenter it has many other uses, but these are easily explained, even to a neophyte.

Conversely, most people have different expectations of a computer. To the technician, it has many more uses than an average nontechnical user can comprehend. This problem only increases as computer types, complexity, and uses increase. To many people the problem is heightened by the many different computers available, each with unique attributes and uses. Some users' differing perceptions of technology relate to the myriad tasks that just one computer can do. But all of these differences reflect the variations in personal experiences.

The following are examples of attitudes toward and perceptions about this familiar form of IT. They are intended to show the range of dissimilarities.

Mabel, our computer user example and payroll clerk, wants nothing more than to get today's work done today.

The computer professional is concerned about how to keep the computer up and running.

A middle manager, using a PC, wants to learn how to use a new spreadsheet application to create statistical reports for a coming management meeting.

The vice president of information systems wants more freedom to purchase the latest equipment so that more computing demands can be met.

The chief operating officer wonders if the company's computer operation is benefiting all of the business and its bottom line.

The CEO blocks all attempts to place a PC in his office.

Computer vendors aim to make their quarterly sales quota.

These characterizations are meant to exaggerate the situation in order to demonstrate the point. One's view of a computer depends on where one stands. All people bring to their perceptions of the computer those circumstances which are most important to them. As individuals, they are heavily influenced by their experiences, knowledge, and personal circumstances. Our individual expectations and experiences with the computer shape our attitudes toward automation. Organizations, on the other hand, need more than a collection of individual employee attitudes. They need to rally everyone in the organization to a common starting point regarding the use of technology.

Tools: A Starting Point for Expectation Management

Developing common expectations is somewhat like arriving at the same place at the end of a journey. It is easier to do if everybody starts at the same spot. A common starting point for a journey into the technological future is the realization that ITs are human tools. In their book *The Fifth Generation*, Edward Feigenbaum and Pamela McCorduck (1983) trace the development of human communication from speech to writing, from writing to printing, and from printing to electronic storage. By tracing this journey, they place the new technology back into its proper category. It is a tool that extends human capabilities. The problem is that this tool is so extraordinary that its connection back to its human user can be missed.

When we miss the connection between tool and human, we inevitably misunderstand the nature of the relationship between them. During the writing of this book, an article appeared in the *Columbus Dispatch*, with the headline, "Robots May Make Human Worker Obsolete." Such popular accounts do a disservice by their shallow approach to this subject. The tools that extend human capabilities of mind and body do not make humans obsolete. People make themselves obsolete whenever they dissociate themselves from the tools. These are our tools. Tools can be rendered obsolete by people. But tools cannot make people obsolete. Only people can make themselves obsolete, unable to survive in a world they have created. And that is the present reality surrounding automation.

Similarly, ITs do not make people or their thought processes extinct. Rather, they extend the human process of thought. They add new dimensions. They aid people in their thinking. They allow people to think more quickly. They make it possible to think without distraction and with an accuracy that is unmatched in their creators. But these technologies do not think better than people do. They think differently, and they help people to think better with them. And that is the true perspective concerning automation.

A tool should never be separated from its human user, no matter how it performs. In fact, a well-used tool is often indistinguishable from its user. A user can often describe the bonding that occurs between them. "Where does the concert violinist's arm stop and the violin begin?" Even the concert listener cannot distinguish between them as the concerto is played. A partnership develops between the two, so that each enhances the other. Both end up doing things they never did before. The solid base needed for that partnership is the user's understanding of the tool.

The starting point for common expectations is understanding the technology as a tool, inseparable from its human creator. The next step is to understand the nature of the tool. Understanding the new IT requires a balanced viewpoint. It must be viewed as a tool that cannot do certain things, yet as a tool that can amaze and surprise its user in the very next instant. This is an expectation that applies to most modern tools. But the computer is also an uncommon tool.

There is a dynamic to the computer, literally a power, that defies definition. It mimics human qualities so well that it almost seems human. It will be seen as a constant innovator, always expanding its horizons. Yet it constantly disappoints us, often because we simply fail in our use of it. Because of this variability in what the technology can be for us, it needs a steadying hand. Like a high-strung thoroughbred, it needs a jockey. But not any jockey will do. A competent one is required. And this is why the development of the people who use it is so important.

Control the Technology Through People Management

The tendency of IT to "blow hot and cold" requires an improved use of our human resources. This volatile technology can enhance or harm its human users. It is the leading force in a technological revolution that is changing the shape of work forever. And whenever technological revolutions occurred, some human systems survived and prospered; some did not. Those that survived did so on the strength of their human resources. They were able to assemble and manage the human resources needed to control and use the new technology. Those that failed did not lack access to the technology. They lacked the human means to exploit it.

The key characteristics of those who learned to exploit new technologies were leadership and cohesiveness. These human systems survived because they developed the people skills to manage the new technology. They connected the tool back to the human. They brought the tool under their control. We propose that three things can control the technology: user management, user education, and user training.

User management can control the technology by setting reasonable parameters and expectations which control its extension and expansion. User education can control it by demystifying the technology while developing a sense of openness to its possibilities. User training can control technology by focusing on functional and productive uses first, and later by encouraging human creativity in the development of new uses (Table 8-2).

Table 8-2
Control of Computer Technology

1. Management controls
   a. Reasonable parameters and expectations
   b. Reasonable extension and expansion
2. Education controls
   a. Remove technological mysteries
   b. Develop technological possibilities
3. Training controls
   a. Focus on functional and productive uses
   b. Encourage creative applications

This thoroughness is necessary if organizations are to benefit from technology. Organizations and technologies must learn to live and work together. We know that the technology can be changed to make it more compatible with people. The question that remains is, can people, and their human institutions, be changed to make better use of technology? Can human institutions adapt, grow, and become better equipped to use technology? These questions are urgent, for automation is upon us all.

Recognize the Trends in Technology Development

From presentations before IBM's large computer user group, Guide International (1977-1982), to a recent speech at the Gulf States Technology Conference, United Arab Emirate (1988), Vicki has described computerization as a runaway train on a downhill track with no brakes. This comment was intended to convey the opinion that there will always be more technology, not less. In addition, the speed with which it enters our lives constantly increases. This is why the big money brokers of the world and the emergent industrial nations have fashioned policies of expansion into the computer market.

At present, no one can identify all the areas of our lives affected by IT. There are too many. Nor can any person predict, at any one time, where a new technology will occur next. There are too many options. But all enterprises need to have their own study and research on the emerging technologies that affect them. We cannot provide them in this book. However, we can provide some general observations that fit most, if not all, organizations. We see the following as significant trends that affect the way management leads organizations into new technology use.

Information In, Data Out

Information management is the new thrust; data is the old one. There is a movement away from the oxymoron of "data management" to the reality of information resource management. Organizations have begun to grasp the difference between data and information. They have begun to grapple with the range and complexity of inferences that flow out of this concept. Now it is no longer the numbers that matter; it is the thinking.

IT is now inviting managers to think. It continues to challenge their minds in two ways. It forces them to follow its line of logic—its functional path. In order to evaluate its output, it forces them to reexamine their own fundamental questions. It even casts them back upon themselves, forcing them to reconnect to things that matter. It will force them to deal with creativeness and the rights of others. And as it continues to develop, the technology will force managers to reconsider human values.

There are levels of human thought that move from data to information to knowledge and to wisdom. Each level of thought has its own values, the criteria by which it operates. The technology is developing its ability to operate at each of these successive levels. As it does so, it raises the issue of human values. Values must be examined as the technology moves through each step from data to wisdom. At each step, there is the challenge of applying appropriate human values to the thought process that the technology initiates.

Individualization of the Workplace

At present, all of us are witnesses to a remarkable change in the manner in which work is done. Both computerization and robotization are putting more power into the hands of the individual worker. As the span of an individual's control broadens, the need for teamwork may appear to decline. The more an individual can use a machine to get things done, the less that person may appear to need the specific skills and talents of others. The PC revolution is leading to such individualization. Even the physical design of the workplace suggests a privatization of labor as the computer area takes on more of the look of a monk's chamber than a shared work space.

This process introduces elements of risk to both the worker and the organization. The worker runs the risk of assuming sole responsibility for decisions and behaviors. Team decisions at least have the advantage of shared risk. The enterprise runs the risk of taking unexamined or poorly examined decisions and actions. After all, the crucible of interpersonal discussion and debate is a powerful means of examining decisions and actions.

The process also introduces an element of psychological distance as workers feel isolated from one another. Social interaction alone does not meet workers' needs. The sharing of common tasks is one of the greatest bonds in the workplace. It builds a sense of community and commitment. Those who have experienced the quality circle style of work can vouch for the way teamwork changes their perception of work and of working relationships. They can also vouch for its impact on productivity, the quality of product or service, and the bottom line.

Ultimately, it is not individualism that is the danger. Individualism can be thought of as empowering individuals to achieve greater productivity and value in their work. Strengthening and empowering the individual can be done in such a way that the community of individuals is also strengthened. Privatization of the worker is the problem. Privatization is the creation of psychological and social isolation between workers. However, even when privatization has occurred, there is no reason why it cannot be reversed. The shift from individualization to privatization occurs only when management allows the technology, or other circumstances, to assume control over the organization.

Downsizing and Proliferating

The remarkable evolution of the computer chip has led to a downsizing and proliferation of the technology. One might have hoped the new abundance of technology would have created an equally generous sharing of technology across all social and economic strata. But that is not the case.

The computer's downsizing did lead to cost reductions that placed the technology in the hands of many more people. But it is still not equally available to all. In addition, the growth in the number and kind of peripherals has added costs back onto the technology. The fact is that only the economically advantaged have access to the full range of IT.

As a result, some people will be unable to afford the new technologies or will not advance in their use as rapidly as others. The availability of the technology varies among school districts, states, and nations. Even where technology is accessible, people differ in their ability to develop skills in its use. These are technological gaps, differences that exist between people, often due to circumstances beyond their control.

The potential danger in these technological gaps dare not be overlooked just because past experiences have not been a threat. For instance, the gap between upper and lower economic levels is not as significant in some forms of technology. An inexpensive automobile and an expensive automobile perform the same tasks; the main difference is between their comfort levels. Many gaps in technology are only symbolic of economic and cultural differences. However, gaps in IT generate new economic and cultural distortions both in kind and in scope.

The presence of these technological gaps creates the potential for a world in continual disarray, as now one, then another part takes dominance over others through IT. And although this happens between nations, a similar scenario can occur within countries by social classes and economic strata. This does not bode well for the conduct of "business as usual."

These problems require a multidimensional solution. Countries and businesses must extend their efforts to make technology available and usable to all. Each of us has a stake in this problem's solution. We are technology's "stakeholders." A business planning its technological future needs workers who are technically competent. The society trying to serve its citizens in this age of automation needs citizens who can use technology. All of us have to make sure that part of "business as usual" is the continual education and training of all citizens in the use of the technologies of our time.

Recognize the Need to Organize the Business to Control the Technology

There is a need to take action, but it must be a planned action and not just a reaction to an isolated situation. There must be a total, planned effort to control and manage the impacts of automation. Three conditions determine success in controlling the impact of an organization's technology use. First, management must be in charge, not the technology. Second, management must select the battlefield in order to win control of the organization. Third, management must kick the dependency habit that says that the technology determines the future.

Condition 1: "Who's in Charge?"

Unfortunately, the perception of a problem is often distorted by the way it is communicated. In a free society, the perception of a technology problem is often determined by the manner in which it is portrayed in the media. American media often describe technology and humans as if they act independently of one another. The previously cited headline, "Robots May Make Human Worker Obsolete," is an example. Doesn't it give the impression that the robot is acting on its own? That kind of talk does two things. It sets a confrontational tone to the historical event, and it takes responsibility for the results out of human hands.

That is not the true situation. If robots are used to displace workers, it's because some other human being made that decision. If workers and robots end up in confrontation, it's because some person decided to have a confrontation rather than a collaboration. It's not robotization that is the problem; it's management. The headlines and the stories do not tell us this. Telling the story the way it really happens is much harder, and it does not sell papers.

It is doubtful that the media can be directly influenced to take a more calm and deliberative approach to technology. Management will have to ignore this "hype" and proceed on the basis of the facts. And the facts are that management can be in charge and can do as it wishes with the technology. Management can institute a more calm and deliberative approach to technology's introduction. Management can eliminate confrontation and competitiveness between people and machines. Management can be in charge because it is already in charge. It just may not be exercising its control in the most effective manner.

Condition 2: Choosing the Battlefield

There is a military axiom that the general who picks the battlefield wins the battle. The technology battle will be won if it can be determined where the battle must be fought. But no battle can be planned until the enemy is known.

Pogo, a favorite comic strip character of Karl's, said it well: "We have met the enemy and they are us." No matter how far off the war is waged, the first battlefield is within. Winning or losing the technology challenge starts within ourselves and our organizations. We have proposed the Technology Implementation Life Cycle as a method and a process for technology implementation. But methods and processes do not work unless the assumptions that lie behind them are addressed.

Table 8-3
Competence Areas to Support Technology Implementation

1. Operational development
2. Technological development
3. Organizational development

Three areas of competence must be addressed by any organization which plans to use the advancing ITs: operational development, technological development, and organizational development (Table 8-3). Operational development includes all the work of delivering a product or service. Technological development includes all areas of research, development, and implementation of technology to accomplish the organization's work. Organizational development includes all human resource development and all strengthening of the organizational structures. These constitute the total battlefield on which the war must be fought.

For a business, there are three "windows of vulnerability" through which the battle of technology will be won or lost. The neglect of any of these: product or service, technology, or human resources loses the battle and the war. To strengthen each of these independently does not win. There must be a synthesis of the three.

We believe that each successful technology implementation ought to be a combination of product or service, technology, and human system in one collaborative effort. This threefold concern should be displayed from the highest levels of the enterprise down to its most basic operations. But in particular, it is critical at the senior executive level.

There has been discussion about the emergence and role of the chief information officer (CIO). Without becoming involved in the details of this discussion, we assert the need for such a position with direct reporting responsibilities to the CEO. The position would be comparable in stature to the office of COO. A third executive position, with equal stature, would be that of chief development officer (CDO). This person would also report to the CEO and would be responsible for all human and organizational development functions.

We state this opinion because of our strong belief in the need for three developmental functions in business today. We must develop the product or service. This is the role of the COO. We must develop the technology. This is the role of the CIO. And we must develop the people and the organization. This is the role of the CDO.

We have no qualms about other ways of structuring these functions. One alternative we have considered is an executive board or operating board serving by appointment of the CEO. The real issue here is not the structure. It is the function.

Condition 3: Kicking the Dependency Habit

Even the best laid plans will fall apart if an old habit rears its head and begins to drive behaviors. Management has, for too long, made strategic automation decisions on the wrong basis. Many automation plans have been driven by strategic planning that focuses on convenience or competition. Convenience is used to describe those instances in which a change in technology occurs mainly because of "convenient" features in the new technology. For example, a new technology is selected because it is faster, provides more data, or eliminates potential human errors in manual systems. Competition-driven changes can occur either because of necessity or because of envy. These changes arise when a company sees a competitor advancing in their shared marketplace and believes it is because the competitor has better technology.

It is not wrong to consider convenience and competition in changing technology. These should be considered as factors. The strategic issue is whether they should ever be determinative factors. If they are used as determinative factors, they will lead to the organization's dependence on technology. If a pattern of such decision making develops, the organization will develop a technology dependency habit. It will be hooked on technology.

For example, the ATM is a remarkably convenient device. There are many stated reasons for adopting this technology. Money can be made available during non-banking hours. Bank customers can access their accounts readily and directly and perform many different kinds of transactions for themselves. Of course, the clincher to the decision is that the competition is doing it. While these are all good points to be raised, they are not the strategic issue. That issue is, "Is this the kind of bank that we choose to be?" Management using good strategic thinking will ask this question from the operational, technical, and human perspectives—and will integrate the answers into one solution.

Ending at the Beginning

The best way to end a book is with the simplest explanation of what it is about. This book is about technological competence—the ability to master and use the next level of technology. This does not imply anything about the types of technology that an organization uses. It simply means preparing the worker for an incremental, natural progression of technological change.

The development of an organization's technical competence requires a change in its strategic philosophy. Current strategic thinking about technological change is often focused on short-term solutions to long-term problems, on the quick fix rather than the final fix. The larger and more significant issues are often ignored. This trend will continue as long as technological change is perceived as a technical issue rather than a management issue.

When strategic thinking is expanded, management will see the need to develop their people, their business, and their organization as they develop their technology. Then technology, this most exciting of all tools, will be back in the hands of its creators. Then they, and their human systems, will be enhanced through its presence and its use.

Technology Implementation Life Cycle Based Upon The McConnell Method

Phase 1: Preimplementation

1. Define the scope of the system and its implementation.
2. Identify, profile, and select an implementation task force.
3. Identify required implementation resources.
4. Prepare a preliminary implementation plan for senior management approval.
5. Assign tasks and deadlines to the implementation task force.
6. Establish times of periodic review and evaluation of the implementation process.
7. Note those steps which need improvement.

Phase 2: Human Design

1. Conduct a workplace impact study.
2. Gather user demographics.
3. Review the organization's criteria/standards for human design.
4. Review the procedures for human design evaluation.
   a. Hardware procedures.
   b. Software procedures.
5. Consult with the human design review committee.
6. Design user screens and reports.
7. Pilot test screens and reports.
8. Periodically review screens and reports.
9. Note those steps which need improvement.

Phase 3: Marketing

1. Gather data on potential technology impacts.
   a. Review and assess previous implementations.
   b. Identify impacts unique to the technology implementation.
   c. Measure and study preimplementation productivity and work styles.
   d. Profile users.
   e. Conduct a reality pretest of the users.
   f. Conduct an IT attitude survey.
   g. Identify the corporate culture and subcultures of user groups.
   h. Form user focus groups.
2. Verify system delivery and installation date.
3. Prepare a marketing plan.
4. Identify required marketing resources.
5. Assign marketing plan tasks.
6. Execute the marketing plan.
7. Evaluate the marketing plan's results.
8. Prepare a marketing report for management.
9. Note those steps which need improvement.

Phase 4: Education

1. Identify user learners.
2. Establish user education criteria.

3. Identify required user education.

4. Conduct user focus groups.

5. Prepare user education objectives.

6. Develop a user education syllabus.

7. Select user education methods.

8. Choose user education media.

9. Develop a user education curriculum.

10. Develop a user education course catalogue.

11. Promote user education courses.

12. Conduct user education.

13. Evaluate user education and courses.

14. Prepare a user education report for management.

15. Revise user education and courses.

16. Note those steps which need improvement.

Phase 5: Training

1. Identify user trainees.

2. Identify user backup personnel.

3. Establish user training criteria.

4. Prepare user training objectives.

5. Select user training approach(es).

6. Identify user training resources.

7. Develop user training lesson plan.

8. Identify user training media.

9. Compare the user training lesson plan to the companion documentation.

10. Develop user training materials and documentation.

11. Pilot test user training.

12. Evaluate and revise user training.

13. Develop a user training course catalogue.

14. Promote user training.

15. Conduct user training.

16. Provide user training and documentation.

17. Evaluate user training and documentation.

18. Revise user training and documentation.

19. Prepare a user training report for management.
20. Note those steps which need improvement.

Phase 6: Documentation

1. Identify required user documentation.
2. Identify user documentation resources.
3. Establish user documentation standards.
4. Outline preliminary user documentation.
5. Determine the user documentation style.
6. Prepare user documentation.
7. Measure the reading and interest levels of user documentation.
8. Pilot test user documentation.
9. Evaluate the user documentation pilot test.
10. Revise/edit user documentation.
11. Package user documentation.
12. Provide user documentation.
13. Train users to use documentation.
14. Evaluate user documentation.
15. Revise user documentation.
16. Maintain a current user documentation roster.
17. Prepare and distribute user documentation updates.
18. Note those steps which need improvement.

Phase 7: Human Communications

1. Identify the internal impacts of IT.
2. Identify the external impacts of IT.
3. Identify and design human communications strategies.
4. Identify the human communications resources required.
5. Develop the human communications plan.
6. Execute the human communications plan.
7. Evaluate the human communications plan.

8. Revise the human communications plan.
9. Prepare a human communications report for management.
10. Note those steps which need improvement.

Phase 8: Postimplementation

1. Administer a user reality posttest.
2. Administer a user postimplementation attitude survey.
3. Conduct a performance measurement study.
4. Develop recommendations to improve the Technology Implementation Life Cycle.
5. Prepare a postimplementation report for management.
6. Revise the Technology Implementation Life Cycle.

The
McConnell Method

Vicki C. McConnell has been developing methods for implementing computer technology since 1972, the year she began working at The Ohio State University Hospitals. Since that time, she has refined this methodology while working at several Fortune 500 corporations and, more lately, as a private consultant.

The McConnell Method is an integrated method built on the assumption that computer technology should be introduced to and not imposed upon the end user. This method recognizes that technology traumatizes many people. They develop strong feelings of awkwardness, fear, or suspicion, encounter a language barrier they do not understand, and develop resentment or resistance to the technology (Fig. B-1).

McConnell recognized very early that each of these traumas required special treatment in order to be controlled and then eliminated. The steps in computer implementation which she developed provide an integrated approach to all of these traumas. They also provide a sequential process of organizational activities which facilitate the productive use of the technology by the end user (Fig. B-2).

McConnell's methodology has been expanded in this book into the Technology Implementation Life Cycle. This latest methodology was co-authored with Karl Koch. It places The McConnell Method into the framework of organizational development and human system processes.

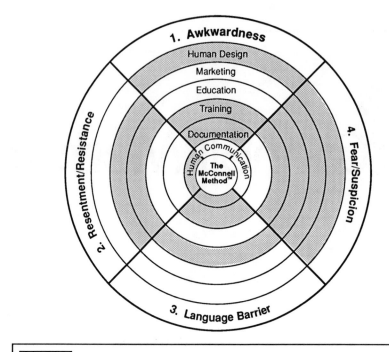

Where The McConnell Method™ has its greatest impact on the traumas of technology.

FIG. B-1   The Traumas of Technology

(1) Awkwardness—discomfort with computer hardware and software. (2) Fear/suspicion—anxiety over job loss to a computer/distrust of computer output. (3) Language barrier—inability to understand technical jargon. (4) Resentment/resistance—dislike of or unwillingness to accept the change created by technology.

STEP	HUMAN SYSTEM	TECHNICAL SYSTEM
1. Human Design		
The creation of technology that balances people's needs with system use	It is people who succeed or fail, not machines	It is flexibility in choosing and designing our technology which helps people succeed
2. Marketing		
Selling the changes created by the installation of new technology	Change can be introduced into any workplace when certain factors are considered	Introduction of new technology always creates social and emotional changes
3. Education		
The study of technological concepts and principles	People will make up their own explanation of a new technology if none is provided	Every possible choice that can be made in a technical system has its own unique requirements for explanation
4. Training		
Instruction on how to operate a technological system	The risk of human failure in learning new skills is reduced by flexibility in training	Introducing a new technology to escalate potential and profits also escalates risks
5. Documentation		
Written information about the new technology, to be used when and where needed	Most people do not know technical language concepts	All technical languages and concepts require translation to be understood and used by people
6. Human Communications		
Effective and ongoing interaction between nontechnical people and technology/technicians	We must responsibly control the human and technical forms through which we communicate	Machines do not communicate, but they can drastically alter the way people do

FIG. B-2   The McConnell Method

Personality, Behavior, and Change

Karl Koch has been doing organizational development (OD) consulting since 1972. Throughout his practice, he has used a variety of personality instruments that assist his clients in understanding their behaviors and their reactions to change. Two of these instruments have been found to be very helpful for technology implementations.

The Personal Profile System™

The Personal Profile System is a product of the Carlson Learning Company of Minneapolis, Minnesota. It was developed by professionals in the behavioral sciences and is used to reveal tendencies in behavior that influence the way people relate to one another and to work demands. Among other indicators, it shows whether a person feels more comfortable dealing with a technical or a human problem. It also shows how different personalities respond to technology changes at work.

The Myers/Briggs Type Indicator™

This type indicator is named in honor of the two women who were its primary developers. It is based on the theoretical model of personality types expounded by Carl Jung. It also provides insights into personality and behavioral tendencies.

Karl has used the Myers/Briggs Type Indicator in systems analysis and design classes to aid the analyst in working with end users while gathering system requirements. It is also helpful in identifying management styles, strengths, and weaknesses.

The authors regularly use these instruments in their consulting work and in connection with technology implementations. Both instruments have certification requirements for their purchase and use. Additional information on certification is available from the authors at:

The MENTOR Group
700 Ackerman Road, Suite 110
Columbus, OH 43202
(614) 251-3552

Similar information may be acquired directly from the following:

Personal Profile System: Carlson Learning Corp/Performax
    Systems International, Inc.
    12755 State Highway 55
    Minneapolis, MN 55441
    (612) 449-2856

Myers/Briggs Type Indicator
    Center for the Application of Psychological Type (CAPT)
    2720 N.W. 6th Street
    Gainesville, FL 32609
    (904) 375-0160

References

Chapter 1

Carlzon, Jan. 1987. *Moments of Truth*. Cambridge, Mass.: Ballinger.

Garson, Barbara. 1988. *The Electronic Sweatshop*. New York: Simon & Schuster.

Hyatt, Joshua. 1989. The last shift. *Inc*. 11(2):74–80.

Mankin, Don, et al. 1988. Managing technological change: the process is key. *Datamation*. 34(18):69–77.

Notowidigdo, M.H. 1987. To neglect maintenance is to neglect a strategic resource. *InformationWEEK*. Issue 110:49.

Vincent, David. 1989. *The Information–Based Corporation*. Homewood, Ill.: Dow Jones-Irwin.

Chapter 2

Albrecht, Karl. 1983. *Organization Development*. Englewood Cliffs, N.J.: Prentice-Hall.

Deal, Terrence E., and Allan A. Kennedy. 1982. *Corporate Cultures, the Rites and Rituals of Corporate Life*. Reading, Mass.: Addison-Wesley.

Gilbert, Thomas F. 1978. *Human Competence, Engineering Worthy Performance*, New York: McGraw-Hill.

Knowles, Malcolm. 1973. *The Adult Learner: A Neglected Species*. Houston, Tex.: Gulf.

MacGregor, Douglas. 1960. *The Human Side of Enterprise*. New York: McGraw-Hill.

Pinchot, Gifford, III. 1988. *Intrapreneuring*. New York: Harper & Row.

Chapter 3

Carlzon, Jan. 1987. *Moments of Truth*. Cambridge, Mass.: Ballinger.

Carroll, Paul B. 1988. Computer glitch. *The Wall Street Journal*. January 22, 1988.

Drucker, Peter. 1973. *Management: Tasks - Responsibilities - Practices.* New York: Harper & Row.

Maccoby, Michael. 1976. *Gamesmen.* New York: Simon & Schuster.

Peters, Thomas, J. and Robert H. Waterman, Jr. 1982. *In Search of Excellence.* New York: Harper & Row.

Rogers, Everett M. 1983. *Diffusion of Innovations.* New York: Free Press.

Spicer, Robert H., II. 1988. Total branch architecture: are we ready? *Banking Systems and Equipment.* 25(8):139–140.

Strassman, Paul. 1988. Face-to-face. *Inc.* 10(3):27–40.

Chapter 4

McGill, Michael. 1988. *American Business and the Quick Fix.* New York: Holt, Rinehart & Winston.

Peters, Thomas, and Robert H. Waterman. 1982. *In Search of Excellence.* New York: Harper & Row.

Chapter 5

Chapanis, Alphonse. 1984. Taming and civilizing computers. Computer culture. *Annals of the New York Academy of Sciences.* 426:202–219.

Deal, Terrence E., and Allan A. Kennedy. 1982. *Corporate Cultures.* Reading, Mass.: Addison-Wesley.

Longley, Dennis, and Michael Shain. 1989. *Van Nostrand Reinhold Dictionary of Information Technology.* Third Edition. New York: Van Nostrand Reinhold.

Chapter 6

Gilbert, Thomas F. 1978. *Human Competence.* New York: McGraw-Hill.

Chapter 7

Carlsson, Barbara, Peter Keane, and J. Bruce Martin. 1976. R&D organizations as learning systems. *Sloan Management Review.* 17(3):1–16.

Carroll, John. 1984. Minimalist training, *Datamation.* 30(18):125–136.

Kanter, Rosabeth Moss. 1983. *The Change Masters.* New York: Simon & Schuster.

Kolb, David. 1984. *Experiential Learning: Experience Is the Source of Learning.* Englewood Cliffs, N.J.: Prentice-Hall.

Mantei, Marilyn M., and Toby J. Teorey. 1988. Cost/benefit analysis for incorporating human factors in the software life cycle. *Computing Practices.* 31(4):428–439.

Chapter 8

Feigenbaum, Edward A., and Pamela McCorduck. 1983. *The Fifth Generation.* Reading, Mass: Addison-Wesley.

Index

About The MENTOR Group

The MENTOR Group, of Columbus, Ohio, was founded by Vicki C. McConnell and Karl Wm. Koch. The services of the firm are based on the premise that information technology (IT) is advancing into all areas of work. This creates a need for better working relationships between information systems (IS) professionals and nontechnical IT users.

The MENTOR Group provides assistance to corporate management in controlling its use of information technology. It also offers services and seminars for IS personnel which improve their management skills and working relationships with IT users. This book, *Computerizing the Corporation,* is the culmination of efforts by The MENTOR Group to integrate its concerns for management control of information technology and IS personnel development needs.

Vicki McConnell is the co-founder and principal officer of The MENTOR Group in Columbus, Ohio, and previous head of The McConnell Group, Los Angeles, California.

Her career focuses on the human concerns of the Information Age. She is the originator of an effective method, The McConnell Method™, designed to introduce information technology to non-technical people (see Appendix B).

For nearly 20 years she has been associated with major organizations where she developed and managed departments devoted to the non-technical IT user. These organizations include: The Ohio State University Hospital Computer Center in Columbus and Carter, Hawley, Hale Stores, Inc. and Crocker National Bank of Los Angeles. McConnell also held the position of Los Angeles commercial district marketing manager for WANG Laboratories.

An adjunct faculty member, she teaches for The Ohio State University's College of Business, Department of Accounting/MIS and the University of Dayton, Department of MIS & Decision Sciences's MBA program. She has served as a member of the faculty for UCLA Business School's Extension Program and Pepperdine University's Communications School in Malibu.

For several years, McConnell directed the end user training project for GUIDE International, an association for large-scale IBM customers.

She has co-developed a basic computer concepts CBT course, "Introduction to Computers: A Guide for the Workplace" with Goal Systems International Inc.

A nationally-known authority on computerization and frequent guest speaker, McConnell has addressed numerous corporate and professional symposiums throughout North America including National Computer Conference, Association for Women in Computing, GUIDE International, Data Processing Management Association, Association for Systems Management, American Society for Training and Development, IBM, Honeywell Large Systems Users Group, NCR Users Group, American Management Association, World Future Society, and Training Magazine Annual Conference.

She addressed the eighth annual Gulf Technology Conference in Dubai, United Arab Emirates in October, 1988. Her topic was, "Computer Education and Training, Distinctions and Contrasts". She was the first woman speaker invited to address this conference.

She is a Columbus, Ohio native and a graduate of The Ohio State University School of Journalism.

Karl Wm. Koch

Karl Koch is the co-founder and principal officer of The MENTOR Group in Columbus, Ohio.

His career is focused on the management concerns of the Information Age. He is one of the developers of "The Power Cycle"™, a cyclical process for understanding management systems. He has integrated this method of management to human learning systems, to change management, to personality types, and to the process of integrating technical systems into human systems.

Koch completed his Master of Arts degree in Sociology at the University of Cincinnati. At that time he also completed training as an associate of Management Design, Inc., a management and organizational development consulting company.

An experienced developer of training programs, under Law Enforcement Assistance Agency (LEAA) grants he developed an eight-state regional training program in organized crime and white collar crime investigative techniques. He has participated in national organized crime conferences and in national planning meetings on training to develop investigative skills. Koch has also developed and conducted training programs for Ohio's Community Action Agencies.

He is an Adjunct Professor in the College of Business, Franklin University in Columbus. He teaches courses in statistics and applied research techniques.

In 1980 Koch was appointed special manager of the Ohio Home Energy Assistance Program for its initial year of development and operation. Among other duties, he was responsible for the development of its on-line computer system serving 350,000 users.

An ordained Lutheran minister, Koch also conducts national seminars on leadership and management for clergy and laity.

He is a certified user of the training materials of Performax Corporation, Carlson Learning Companies, Minneapolis, Minnesota and of the Myers/Briggs Type Indicator™. He has developed a wide range of training materials for the improvement of management skills.

Koch is a native of Seattle, Washington.